selling
the movie

WINNER · BEST PICTURE · 1994 CANNES FILM FESTIVAL

PULP FICTION

a Quentin Tarantino film

10¢

produced by
Lawrence Bender

JOHN TRAVOLTA
SAMUEL L. JACKSON
UMA THURMAN
HARVEY KEITEL
TIM ROTH
AMANDA PLUMMER
MARIA de MEDEIROS
VING RHAMES
ERIC STOLTZ
ROSANNA ARQUETTE
CHRISTOPHER WALKEN
and
BRUCE WILLIS

MIRAMAX FILMS PRESENTS A BAND APART AND JERSEY FILMS PRODUCTION A FILM BY QUENTIN TARANTINO PULP FICTION MUSIC SUPERVISOR KARYN RACHTMAN
COSTUME DESIGNER BETSY HEIMANN PRODUCTION DESIGNER DAVID WASCO EDITOR SALLY MENKE DIRECTOR OF PHOTOGRAPHY ANDRZEJ SEKULA
CO-EXECUTIVE PRODUCERS BOB WEINSTEIN HARVEY WEINSTEIN RICHARD N. GLADSTEIN EXECUTIVE PRODUCERS DANNY DEVITO MICHAEL SHAMBERG
STACEY SHER STORIES BY QUENTIN TARANTINO & ROGER AVARY PRODUCED BY LAWRENCE BENDER WRITTEN AND DIRECTED BY QUENTIN TARANTINO

selling
the movie
the art of the film poster

ian haydn smith

WHITE LION
PUBLISHING

Brimming with creative inspiration, how-to projects and useful information to enrich your everyday life, Quarto Knows is a favourite destination for those pursuing their interests and passions. Visit our site and dig deeper with our books into your area of interest: Quarto Creates, Quarto Cooks, Quarto Homes, Quarto Lives, Quarto Drives, Quarto Explores, QuartoGifts, or Quarto Kids.

First published in 2018 by White Lion Publishing,
an imprint of The Quarto Group.
The Old Brewery, 6 Blundell Street,
London, N7 9BH,
United Kingdom
T (0)20 7700 6700 F (0)20 7700 8066
www.QuartoKnows.com

A catalogue record for this book is available from the British Library.

ISBN 978 0 71124 024 7
Ebook ISBN 978 1 71124 025 4

10 9 8 7 6 5 4 3 2

Design by Josse Pickard

Printed in Slovenia by GPS Group

CONTENTS

INTRODUCTION

Before the Internet and streaming; before television, DVD, and video; before the trailer, electronic press kits, celebrity interviews, film journals, and fan magazines; even before film stars, the movies had posters. The simplest form of film promotion has remained its most effective for more than one hundred years. Its size has varied and its style has bowed to changing fashions, but the function of a film poster has remained the same: to sell a movie.

The rise of the movie poster collector has given many of these artworks a second life. Poster collecting began in the late nineteenth century, when Jules Chéret created beautiful lithographs of the Parisian social scene, but the enthusiasm for collecting dwindled as art nouveau's popularity diminished. Interest was rekindled in the 1960s, when the emphasis shifted to movie posters. The market for genuine posters became lucrative.

Some posters have no monetary value but their cultural importance is great, often acting as a signpost

to shifting attitudes. A slight alteration in the emphasis of a design can affect the way we look at a specific era in cinema. Even the size of a poster denotes changing tastes within the world of exhibition. The moment framing was introduced, size became standardized. In the United States, the one sheet was set at 27 × 41 inches (69 × 104 cm). Outside a cinema, a three sheet, spanning 41 × 81 inches (104 × 206 cm), was the usual size displayed, but a poster could reach the scale of a twenty-four sheet (246 × 108 inches, 625 × 274 cm). In Britain, the single sheet or double crown measured 20 × 30 inches (51 × 76 cm), although the more popular size today is the quad, which comes in at 40 × 30 inches (102 × 76 cm). Specific sizes in other countries vary.

Posters from any era are fascinating to look at, but the reasons for their importance are many. The gradual recognition of actors in early cinema hints at the infancy of the star system. Whereas posters once showed a scene with no credits, audience interest in performers resulted in popular actors being named, and demand grew for

BELOW
The artwork for Tom Browning's *Freaks* (1932) offers a subversion of a classical Hollywood poster.

OPPOSITE
CLOCKWISE FROM TOP LEFT
Georgy Stenberg's design for Sergei Eisenstein's epic *October* (1927) exemplifies the Soviet Constructivist movement.

Blending expressionistic elements with a style that audiences would recognize from the 1930s Universal horror films, *I Walked with a Zombie's* (1943) poster hints at something different.

The typewriter replacing the human face underpins David Cronenberg's blurring the lines between reality and creativity in his adaptation of William Burroughs's *Naked Lunch* (1991).

Minimalism lay at the heart of Robert Bresson's films and is key to the power of the image used for the *Pickpocket* (1959) poster design.

ОКТЯБРЬ
OCTOBER

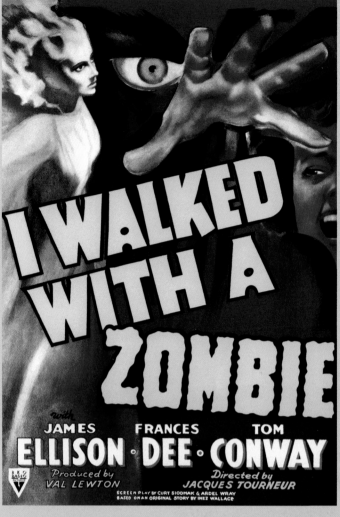

I WALKED WITH A ZOMBIE

with
JAMES FRANCES TOM
ELLISON · DEE · CONWAY

Produced by
VAL LEWTON

Directed by
JACQUES TOURNEUR

SCREEN PLAY BY CURT SIODMAK & ARDEL WRAY
BASED ON AN ORIGINAL STORY BY INEZ WALLACE

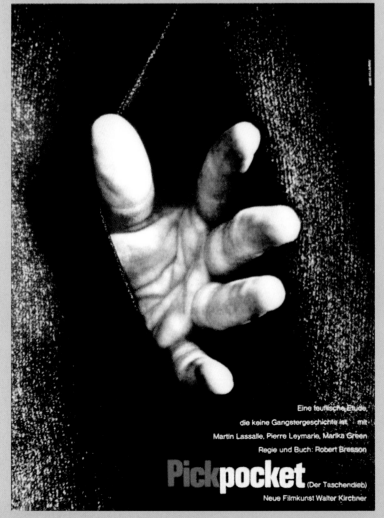

Eine teuflische Etude,
die keine Gangstergeschichte ist, mit

Martin Lassalle, Pierre Leymarie, Marika Green

Regie und Buch: Robert Bresson

Pickpocket
(Der Taschendieb)

Neue Filmkunst Walter Kirchner

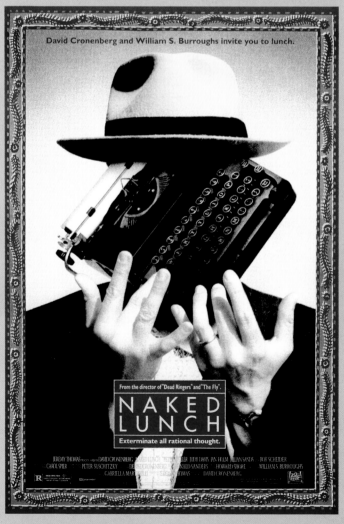

David Cronenberg and William S. Burroughs invite you to lunch.

From the director of "Dead Ringers" and "The Fly".

NAKED LUNCH
Exterminate all rational thought.

JEREMY THOMAS
CAROL SPIER PETER SUSCHITZKY
GABRIELLA MARTINELLI
DAVID CRONENBERG
WILLIAM S. BURROUGHS

films that featured them. Subsequently, an actor's billing on a poster charted both their rise and fall.

Attitudes to sex across decades and cultures can also be evinced through a cursory glance at posters from different periods. The silent era reflected permissive and censorial responses. US attitudes to sex were wildly different to those of the French, while the more open-minded views exhibited in the cinema of Germany's Weimar Republic were in direct contrast to the strict rules imposed by the Nazi regime only a few years later.

Movie posters reveal how cinema and societies responded to race, gender, and class. They show how propaganda influenced opinions and how some governments saw the medium as a tool of the state, while others regarded it as a lucrative source of commerce. Most of all, posters exist as a way of convincing an audience to watch a film. How they do that is the subject of this book.

To present an exhaustive history of movie posters around the world would be a herculean task that would require more than one slim volume. Some cinemas, such as Bollywood, warrant a separate—and sizable—study. The section on the 1970s action movie is the briefest dip into an ocean that is as expansive as it is richly rewarding. Instead, *Selling the Movie* presents a brief history of cinema and its key moments told through film posters. It is divided into decades, but the topics in each section often span a longer period.

These topics cover cultural, economic, societal, and political aspects of cinema, as well as the medium's position as the most popular form of mass entertainment. They range from influential genres to the changing faces of stardom and how each generation's icons are presented. Naturally, there are posters that helped to define a particular decade in cinema, and individual films or actors whose presence made an indelible impact on both the medium and the world stage.

Hollywood has dominated cinema and the movie poster market since the early days, so it plays a significant role in this book. However, each and every section illuminates the influences that have affected the way that movies are sold.

BELOW

If the poster for *Baby Driver* (2017, below left) hints at the film's kinetic energy, the steps Meryl Streep and Tom Hanks' characters face in the equally minimalist artwork for *The Post* (2017, below right) are a metaphor for the obstacles they face in challenging the power of government.

OPPOSITE
CLOCKWISE FROM TOP LEFT

The main protagonists form part of a gun in the poster for *The Mackintosh Man* (1973), playing to classic spy tropes where relationships are intertwined with espionage, albeit starkly rendered here.

John Frankenheimer's *Seconds* (1966) explores the notion of a man starting his life anew, hence Saul Bass' design of a machine that produces humans.

Andrzej Pagowski's poster for Krzysztof Kieślowski's *A Short Film About Killing* (1988) emphasizes the film's uncompromising account of a murder and the repercussions that result from it.

This German poster for the early Chaplin short *Shanghied* (1916) finds the comic star dressed up as a sailor, although by this time his Tramp persona was being developed.

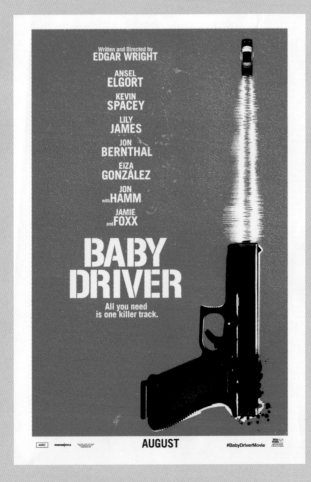

PAUL NEWMAN
THE MACKINTOSH MAN

whoever he is he's not what you think.

Celebrating Warner Bros. 50th Anniversary. A Warner Communications Company

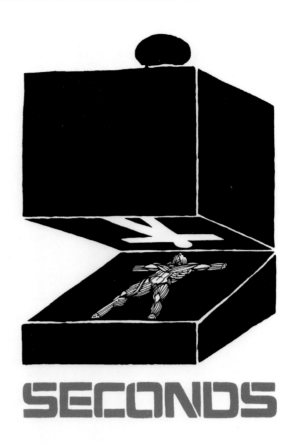

SECONDS

A JOHN FRANKENHEIMER FILM · ROCK HUDSON · SALOME JENS · WILL GEER · JOHN RANDOLPH · JEFF CORY
WESLEY ADDY · MURRAY HAMILTON · KARL SWENSON · KHIGH DHIGH · FRANCIS REID · RICHARD ANDERSON
SCREENPLAY BY LEWIS JOHN CARLINO · BASED ON A NOVEL BY DAVID ELY · MUSIC BY JERRY GOLDSMITH
PRODUCED BY EDWARD LEWIS · DIRECTED BY JOHN FRANKENHEIMER · A JOEL PRODUCTIONS RELEASE

CHAPLINS ÄVENTYR

LAND OCH SJÖSS

ENSAMRÄTT: FILMBYRÅN S. B. D. STOCKHOLM

KRÓTKI FILM O ZABIJANIU

CLOCKWISE FROM TOP LEFT

Aristide Bruant, in His Cabaret (1893)
A singer and owner of a cabaret in Montmartre, Aristide Bruant approached Henri de Toulouse-Lautrec with the commission of improving his image so that he could be advertised in more upmarket cafés and bars around the city.

Gismonda (1894)
First appearing on January 1, 1895, Alphonse Mucha's poster was radical in both shape and design. The sleek long form was new and the use of pastels was radical, capturing Sarah Bernhardt in a moment of tranquility.

Moulin Rouge: La Goulue (1891)
This four-color lithograph remains one of Toulouse-Lautrec's most famous posters, capturing legendary can-can dancer La Goulue and her partner Valentin le Désossé. The use of silhouette is particularly striking.

THE ORIGINS OF THE MOVIE POSTER

Posters have been in existence in various forms for hundreds of years. They were first used as public announcements or notices, and advertisements followed. One of the earliest posters on record was created by English merchant, diplomat, and printer William Caxton in the fifteenth century. The posting of notices on walls became so rife in France that in the seventeenth century the practice was banned unless prior permission had been obtained. By the middle of the eighteenth century, signboards started to appear in Paris, which were a precursor to billboards. However, it would be another century before posters began to be designed to the point where they achieved the status of art.

A rudimentary version of lithography, which allowed for a cheap and rapid duplication of a print, was invented by German actor and playwright Alois Senefelder in the late eighteenth century. Further modifications followed, and by the mid nineteenth century, the young French artist Jules Chéret had started to create his graphic designs employing the process. The age of the modern poster began with him.

Chéret started an apprenticeship with a lithographer when he was only thirteen years of age. In 1858, he produced his earliest known poster, for the Parisian Théâtre des Bouffes' production of Jacques Offenbach's *Orpheus in the Underworld*. The following year, the designer traveled to England where he spent seven years developing his craft.

Upon returning to Paris, Chéret set up his own press and began work of such refinement that it took art out of the gallery and onto the street. He became the leading figure in belle époque poster art, capturing the thrill and atmosphere of Paris' various cabarets, theaters, and music halls. *Bal Valentino* (1869) was one of Chéret's earliest works from this period to draw acclaim. His style embraced popular folk art, but added the sophistication of city life. Women dominated his poster designs—Danish actress and dancer Charlotte Wiehe was Chéret's favorite model—and they were portrayed as joyous, dancing, and happy. These figures became known as "Chérettes," and they encouraged women to socialize in a way that might have been deemed unthinkable in an earlier decade.

ABOVE

Bal Valentino (1869)
Jules Chéret's first major success is a celebration of the high life in late nineteenth-century Paris and features his signature "Chérette"—a young woman enjoying a world of dance.

Prochainement
Tournée
du
Chat Noir
avec
Rodolphe Salis
Imp. Charles Verneau, 114. Rue Oberkampf. Paris (Déposé)
Steinlen

Chéret undoubtedly elevated posters to an art form, and it wasn't long before some artists took notice. Throughout his career, the designer produced more than 2,000 posters. Although the output of Henri de Toulouse-Lautrec paled in comparison—just thirty-one designs in total—his work was no less impressive. Toulouse-Lautrec's first poster was commissioned in 1891 by impresario Charles Zidler for the reopening of his club, the Moulin Rouge. Further commissions followed, including a poster for another club, Le Divan Japonais, and an advertisement for the satirical singer Aristide Bruant, a friend of the artist, who performed at Les Ambassadeurs. Toulouse-Lautrec took inspiration from a wide variety of sources. These included an exhibition of Japanese woodblock prints that he viewed in Paris, which was part of a much larger wave of Japonisme (an enthusiasm for Japanese design).

Other artists produced outstanding work during this period, too. The Swiss-born painter and printmaker Théophile-Alexandre Steinlen is arguably most famous for his poster of 1896 titled "Tournée du Chat Noir," which advertised the popular Parisian bar's reopening. In style, it echoes the work of Toulouse-Lautrec, but it has a stronger contrast between the image of the cat and the decorative lettering adjacent to it. Even more decorative was the work of Alphonse Mucha.

Mucha traveled to Paris to study at the Académie Julian in 1887. Originally from Moravia (now part of the Czech Republic), he had previously worked for a theater company in Vienna and then undertook formal training at the Munich Academy of Fine Arts. In 1894, while visiting a print shop, he learned of the need for a poster to advertise an upcoming show at Théâtre de la Renaissance, Paris, directed by and starring the darling of French theater Sarah Bernhardt. After delivering a poster for the play *Gismonda* within two weeks, which impressed Bernhardt, he entered into a six-year collaboration and friendship with the actor. His paintings were delicately detailed and were initially referred to as the Mucha style; later they became part of the much larger art nouveau movement.

Art nouveau was reaching the apex of its popularity when the Exposition Universelle was held in Paris in 1900. At the same time, cinema was gradually transforming from a sideshow entertainment into something more substantial. Within fifteen years, it became the dominant form of mass entertainment around the world. Toulouse-Lautrec died in 1901, at only thirty-seven years of age, so he may have seen the earliest examples of filmmaking. He is generally regarded as the last great French poster artist of his era, but the poster as a medium for promoting film was only just beginning.

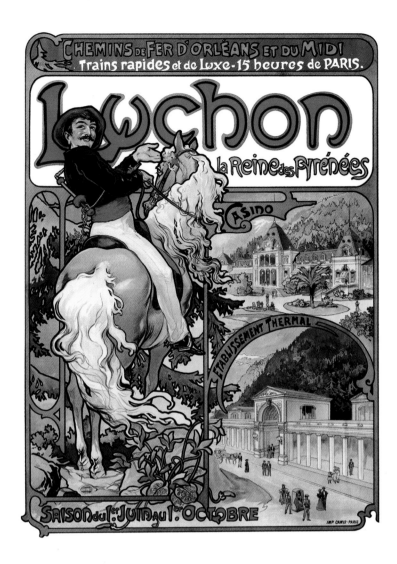

THE FIRST FILM POSTERS

Jules Chéret did not design the first film poster, but he did create the artwork for an early form of moving image. In 1877, Emile Reynaud invented the praxinoscope, a device used to project a series of images, which had been drawn onto celluloid, onto a screen. His show, *Pantomimes Lumineuses*, received its first public audience in October 1892, and Chéret's poster design was intended to entice the public to attend this new form of entertainment.

Two years later, Thomas Edison showcased his Kinetoscope in Paris. Impressed by this invention, which allowed an individual to view a film through a peephole, Louis Lumière began to develop the Cinématographe with his brother Auguste. On December 28, 1895, the Lumières gave the first public screening of their films to a paying audience. Chéret had designed a poster for the brothers, but they turned it down, instead opting for a design by Marcellin Auzolle, a commercial artist. This work is believed to be the first poster ever produced for an individual film.

What is noticeable about Auzolle's design, when compared with Chéret's poster for *Pantomimes Lumineuses*, or any of the artworks that adorned the streets of Paris over the previous thirty years, is the inclusion of the audience. They are shown to be enjoying the spectacle of a man spraying himself in the face with his own hose pipe, in a scene taken from Louis Lumière's *L'Arroseur arrosé* (*The Waterer Watered*, 1895). This encapsulated the selling point—that audiences would have a good time if they took a chance on this new form of entertainment.

Not to be outdone, in 1896 the Edison Company unveiled a motion picture projector called the Vitascope. It was accompanied by a similar image to the one designed by Auzolle, albeit on a much larger scale. Here, audiences were being sold an entertainment that was not a world away from the music halls with which they were familiar.

Short films soon followed, although initially the actors were not credited. However, when audience members began to send correspondence asking about their favorite players, the owners of the small film production companies responded and a movie industry started to take shape.

Cinématographie Lumière (1895)
Marcellin Auzolle's design not only includes an audience watching a Lumière film, but also emphasizes their active engagement with the action on screen, exhibiting a sense of wonder and joy.

BELOW

The Vitascope (1896)
Like everything Edison did, the Vitascope had to be bigger and better. Here an orchestra accompanies the images on the screen and, unlike in Auzolle's image, the picture the audience is watching is in color.

1910s

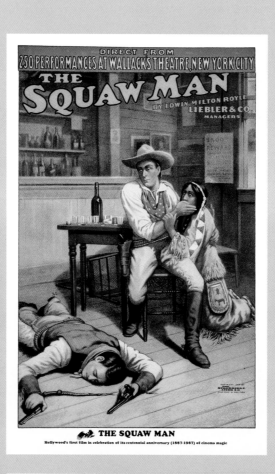

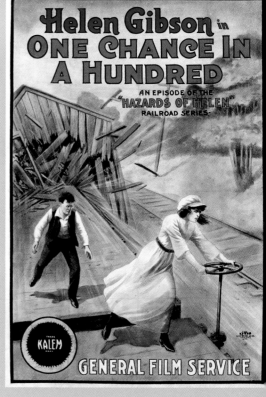

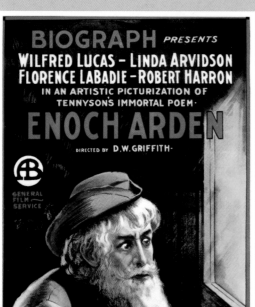

Cinema was little more than a curio following its first screenings in 1895, seen as part of a bill of entertainment in a music hall or at a traveling road show. However, the rapid growth of the filmmaking industry, the move toward feature-length films, and increased audience attendance in cinema's second full decade of existence saw it become the most popular form of entertainment.

Although watching a motion picture was seen as a working-class pastime at the beginning of the twentieth century in the United States, by 1910 the enthusiasm for movies had stretched to the middle class. Storefront cinemas and nickelodeons were attracting enough revenue for some entrepreneurs to consider establishing a dedicated building that could show an advertised program of films. One of the first movie houses was Tally's Broadway Theater in Los Angeles. Its popularity led to larger ambitions of a movie palace that would cater to all walks of life. The first was the Regent Theater, designed by Thomas Lamb, which opened in Harlem in 1913. More movie palaces followed, including Sid Grauman's first West Coast venue, Million Dollar Theater, which opened

its doors in Downtown Los Angeles in 1918. In Europe, film production and cinemas also expanded, with France leading the way. However, World War I had a detrimental impact on cinema production, as it did on most aspects of life. By the conflict's end, Hollywood's monopoly of the international film landscape was assured.

As movie theaters increased in size and films grew in length, scale, and budget, there was a greater need to attract audiences. Film production was not cheap, and the landscape had shifted dramatically from small pockets of innovators to a growth industry that employed thousands. The promotion of films became key, and film posters developed from their rudimentary origins to become important components in selling a movie. Large-scale, epic cinema enabled designers to capture the thrill of action scenes and spectacular set designs, while the emergence of screen stars offered an opportunity for studios to create a brand that audiences would return to. The role of the poster in World War I made clear its power to influence, and as the decade progressed film studios became more adept at working with designers to create images that would entice audiences into the cinema.

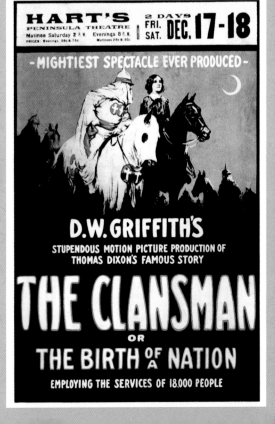

EARLY HOLLYWOOD

Cinema developed at a rapid pace in its early years, as did the way in which films were promoted. Often, audiences were drawn to a selection of short films not by their content but by the novelty and spectacle of this relatively new entertainment. However, as the medium entered its second full decade, its commercial value began to be recognized and out of it an industry started to take shape.

Those profiting from filmmaking in cinema's nascent years were the technicians and businesspeople responsible for making and selling the equipment to film and project. This balance soon shifted to the industries that were more focused on creating a product that people would pay to see. And with the constant demand for entertainment came the medium's development, expanding from short films to features.

In 1910, Hollywood was a small rural community of 5,000. Within ten years, it had burgeoned to 35,000. With its growing network of producers, technicians, and performers, by 1915 the Los Angeles/Hollywood area accounted for 60 percent of all filmmaking in the United States, and the area was the thriving hub of a nascent but already profitable industry.

Promotion for the majority of films at the beginning of the decade was rudimentary, mostly comprised of hand-drawn posters that featured a scene from the film that encapsulated its theme or genre. The serial films were a good example of this. Each episode, which was often no longer than one reel, featured a dominant situation.

As films increased in length and audiences were given more choice, so promotional posters became more detailed, played to trends, and highlighted elements that would appeal to the masses. Mack Sennett's studio, for example, identified the popularity of knockabout comedies and so became known for that style of film. Charles Chaplin had worked his way through Sennett's ranks and understood the power of promotion in developing an image. He became one of the first great stars of cinema because he focused on developing the screen persona of an amiable tramp. Promoting that image led to audience recognition and the demand to see more of him. Studios also recognized the possibility of developing actors' screen personas as a draw for audiences, and out of this grew the star system.

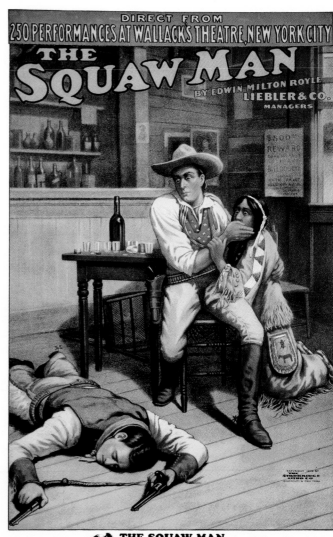

THE SQUAW MAN
Hollywood's first film in celebration of its centennial anniversary (1887-1987) of cinema magic

THE KID AUTO RACE
FEATURING
CHARLIE CHAPLIN

TRAFFIC IN SOULS
OR WHILE NEW YORK SLEEPS
A POWERFUL PHOTO-DRAMA
OF TODAY
SIX REELS OF THRILLING REALITIES
UNIVERSAL FILM MFG. CO.

Helen Gibson in
ONE CHANCE IN A HUNDRED
AN EPISODE OF THE
"HAZARDS OF HELEN"
RAILROAD SERIES.
KALEM
GENERAL FILM SERVICE

NEW CENTER THEATRE
Fifteenth St. and Troost Avenue
ONE WEEK
COMMENCING SUNDAY, MAR. 2

COLORED PEOPLE SEATED ANYWHERE IN THE HOUSE
TWICE DAILY, 2:30 AND 8:15 P. M.

Oscar Micheaux's Mammoth Photo-Play
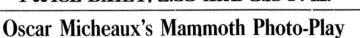
"The Homesteader"

A powerful Drama of the Great American North-west; adapted for the screen by the author from his popular new novel of the same name.

FEATURING

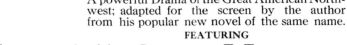
An All-Star Negro Cast!
At Popular Prices

ALSO
The Return of the "Fighting 8th"
The crack Chicago Regiment who pushed the Huns back across the Rhine and sent the Kaiser into oblivion.

AND
GEORGE GARNER, Jr.
Greatest Negro Tenor,
will sing at each performance

NOTE---This wonderful and spectacular production, the first great creation from the pen of a Negro ever screened was held up by the Board of Censors for the city of Chicago, owing to a vicious attack by three well known Negro ministers of that city, until reviewed by a committee of the better class of both races, who unanimously proclaimed it to be the most masterful portrayal for many a day. The part objected to by these three ministers was, that it attacked the moral conduct of a certain well known minister—one of the three happening to be the one attacked. Needless to say the production was duly released and is now playing to great crowds at more than a dozen houses in that city, black and white.

Beautiful EVELYN PREER
Appearing as "Orlean," whose Characterization is Complete.

OSCAR MICHEAUX
Author of "THE HOMESTEADER"

MISS INEZ SMITH
Portraying the Evil "Ethel," Whose "Close-ups" Will Long Be Remembered.

CHAS. D. LUCAS
Whose vivid portrayal of "Jean Baptiste," the man who went, is without doubt the most perfect work ever done by a Negro.

MISS IRIS HALL
As "Agnes," the Tenderest Little Heroine Ever Created.

GEORGE R. GARNER, JR.
The Race's Greatest Tenor, who will sing at each performance.

TOP LEFT

Kid Auto Races at Venice (1914)
Chaplin's Tramp made his first public appearance in this film, produced by Mack Sennett. All the elements are there, but they were refined in subsequent appearances.

TOP MIDDLE

Traffic in Souls (1913)
The artwork highlights the film's length (six reels, or 88 minutes), which was longer than most US films at that time. It also employs clever frame-within-a-frame artwork to suggest the arrival of the police.

TOP RIGHT

The Hazards of Helen (1915)
Just one of the predicaments Helen Holmes' character finds herself in over the course of her hugely successful three-year run. The artwork for each adventure sums up what audiences can expect.

ABOVE

The Homesteader (1919)
This newspaper ad is an important artifact that highlights the existence of African American cinema, and the small industry making it, outside of mainstream Hollywood.

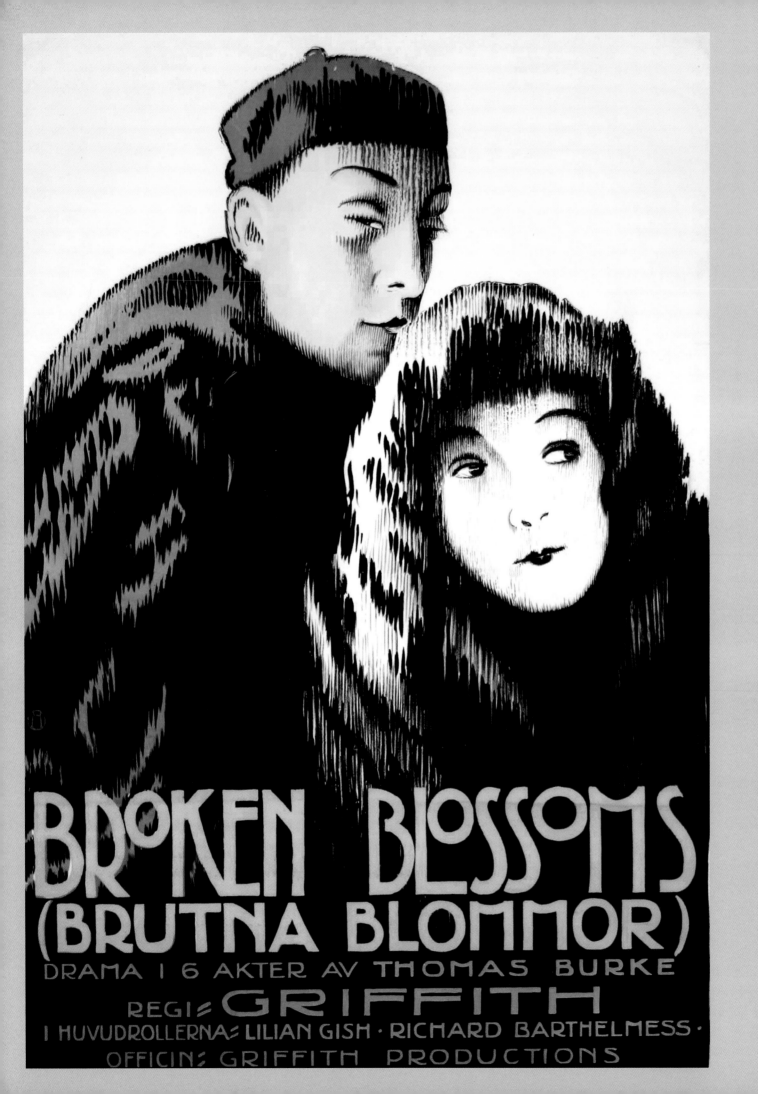

BROKEN BLOSSOMS
(BRUTNA BLOMMOR)
DRAMA I 6 AKTER AV THOMAS BURKE
REGI: GRIFFITH
I HUVUDROLLERNA: LILIAN GISH · RICHARD BARTHELMESS ·
OFFICIN: GRIFFITH PRODUCTIONS

D. W. GRIFFITH

As a pioneer of early cinema and the style of filmmaking that became the bedrock of classical Hollywood, D. W. Griffith is a key figure. He not only developed advanced camera, narrative, and editing techniques, but he also understood the power of promotion and went to great lengths to publicize his work.

He entered the industry in 1908, initially as a stage extra, but by the end of the year he had directed almost fifty shorts. *Old California* (1910) was the first film shot in Hollywood, and in 1914 he directed his first feature, *Judith of Bethulia* (1914). A year later, he made his name with *The Birth of a Nation* (1915). Its dubious subject matter and influence notwithstanding (see pages 24-25), the film was an extraordinary achievement and a huge success.

Unlike those of his peers, Griffith's name as a director had now become a commodity. He was not merely the man behind his films, but a public figure whose initials appeared on intertitles. His fame spread with his subsequent epic *Intolerance* (1916). Aside from the conventional artwork for the film, he embarked on an elaborate road show to promote it. Although *Intolerance* was critically acclaimed and performed well, the cost of production and promotion dwarfed any box office revenue. Griffith had personally invested in the film and its promotion, which left him in dire financial straits for the remainder of his life.

Although the rest of Griffith's career never achieved the commercial heights of these earlier features, his ambition and innovation remained undiminished into the 1920s. *Broken Blossoms* (1919) began a string of dramas featuring impressive set pieces. Moreover, it was a sign of Griffith's position in the public eye that his name on a poster for a film would likely attract a larger audience than the stars who appeared in it. This is evinced by the poster for *Orphans of the Storm* (1921), an epic set before and during the French Revolution. Lillian and Dorothy Gish, who were popular actors at the time, appear beneath the film's title, while Griffith's signature dominates the upper third of the poster. His name may not take up as much space on the posters for *Way Down East* (1920) or *Broken Blossoms*, but it nevertheless looms large.

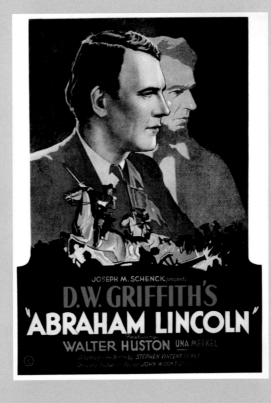

THE EARLY EPIC

Cinema is spectacle. With the emergence of the feature-length film, the industry grew rapidly in scale. Although Hollywood later dominated the majority of epic films, the earliest examples came from Italy. Drawing on ancient history, their directors cast thousands of extras and built immense sets in order to create the most lavish spectacles.

The pioneers of these Italian films were Enrico Guazzoni and Giovanni Pastrone. Guazzoni's *Quo Vadis?* (1912) unfolds in early Christian Rome. It was the first film to run for longer than two hours and featured a cast of 5,000 extras. Pastrone had already whet his appetite for the historical epic with his short *The Fall of Troy* (1911). However, *Cabiria* (1914) was on a scale few filmmakers of the time could imagine. Shot in Turin, but set in Sicily, Carthage, and Cirta at the time of the Second Punic War, this early example of the blockbuster features operatic religious ceremonies, Hannibal's trek across the Alps, sieges, battles, and even the eruption of Mount Etna. Generally credited with creating the "epic" movie, Pastrone also used moving cameras in a way that had not been seen before.

The posters for *Cabiria* are no less impressive. A particular focus is the entrance to the Temple of Moloch. Rising above it is the statue of a figure with three eyes. Surrounded by fire, it is a monstrous, unearthly sight—exactly the kind of image to attract an audience clamoring for something new.

After his success with the divisive *The Birth of a Nation* (1915) and clearly having seen Pastrone's epic, D. W. Griffith embarked on his own multi-narrative historical drama. *Intolerance* (1916) unfolds in ancient Babylonia, during the time of Jesus, the lead-up to the St. Bartholomew's Day Massacre in sixteenth-century France, and the present day. Promotional artwork for the film either used individual characters from the four segments in dramatic postures, or took selections of stills from the film that emphasized the vast scale of Griffith's undertaking. At the same time, the director toured the United States to promote the film—an early example of the press circuit that accompanies the release of films today. Other directors soon followed Pastrone and Griffith's example, and the epic became a staple of silent cinema.

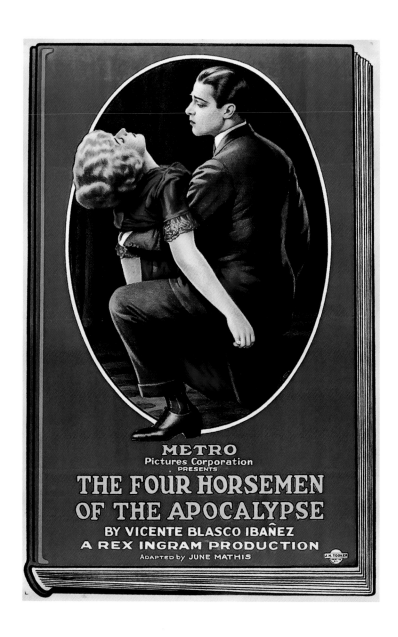

ABOVE

The Four Horsemen of the Apocalypse (1921)
Rex Ingram's World War I drama was one of the first epics of the 1920s. Rather than emphasize scale, this poster hints at the film's literary origins.

OPPOSITE

Cabiria (1914)
This poster promoting a restored version of Pastrone's historical drama emphasizes the scale of his endeavor, hints at the size of the cast, and highlights the film's most memorable set.

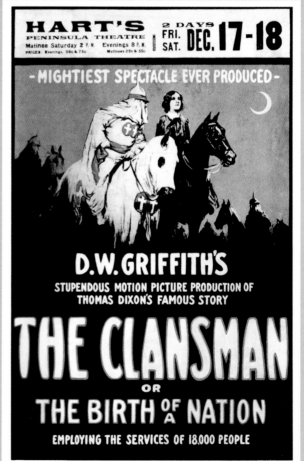

POSTERS OF THE DECADE

By the end of the 1910s, following significant developments in the medium, two films had made a huge impact on the psyches of cinemagoers. One was a plea for peace in the world after years of savage conflict. The other was an attempt to rewrite history, defame an entire race, and, intentionally or otherwise, encourage the resurgence of an organization fueled by prejudice and hate.

The Birth of a Nation (1915) is an extraordinary film on a technical level. It introduced a grammar to cinema that had previously only been toyed with. Furthermore, the complexity of its editing and narrative storytelling were far beyond the reach of most films of that time. But it is racist, revisionist, and untruthful. It was adapted from Southern Baptist minister and North Carolina state legislator Reverend Thomas Dixon Jr.'s novel and stage play *The Clansman* (1905). Along with his earlier novel, *The Leopard's Spots: A Romance of the White Man's Burden—1865–1900* (1905), it lionizes the Ku Klux Klan and resistance to the Reconstruction era that followed in the wake of the South's defeat in the American Civil War. Griffith's film is divided into two sections. The first

details history as it happened and the events that led to the outbreak of conflict. But after the assassination of President Abraham Lincoln in the film, Griffith presents an alternative account of events, vilifying the emancipated black population and portraying the Klan as the saviors of white women's virtue.

The posters advertising Griffith's epic mirror the film's politics. The Klansmen are the knights in white. In one image, an American flag is draped around a naked white woman in bondage, while the featured still from the film shows the official surrender of the Confederates at the Appomattox Court House. It is an early example of the power of propaganda.

Abel Gance's *J'accuse!* (1919) is suffused with the suffering that mainland Europe experienced during World War I. It was the first of his epics, which culminated in the extraordinary *Napoleon* (1927). With its powerful final sequence of the ghosts of the dead rising from the battlefields, Gance's film presents a staunchly forthright plea for peace. The film was promoted through the images of the suffering of men, haunted by the horror they had witnessed.

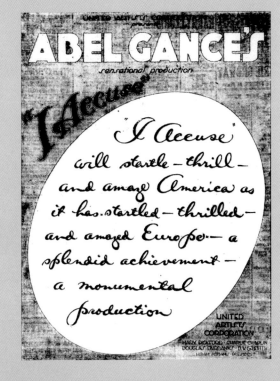

1920s

Arguably more than any other decade, the 1920s saw various art movements converge with movie poster design to create extraordinary images for films, drawing out their psychological, social, and political themes. It also witnessed Hollywood increase its foothold as the world's largest film industry.

German expressionism and Soviet constructivism had a profound effect upon cinema. The former did not influence international cinema initially, but by the 1930s and 1940s the use of light and shadow could be seen in horror, film noir, and the thriller genre in general. Fritz Lang's *Metropolis* (1927) drew from elements of expressionism, and its impact upon world cinema, along with that of F. W. Murnau's films, ensured that the movement remained a landmark in film history. In addition, the poster for Lang's science fiction epic became one of the designs most sought after by collectors.

The Russian Revolution changed every aspect of that country's life and culture. Lenin was an enthusiastic supporter of cinema and saw in it the first art form that could represent the masses. Artists such as Alexander Rodchenko and the Stenberg brothers worked with major

Soviet filmmakers in promoting this new kind of cinema. As Sergei Eisenstein, Dziga Vertov, Lev Kuleshov, and Vsevolod Pudovkin transformed the language of film, the artists designing posters for their films moved away from representation and more toward interpretation. In doing so, they created some of the most striking images in the history of movie poster design.

Charles Chaplin's Tramp is arguably the first globally recognized film character and Chaplin one of the most important stars of the decade. However, he was not alone, as each studio—and studios in every film-producing country—rushed to promote its stars in order to dominate the box office. Rudolph Valentino, Asta Nielsen, and Greta Garbo proved that sex sells, and designers went as far as was permissible in promoting these actors as sex symbols. At the same time, moral groups became more vocal in decrying the immorality of cinema.

Cinema itself became increasingly vocal toward the end of the decade, as synchronized sound was introduced. It wasn't perfect at first, but this development would forever change the experience of going to the movies.

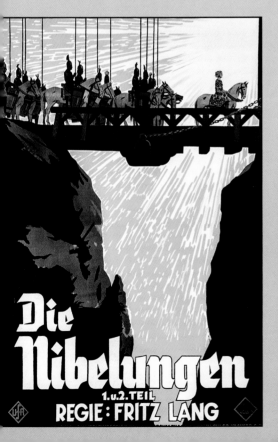

THE RISE OF THE STAR

The movie star was born the moment producers realized that an audience would pay to see their favorite actor as keenly as they would a genre they enjoyed. Over subsequent decades, the way a star was sold became increasingly complex, but in the nascent years of silent features the methodology was simple: if the audience likes the actor, they will want to see more of them. Moreover, people began to associate stars with a particular kind of filmmaking. They were no longer just a name or a face that the audience recognized; they came to represent a brand with which people could identify.

Lon Chaney was an early example of a star associated not so much with the way he looked, but with the kind of characters he played and the genre of film he appeared in. A vaudeville performer, Chaney became known for his mastery with makeup. After his breakthrough performance in *The Miracle Man* (1919), the actor took on more daring roles, most notably in *The Hunchback of Notre Dame* (1923) and *The Phantom of the Opera* (1925), both of which Universal sold on his ability to transform into character.

   As evinced by their performances opposite one another in *He Who Gets Slapped* (1924), Chaney and John Gilbert existed on different sides of the acting spectrum. Known as "the Great Lover," Gilbert was one of silent Hollywood's great romantic leads—a dashing star with a silky presence. He started out in film in 1915, and roles in serious dramas toward the end of the decade attracted praise. However, it was his move to MGM and his collaboration with Greta Garbo (see pages 32–33) that earned him his stellar reputation.

   Douglas Fairbanks was the audience's action star. His persona was that of the unruffled hero, able to carry out any mission—usually in the name of love—while maintaining a smile and an easy manner throughout. An actor since the age of fifteen, he dominated the adventure genre in the 1920s with his athletic performances. Fairbanks' marriage to Mary Pickford made the pair Hollywood royalty, and it also transformed them both into superstars.

   Pickford was the bigger star before she and Fairbanks were married. She had been acting in film since 1909, but it wasn't until she took control of her own career while

The Phantom of the Opera (1925)
In many of the posters promoting Chaney's most iconic roles, his appearance is either disfigured or masked. Here, the flow of water hints at an almost supernatural presence.

ABOVE

The Taming of the Shrew (1929)
The only film to feature the husband and wife stars was not a success, but the artwork perfectly captures their screen personas: the laid-back, easygoing action figure and the more dramatic actress.

TOP RIGHT

The Wind (1928)
Lillian Gish was the dramatic icon of her generation, and the posters for her films always feature her in a state of unease or distress—often one of the more suspenseful moments from the film.

BOTTOM RIGHT

The Big Parade (1925)
There is war and drama in King Vidor's film. But John Gilbert was one of the era's great screen lovers, so the poster's central image is the actor in a pose with which most audiences identify him.

under contract with what would become Paramount Pictures that she achieved stardom. She was known for playing much younger characters, of both sexes, and feisty young female roles. She and Fairbanks appeared together on screen only once, as their careers were in decline, in an adaptation of *The Taming of the Shrew* (1929). Although the film was poorly received, its artwork perfectly captures their screen personas.

Lillian Gish and Gloria Swanson also existed at opposite ends of the scale in terms of their star personas. Gish's career would eventually span seventy-five years. Known as "the First Lady of American Cinema," she was also regarded as one of its finest actors. Her fame initially came through a series of performances she gave for D. W. Griffith, from *An Unseen Enemy* (1912) to *Orphans of the Storm* (1921), in the latter of which she is credited with developing screen acting techniques. Gish then moved to MGM in order to have more creative control, and there she oversaw and starred in *La Bohème* (1926), *The Scarlet Letter* (1926), and *The Wind* (1928). The artwork for these, like for her earlier roles, tends to focus on the actor in a moment of high drama.

Swanson, by contrast, was known as much for the outfits that she wore as for her performances. Originally starring in Keystone comedies, she moved to Paramount Pictures, where Cecil B. DeMille transformed her screen persona. Swanson starred in six films for him, from *Don't Change Your Husband* (1919) to *The Affairs of Anatol* (1921), and enjoyed an equally lucrative partnership with Sam Wood. *Sadie Thompson* (1928) saw Swanson become her own producer, but style remained key to her image.

Of the international stars, Asta Nielsen and Emil Jannings possessed two of the strongest screen personas. Nielsen was born in Denmark, but the majority of her career took place in Germany, where she was simply referred to as "the Asta." She was the tragic star, but she also gave performances that were sexually frank for the time. The subtlety of Nielsen's performances also helped shift screen acting from a more declamatory style to the nuanced approach that became the norm when sound was first introduced.

Jannings was one of the more problematic screen figures of the era. He was awarded the very first Academy Award for Best Actor in 1929 for his work in *The Way of All Flesh* (1927) and *The Last Command* (1928). They were his first films for Paramount, and followed a stunning career in Germany. Jannings' most notable work includes three films directed by F. W. Murnau: *The Last Laugh* (1924), *Tartuffe* (1925), and *Faust* (1926), as well as starring opposite Marlene Dietrich in *The Blue Angel* (1930). However, his association with the Nazis forever marred his reputation.

ABOVE

The Way of All Flesh (1927)
Although Victor Fleming's film is now lost, the artwork highlights Emil Jannings' versatility as an actor, playing two distinct roles. The religious element is played down by its appearance behind the credits.

OPPOSITE

The Joyless Street (1925)
A beautifully designed artwork for G. W. Pabst's tragic melodrama, one of the first films of the New Objectivity movement that sought realism in art, offers a suitably iconic portrait of Asta Nielsen.

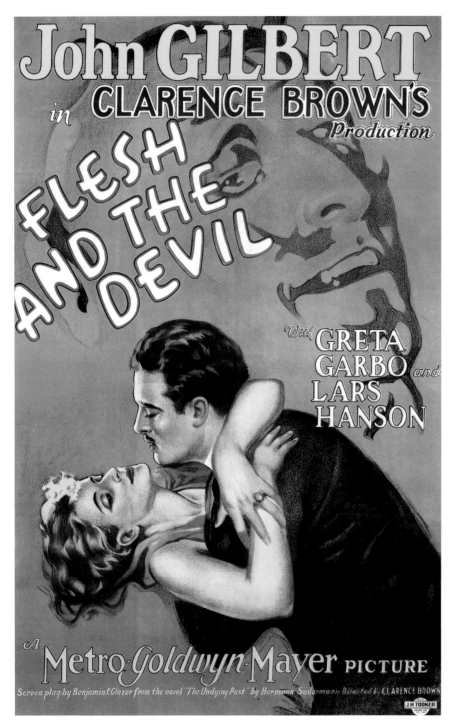

ABOVE

Flesh and the Devil (1926)
Audiences knew what to expect from John Gilbert, but even by his standards sparks flew when he played opposite Greta Garbo. The title of the film adds extra frisson to the sexual chemistry between them.

TOP RIGHT

The Son of the Sheik (1926)
The bared chest is a classic Valentino pose—one that appears on a number of the posters for his most famous films. As the star, he is facing the audience as much as he is his captive.

BOTTOM RIGHT

She Done Him Wrong (1933)
Mae West came from vaudeville and took early sound cinema by storm. This poster is provocative, and the way in which West is portrayed highlights the early sound era's ability to explore sexuality frankly.

SEX AND THE CINEMA

Sex has always played a significant role in cinema and, along with it, censorial attitudes toward what should be allowed on the screen. *The Kiss* (1896) was the first film to show a man and woman kissing, and it caused uproar among moral and religious groups.

By the 1920s it was clear that sex sold. Outside of the illicit industry producing "stag" or "risque" films that featured unsimulated sex acts, Hollywood saw box office potential in pushing the envelope of what was morally acceptable. D. W. Griffith featured a seduction scene in *Way Down East* (1920), while in *Manslaughter* (1922) Cecil B. DeMille included an extraordinary orgy scene. Both films justified these inclusions by having their characters face moral consequences. Likewise, DeMille's subsequent biblical epics were able to indulge in debauched excess because the participants would soon face the wrath of God.

Rudolph Valentino's breakthrough performance in *The Sheik* (1921) not only made him the biggest star of the silent era, but he also became cinema's first sex symbol, with posters promoting his physical beauty. A romantic melodrama and adventure that hasn't quite stood the test of time, *The Sheik* caused a sensation when it was released. *Blood and Sand* (1922) cemented Valentino's position as the romantic lead of the era, this time playing a Spanish matador whose conquests behind closed doors were as furious as those inside the ring. However, it was the actor's final film, *The Son of the Sheik* (1926), that— along with the earlier *The Eagle* (1925)—produced his best work and forever defined his image.

In the same year, Greta Garbo provoked audiences in *Flesh and the Devil* (1926), as part of a romantic triangle that features a subtle homosexual subtext. The on-screen chemistry between Garbo and costar John Gilbert was clear, and they began a much-publicized affair, which only helped to promote the film. *Flesh and the Devil* was noted at the time for the intensity of its lovemaking scenes, but they soon appeared modest to audiences.

Other stars of the 1920s attracted similar attention for the sexualized roles they took on, most notably Louise Brooks in G. W. Pabst's *Pandora's Box* and *Diary of a Lost Girl* (both 1929). With the arrival of sound, Mae West caused uproar with her frankness, but the Hays Code soon took control of what audiences saw and heard at the movies.

THE COMEDY STAR

The first comedy was Louis Lumière's *L'arroseur arrosé* or *The Waterer Watered* (1895), in which a man is sprayed in the face by a hose pipe. Although rudimentary, it perfectly encapsulates the style of physical comedy that dominated pre-sound cinema.

The 1910s saw an industry develop around comedy shorts, with Mack Sennett's Keystone Cops offering their own brand of madcap sketches and chases. Following Charles Chaplin's creation of a recognizable persona (see overleaf), which had already been pioneered by Max Linder in France, various comedy actors made a break for stardom. Some remained in supporting roles, while others found greater fame with the arrival of sound. However, in the 1920s, three figures achieved stardom comparable to Chaplin's, particularly in the way they were promoted.

Harry Langdon is the least remembered. Yet in the 1920s he was easily recognized, playing a man with an innocent, almost child-like view of the world. His style of physical comedy was less furious than that of his peers. A late starter in film, which he entered in the early 1920s, he became a star through his work at Keystone. *Tramp, Tramp, Tramp* (1926) is a typical example of his relaxed style on screen, playing a loser who dreams of marrying Joan Crawford's billboard model. In the same year, he appeared in his most acclaimed film, *The Strong Man* (1926), directed by Frank Capra.

By the time Harold Lloyd made *The Freshman* (1925), he had been playing his bespectacled hero for five years. His films were not as successful as those of Chaplin but he was far more prolific in his output, which made him the bigger box office star in the 1920s. Key to Lloyd's appeal was the inventively choreographed chase sequences that appeared in each film and a persona that was eminently likable.

Buster Keaton also performed extraordinary stunts, often at great personal risk, in his films. He was the deadpan genius. Once a sidekick, gag writer, and unofficial second director to Fatty Arbuckle, in 1920 Keaton broke away, first appearing in a combination of comedy shorts and features for the first few years before focusing on more complex films. His serious expression was used to brilliant effect throughout his best work in the 1920s, which includes *Sherlock Jr.* (1924), *The General* (1926), and *The Cameraman* (1928).

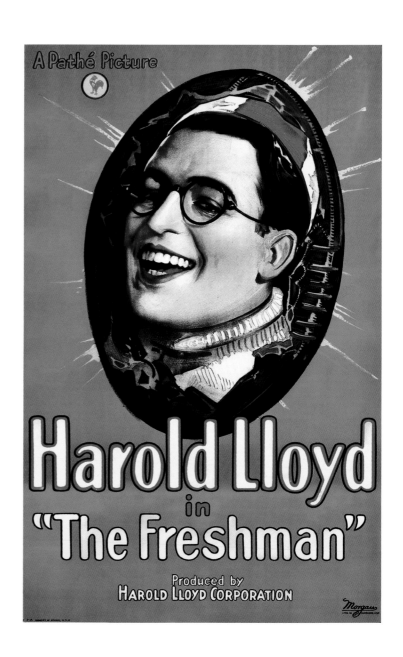

TOP
Steamboat Bill, Jr. (1928)
Buster Keaton looks typically deadpan in this poster for his comedy, the last produced by Keaton's own company. The other version of the poster features costar Marion Byron with fiery red hair.

BOTTOM
Tramp, Tramp, Tramp (1926)
Harry Langdon's guileless expression sums up the character he played in his most famous films: an innocent caught up in a hectic world. That world, denoted here by the shapeless map of America, is the country's open roads.

ZLATÉ OPOJENÍ

KLASICKÝ FILM CHARLIE CHAPLINA

AMERICKÝ FILM

© GRYGAR 73

Vydala Ústřední půjčovna filmů - Výstřky OTK 23

CHARLES CHAPLIN

CHAPLIN AROUND THE WORLD

OPPOSITE

The Gold Rush
(1925/1973)
This could be read as
Chaplin's world turned
upside down. The presence
of the bear is the only
direct link to the film.
More important is the
sense that the Tramp is
the key selling point. The
setting is secondary.

BELOW LEFT

The Great Dictator
(1940/1968)
This French poster
from the 1960s cleverly
employs a blank face
—save the mustache—
for the dictator, thus
suggesting both Chaplin
and Hitler. The star
appears to be the person
cultivating the image.

BELOW RIGHT

The Kid (1921)
This beautiful, simple
design for the original
release of Chaplin's first
feature needs nothing
more than Chaplin
standing guard over
Jackie Coogan. The
backdrop includes few
details, hinting at the
world without possessions
in which they exist.

Charles Chaplin might not have been the first film star, but he became the most recognized screen presence in cinema by understanding the power of an easily identifiable public persona. He learned it during his time on the London stage, and it didn't take him long to work out what would appeal to cinema audiences.

Chaplin was offered a job with the New York Motion Picture Company during his second US stage tour. He initially worked for Mack Sennett at Keystone before switching to Essanay, then Mutual, and First National. Finally, he formed United Artists with Douglas Fairbanks, Mary Pickford, and D. W. Griffith, which allowed him artistic freedom over the films he made.

Chaplin first appeared on film in the one-reeler *Making a Living* (1914). Although he received positive notices, he disliked the experience. For his second appearance, he selected his own outfit, which included baggy trousers, a tight jacket, a hat that was too small for him, and oversized shoes. The film was *Mabel's Strange Predicament* (1914), although audiences first saw the Tramp costume in *Kid Auto Races at Venice* (1914, see page 19), by which

time the look had developed further. Chaplin's appearance in *The Tramp* and *The Bank* (both 1915) molded the characteristics of his persona, particularly his optimism for a happier life and his acceptance of his failure to achieve it. He quickly became the most popular character in Sennett's retinue of performers.

The Kid (1921) was Chaplin's first feature as an actor and director. His intention was to make a film that balanced comedy and drama. Apparently inspired by the death of his baby son just ten days before production began, Chaplin's decision to introduce more pathos into his work chimed with audiences who flocked to see the film. It ended the year second only to *The Four Horsemen of the Apocalypse* (1921) at the US box office, and by the middle of the decade it had been screened to great success in more than fifty countries.

Chaplin continued to play the Tramp character in shorts and features until *Modern Times* (1936). Since then, his persona has resonated across cultures and generations, viewed as an everyman figure striving to make his way in the world.

THE INFLUENCE OF ART

Various art movements intersected, clashed, and emerged throughout the first two decades of the twentieth century. Their impact upon cinema often depended on a particular country, with some movements having a profound and long-lasting effect, while others burned brightly for a short time before fading. Beyond the obvious influence of German expressionism and Soviet constructivism, dadaism, futurism, precisionism, suprematism, surrealism, Bauhaus, and art nouveau all played varying roles in cinema and poster design.

Both Pablo Picasso and Georges Braque were fascinated by early film, with its accentuation of movement and multiple perspectives. If the link remained little more than tangential, three derivatives of cubism—futurism, precisionism, and suprematism—played a more significant role, particularly among avant-garde filmmakers. One of the finest examples from this period is Fernand Léger and Dudley Murphy's *Ballet mécanique* (1924). In particular, the film's play with the movement of humans and machines can be seen to reflect futurist notions of the mechanization of society.

The term "art deco" wasn't coined until the 1960s, when the movement was revived. But the style came to prominence in the 1920s, occupying a commanding position in Western culture. It was never one specific style, but a mixture of many different sources and influences. These ranged from art nouveau (see page 13) and cubism to recent archeological discoveries from Egypt and art from both Africa and East Asia. A key event was L'Exposition Internationale des Arts Décoratifs et Industriels Modernes (the International Exhibition of Modern Decorative and Industrial Arts), which took place in Paris from April to October 1925. It celebrated what was then referred to as the "style moderne" and brought together designers from across Europe who displayed examples of their work, including clothing, jewelry, and artworks.

Art deco was arguably the most popular art form of the 1920s. In New York, its influence rose above all others as skyscrapers were built in the style. The American Radiator Building (1924), Chrysler Building (1928–1930), and Rockefeller Center (1933) were all designed in the art deco style. It seemed to fuse with jazz, pushing

ABOVE

The Cabinet of Dr. Caligari (1920)
A wildly different, yet stylish, interpretation of Robert Wiene's German expressionist classic finds the titular character filtered through the prism of art deco design.

OPPOSITE

Hallelujah (1929)
Art deco meets the jazz age in this poster for King Vidor's film, which was one of the major Hollywood studios' first all-black movies. The poster captures the musicality of the film and the hedonism of the age.

the music into the mainstream and promoting it as part of a lifestyle that encompassed all aspects of design. Art deco was also present in graphic design. One pioneer was George Barbier, who first exhibited his illustrations in 1911 and was later celebrated for his work in the French fashion magazines *Gazette du Bon Ton* and *L'Illustration*. He didn't so much reflect a world with his immaculately detailed illustrations as help to define it.

Other designers celebrated the modern age of transport, with posters highlighting the luxury of travel by steamship or airplane. Cabarets and nightclubs were portrayed with hedonistic glee, and cinema was sold as the era's pre-eminent form of entertainment. The art deco posters created for film appeared in two forms. First, there were the posters that fitted the style, no matter the film. As such, they were not dissimilar to the Soviet constructivist designs, which elevated form over content. These art deco designs may not have been as radical as the Soviet constructivist artworks, but they were more expressive than representative. Second, there were the posters created for films that were themselves imbued with art deco style. More often than not this would take the form of set design or costume. However, it could also reflect the tone of the film, which the posters would capture in order to "sell" a particular film's lifestyle to cinema audiences.

The Bauhaus skirted the fringes of film (László Moholy-Nagy had for years tried to establish an "Experimental Station for Cinema"), although there was an occasional attempt to engage with the form. In 1929, a small selection of films was screened at the groundbreaking Film und Foto (International Exhibition of the German Industrial Confederation) in Stuttgart. Although photography was its main focus, the emphasis placed on typography impacted the way in which posters across all areas of culture and society were designed.

The surrealist movement dabbled only tangentially with film, yet it produced one of the medium's finest filmmakers in Luis Buñuel. His collaboration with Salvador Dalí on *Un chien andalou* (1929) remains one of the high points of avant-garde filmmaking from this era. Buñuel subsequently surpassed it with *L'Age d'or* (1930) and other films that draw on surrealist ideas while carving his own unique path. He also embarked on a successful collaboration with designer René Ferracci, which brought out the surrealist influence in the artwork for his final films (see page 202). Meanwhile, Dalí's only other significant contribution to a film was his short-lived involvement with Alfred Hitchcock on *Spellbound* (1945), during which he helped to design the sets for the sequences that detail the dreams experienced by Gregory Peck's character.

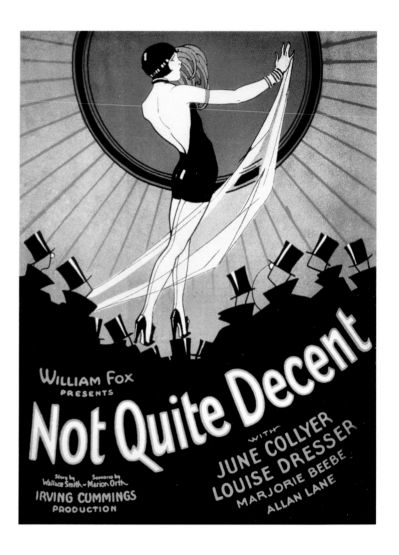

ABOVE

Not Quite Decent (1929)
Designed for one of the earliest films to feature sound, albeit only for part of the film, this poster captures the influence of art deco on fashion and style in the 1920s. It hints at a bright new world.

ABOVE

Film und Foto (1929)
This is the main image for a key exhibition of US and European photography, as well as film and the visual arts. Its oblique angle and the posture of the photographer with his camera make it confrontational.

INTERNATIONALE AUSSTELLUNG
DES DEUTSCHEN WERKBUNDS

FILM UND FOTO

STUTTGART 1929

FOTO-AUSSTELLUNG VOM 18. MAI BIS 7. JULI

IN DEN NEUEN AUSSTELLUNGSHALLEN AUF DEM INTERIMTHEATERPLATZ

FILM-SONDERVORFÜHRUNGEN VOM 13. BIS 26. JUNI

IN DEN KÖNIGSBAULICHTSPIELEN

OFFSETREPRODUKTION DER FA. G. REISACHER STUTTGART   DRUCK DER UNION STUTTGART

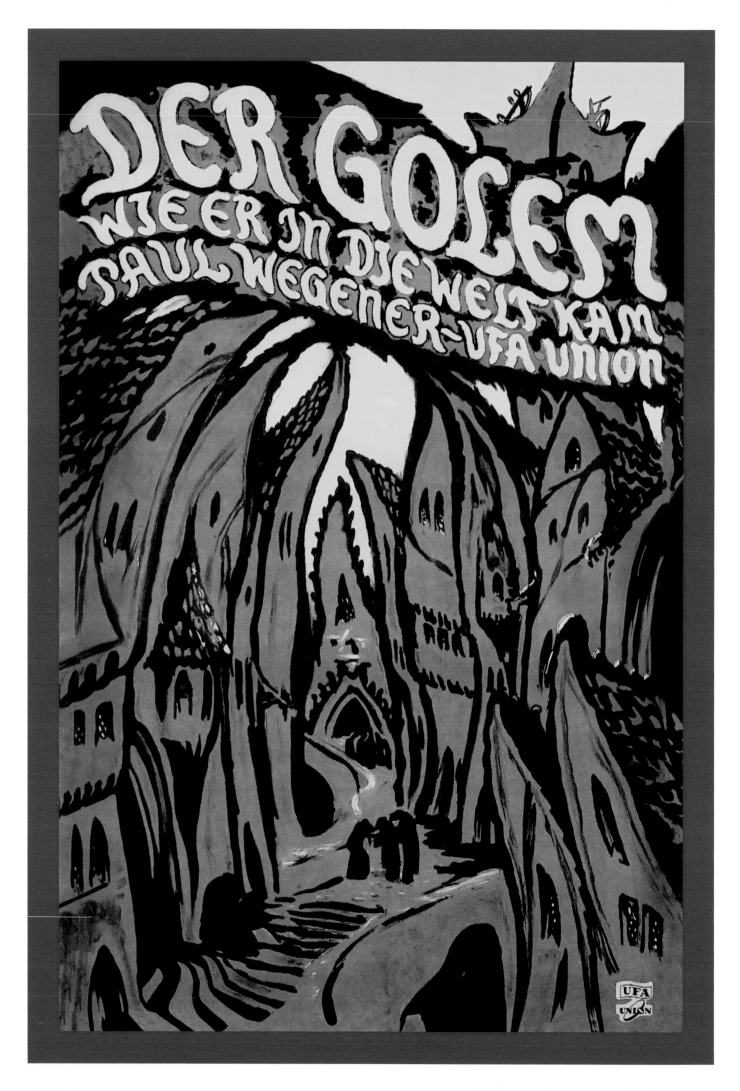

GERMAN EXPRESSIONISM

Unlike other art movements of the time, German expressionism barely traveled beyond the country's own borders, although subsequent decades saw its influence reach far and wide. This was because the country was isolated from much of Europe after World War I. As a result, Germany's domestic film industry grew in scale. By the 1920s, it was regarded as one of the most influential national cinemas, producing films that outstripped those of most other countries in creativity and innovation.

Expressionism is a modernist movement that began around the beginning of the twentieth century. Its origins are found in poetry and painting. Rather than represent reality, expressionism sought a subjective view of the world. For cinema, this meant the outward projection of a character's psyche—the physical transformation of a given world through the manipulation of light, shadow, and architecture.

An early example of a German expressionist film is Stellan Rye and Paul Wegener's *The Student of Prague* (1913), which tells the tale of a poor student who is fooled by a sorcerer who steals his shadow. The poster for the film features the protagonist and differs only slightly from other film posters of the era. But, like the film, its tone hints at the development of a new visual style. By the time Robert Wiene's *The Cabinet of Dr. Caligari* (1920) was released, German expressionism had reached its apex. Accentuating shadows—even painting them onto set walls—and constructing misshapen buildings, the film reflects the tortured mind of its storyteller and the warped nature of his narrative. Stahl-Arpke's poster for the film plays up this oddly shaped world and the horror it contains.

Wegener and Carl Boese's *The Golem* (1920) proved to be no less chilling in its interpretation of the world. The posters designed to accompany the film draw heavily on expressionist art, particularly the work of Norwegian painter Edvard Munch.

Although these films remain the true examples of German expressionism, other films took elements from the style. Many of the practitioners involved in their production made their way to Hollywood in order to escape the Nazis, and their influence can be felt in the way in which horror films and film noir developed.

OPPOSITE

The Golem (1920)
Edvard Munch is an appropriate influence for this artwork. The Norwegian artist specialized in exploring psychological themes, which are also key to many German expressionist films.

ABOVE

The Cabinet of Dr. Caligari (1920)
Stahl-Arpke's design adds color to Robert Wiene's monochrome world. The minimal palette adds to the grotesque nature of this distorted and unsettling environment.

FRITZ LANG

Of all the directors to emerge from the German film industry in the 1920s, Fritz Lang remains the most famous. His work may lack the lyricism and visual poetry of F. W. Murnau, but it was produced on a monumental scale and possesses a grandiosity that is breathtaking to watch. Lang's career can be divided into three periods: silent and early sound films in Berlin; the period he spent in the United States following his flight from the Nazis; and his return in the late 1950s to Germany where he completed his final three films.

Lang first considered a career in film while recovering from wounds received fighting with Austrian forces in 1916. After a brief spell acting on stage in Vienna, he became a writer, eventually moving into direction at the legendary Ufa studio. His early films are mostly lost, but they were predominantly genre fare, particularly adventure stories such as the *Spiders* series (1919–1920). However, *Destiny* (1921) hinted at what was to come. Like Lang's subsequent film, the epic two-part *Dr. Mabuse: The Gambler* (1922), *Destiny* sees the director drawing heavily on German expressionism. That influence is also

apparent in the vast cinematic canvas he created for another two-part film, *Die Nibelungen* (1924), the poster for which presents a Teutonic vision of the world.

It took Lang a further three years to produce the medium's first great science fiction film and a visionary work. *Metropolis* (1927) features an extraordinary array of effects in its creation of a future city. However, it was criticized initially for its storytelling and length, and ultimately failed to recoup its sizable budget at the box office. Nevertheless, *Metropolis* remains one of the finest films of the silent era and features beautiful promotional artwork. The main image (see page 52) is one of the most sought-after posters by collectors. Likewise, the artwork for Lang's lesser known *Woman in the Moon* (1929), another science fiction film, captures the wonder of space travel. And the various artwork that accompanied *The Testament of Dr. Mabuse* (1933), Lang's sequel to his crime epic of 1922, is unsettling. Although the Nazis banned *The Testament of Dr. Mabuse*, the director was offered the job of heading up Ufa. But by that point Lang was preparing to flee to the United States.

BELOW LEFT

The Testament of Dr. Mabuse (1933)
The film opens in an asylum for the insane, and so the artwork for the film hints at the many personalities of its twisted eponymous character.

BELOW RIGHT

Die Nibelungen (1924)
Like the film, this poster channels the iconography of the great German myth. It is a very different world to that depicted in the more expressionist posters of the time, but perfectly captures the epic tone of its subject.

OPPOSITE
LEFT TO RIGHT

Woman in the Moon (1929)
Alfred Herrmann's design captures the wonder and spectacle of space travel. The poster for Fritz Lang's second science fiction adventure employs a pair of shaded bands around the rocket; the yellow and white behind it hint at velocity.

Metropolis (1927)
This is a future world as a dream. A stark contrast to the more popular image for the film (see page 52), this artwork interlays a woman's face with an abstract structure to produce a striking image.

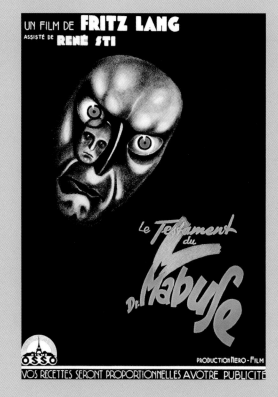

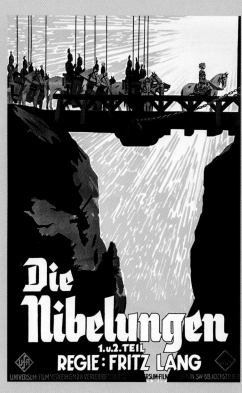

FRAU IM MOND

EIN FILM VON
FRITZ LANG
MANUSKRIPT: THEA v. HARBOU
HAUPTDARSTELLER:
GERDA MAURUS WILLY FRITSCH

METROPOLIS
EIN FILM VON FRITZ LANG
MANUSKRIPT: THEA v. HARBOU ★ MUSIK: GOTTFRIED HUPPERTZ
WOCHENTAGS 5 8³⁰ SONNABENDS u. SONNTAGS 3 6 9
VORVERKAUF FÜR 7 TAGE THEATERKASSEN A. WERTHEIM u. UFA-PAVILLON
UFA-PAVILLON
AM NOLLENDORFPLATZ

TOP LEFT

A Sixth Part of the World (1926)
Dziga Vertov's documentary took him to remote areas of the USSR, as represented by the map and grid lines in this design. The importance of the country is emphasized by it being the only one shown.

TOP RIGHT

Battleship Potemkin (1925)
Alexander Rodchenko's design is one of the most famous Soviet constructivist posters. The image enshrining the military might of the Russian navy notwithstanding, Rodchenko's use of symmetry is striking.

BOTTOM LEFT

Man with a Movie Camera (1929)
One of the most iconic designs by Vladimir and Georgii Stenberg, this poster perfectly encapsulates the dizzying effect of Dziga Vertov's film, which itself captures a day in the life of a city.

BOTTOM RIGHT

A Kiss from Mary Pickford (1927)
Sergey Komarov inserted footage of Mary Pickford and Douglas Fairbanks' visit to the Soviet Union into his comedy. Accordingly, Pickford is a central figure in Semion Semionov's design, next to Igor Ilyinsky.

SOVIET CONSTRUCTIVISM

The radical poster art that accompanied the films
made after the Russian Revolution of 1917 was the
result of the nexus between political and artistic
thought. Eventually identified as constructivism,
it drew on an array of art movements and the
manifestos that defined them.

Unlike the rest of Europe, Russian poster art was not
initially impacted by art nouveau. However, an exhibition
in St. Petersburg in 1908 prompted a significant response
from artists. The influence of cubism was particularly
felt in Moscow's Café Pittoresque, which featured reliefs
designed by Vladimir Tatlin, with the aid of Alexander
Rodchenko. It became one of the key meeting points
for artists in the city.

The reorganization of the Soviet film industry after
the revolution was placed in the hands of Lenin's wife,
Nadezhda Krupskaya. Although film stock was initially
difficult to source, particularly while World War I still
raged, it became more available after the conflict had
ended and by 1923 the state-owned film production
company Goskino was established. It even had its own
poster department, Reklam Film.

Constructivism emerged from the work of Russian
futurism and suprematism, and the development of
photomontage helped create a radically new style of
design. This was unfolding as filmmakers such as Sergei
Eisenstein, Lev Kuleshov, Vsevolod Pudovkin, and Dziga
Vertov were also developing a radically new kind of
cinema. Accentuating the role of editing, they were
searching for what Vertov called "film truth," which was
the splicing together of documentary footage to create a
deeper meaning. This approach was then reflected in the
posters that artists created to promote these films. They
possessed their own form of montage, splicing together
disparate images to create a coherent whole.

Rodchenko was one of the leading artists of the
constructivist movement, and his design for Eisenstein's
Battleship Potemkin (1925) is one of the key film
posters of the era. Along with the Stenberg brothers
(see overleaf), Semion Semionov, Anatoly Belsky, Pyotr
Zhukov, and Grigory Borisov, Rodchenko helped define
this radical poster style. However, the movement's
association with Trotsky and the shift toward socialist
realism saw it draw to a close by the early 1930s.

ABOVE

5 Minutes (1929)
Anatoly Belsky's design is a key work
of Soviet constructivist poster art.
It juxtaposes the head of one of the
characters over a city block with the
typography resembling a bolt of lightning.

THE STENBERG BROTHERS

The film posters of Vladimir and Georgii Stenberg cover the period from 1923 to 1933. They represent the perfect synthesis of the formal and philosophical elements of the Russian avant-garde. In their late teens, while the Russian Revolution was taking place, the brothers established themselves as pioneers in the design of posters, both for Soviet films and international releases.

The Stenberg brothers attended the Stroganov School of Applied Art in Moscow between 1917 and 1922, where they studied military engineering and specialized in bridge and railroad construction. However, upon encountering Alexander Rodchenko and other artists, they became increasingly enmeshed in an art world that was engaging with monumental political and social change. They held their first exhibition, with Konstantin Medunetsky, at a cafe in Moscow in 1921, where the three also launched their manifesto "The Constructivists Address the World." At the same time, they began designing posters and stage sets for local theaters.

In 1923, the brothers created their first film poster for *The Eyes of Love*, which was signed "Sten." Later they signed their work "2 Stenberg 2," which shifted the focus away from single authorship and more toward a collective concept that was in keeping with their ideological beliefs. Subsequent film posters were more complex, but the brothers adhered to a style that ran against the grain of most film poster design. Rather than elaborate on a scene from the film or emphasize the presence of a particular star, the Stenbergs tried to capture the atmosphere or tone of a film. This could involve drawing together disparate elements to create a unique whole or designing an image around one single motif that would nevertheless contrast with more conventional representation.

The Stenbergs' use of photomontage contrasted with that of their peers. They often constructed designs that employed photomontage, but the end result never included photography. Once a design was agreed upon, the photographic aspect would be replaced by a drawing. This allowed for greater freedom with the image and was more effective in implying movement within a design.

In terms of their working practices, the brothers often designed together, alternating their input on an artwork. This ended after Georgii died in a road accident. Vladimir continued to design but his posters lacked the flair of the brothers' collaborations.

BELOW LEFT

The General (1926)
The American North and South during the Civil War are given a Manichaean take, with Buster Keaton's character traversing both worlds. Once again, the design is more interpretive than representative.

BELOW RIGHT

The Three Millions Trial (1926)
Olga Zhizneva, who plays a wife who is planning to rob her husband with the aid of her lover, is the central figure in this design. The Stenbergs' updated signature appears on the right.

OPPOSITE
TOP TO BOTTOM

The Eyes of Love (1923)
The brothers' first poster design is a simple but effective use of block color. The early version of their signature is visible on the right.

Battleship Potemkin (1925/1929)
This image employs the same visual elements as Alexander Rodchenko's earlier design for the film (see page 46), but the perspective is more playful here, in terms of the guns and the positioning of the soldiers.

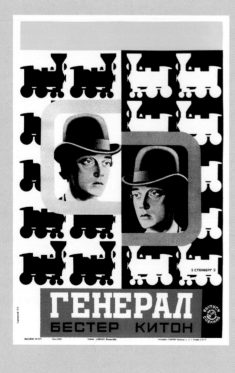

THE ARRIVAL OF SOUND

In 1927, the Warner Bros. publicity machine went into overdrive to proclaim *The Jazz Singer* the first "talkie." Experiments with sound and film had been carried out since the mid 1890s, when Thomas Edison announced the development of the Kinetoscope. Optical sound on film began to appear in 1919 with US inventor Lee de Forest leading the way. In 1923, he gave the first commercial screening of a series of shorts, using his Phonofilm system. Although the Tri-Ergon sound system proved popular in Europe, when Sam Warner witnessed a demonstration of Western Electric's sound-on-disc system, he convinced his brothers that this was the way forward with movies. In 1926, *Don Juan* became the first feature to have a complete synchronized soundtrack, albeit with no dialogue. A year later, *The Jazz Singer* opened.

Alan Crosland's musical, which starred Al Jolson, was a resounding success for Warner Bros., earning the studio US$1 million more than any previous release and saving it from financial ruin. It was the third most successful film of the year, but was bettered by Warner Bros. and Jolson's follow-up feature *The Singing Fool* (1928). In-between, the studio released *Tenderloin*, *Glorious Betsy,* and *The Lion and the Mouse* (all 1928), which each featured segments with synchronous sound. In July 1928, Warner Bros. released *Lights of New York*, which was the first all-talking feature. Again, it was a great success. However, commercial sound cinema still had some way to go, as many venues were not equipped with the right technology to play the films.

Sound began to feature in European films in 1929. The most notable all-talking feature was Alfred Hitchcock's thriller *Blackmail* (1929). The director had already completed a silent version of the film, but re-shot certain scenes in order to include dialogue. It was followed by films from Germany, Sweden, and finally France.

Warner Bros. went one step further in 1929 with the first all-talking, all-color, feature-length film *On with the Show*. Directed once again by Crosland, it employed a two-strip color technique and was a huge box office success. However, it was soon eclipsed by the studio's next color and sound extravaganza, *Gold Diggers of Broadway* (1929), which presaged a decade of musicals on the screen.

The Jazz Singer (1927)
The piano is the key component in this image, along with Al Jolson appearing to sing. This poster shows the film at its most wholesome. Other artworks featured Jolson in blackface makeup.

Blackmail (1929)
The photos in this poster
combine to resemble the
sound emanating from an
amplifier. In a busy design,
the red hints at the danger
faced by Anny Ondra's
protagonist and the film's
title crosses with the
images to form a target.

On with the Show (1929)
The selling points here
are sound and titillation,
as evinced by the dancer
facing away from the
audience with her skirt
raised. It gives a double
meaning to the film's title.

Lights of New York (1928)
The film's use of sound
is intimated here by the
dancers tearing through
the image. The design
also suggests the activity
unfolding behind the doors
of the building, where the
passengers of the car are
about to go.

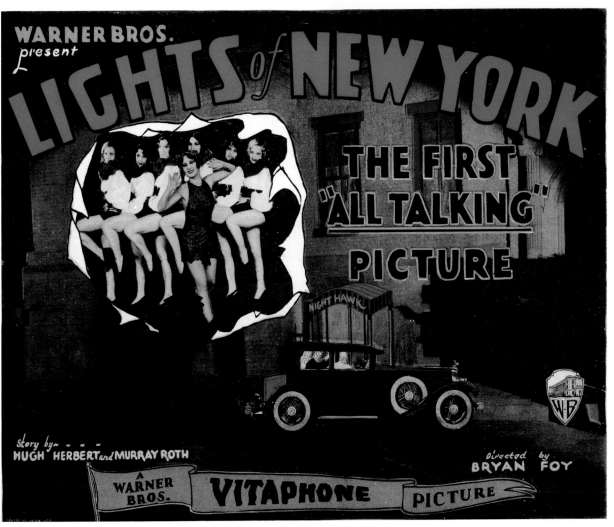

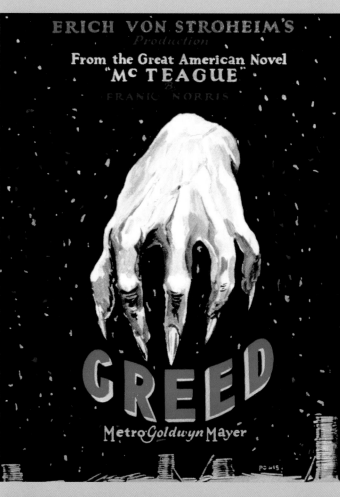

POSTERS OF THE DECADE

OPPOSITE FAR LEFT

Metropolis (1927)
With only four original posters in existence, this image for Fritz Lang's first science fiction film has become one of the most iconic posters of the silent era. The typography hints at the expressionistic elements in the film.

OPPOSITE TOP LEFT

Greed (1924)
This could easily have been the poster for F. W. Murnau's *Nosferatu* (1922), with its inhuman hand. Instead, it hints at how twisted and tortured we can become when driven by avarice.

OPPOSITE BOTTOM LEFT AND BELOW

The Passion of Joan of Arc (1928)
Both posters hint at the suffering experienced by France's young saint. The image on the left highlights her sacrifice, while the one on the right captures Joan's rapture and the cruelty of her captors.

One of the greatest decades for cinema, the 1920s was also extraordinary for the creativity of poster design. For three visionary directors, the artwork for their films was simple, yet it conveyed the power of the images created in their work.

Erich von Stroheim was one of the great directors of the silent era, but his unwillingness to compromise found him battling Hollywood studio heads. He was an actor and assistant director on D. W. Griffith's *Intolerance: Love's Struggle Throughout the Ages* (1916), and then made his directorial debut with *Blind Husbands* (1919). This was followed by the now lost *The Devil's Passkey* (1920) and *Foolish Wives* (1922), the latter of which is purported to be the first film to cost US$1 million to make. However, it is for *Greed* (1924), an adaptation of Frank Norris' novel *McTeague* (1899), that Stroheim will be remembered. The film's original cut was ten hours, which the filmmaker trimmed to six with the idea that it would be shown in two parts. A four-hour version was then created, but the film was taken out of Stroheim's hands and was never seen in a full version again. What remains today, pieced together from surviving remnants, is a shadow of the original, but it is still a striking account of greed, highlighted by the film's unsettling poster.

Carl Theodor Dreyer's austere, minimalist *The Passion of Joan of Arc* (1928) is one of the masterpieces of cinema. He became an influential figure in European cinema, and this film defined his oeuvre. A study in faith, sacrifice, and redemption, it is dominated by Renée Jeanne (Maria) Falconetti's extraordinary performance, without stage makeup, featuring harsh lighting, and predominantly in extreme close-up. René Péron's artwork, which appeared as an immense four-panel poster, captures the future saint in a state of rapture, while her arbiters look on in judgment.

One of the most sought-after film posters is Heinz Schulz-Neudamm's vision of Fritz Lang's future world, which perfectly captures the scale of *Metropolis* (1927). With its elongated buildings, angular design, and play with light, it emphasizes the film's set designers Otto Hunte, Erich Kettelhut, and Karl Vollbracht's desire to convey an essence of German expressionism in their creation of a vast city. It sits on the shoulders of the robot whose creation may be its undoing.

1930s

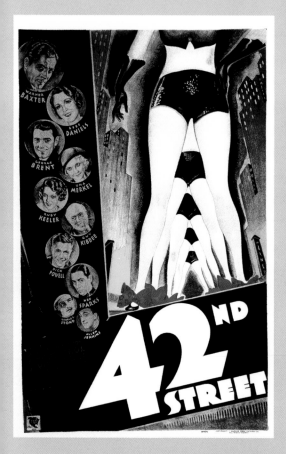

World War I and the newly established Soviet Union recognized the potential of poster design and filmmaking in the dissemination of propaganda, but the Nazi regime in 1930s Germany took it much further. Initially, film was used to promote what was regarded as the excellence and purity of the Aryan race, with Hitler's vast rallies in Nuremberg and the Olympic Games of 1936 in Berlin being of particular interest. However, the focus then turned toward anti-Semitic subject matter and a hatred of all aspects of Jewish culture. The response from countries opposed to Nazi Germany was muted at first, but as Europe and then the United States headed toward war, cinema became an effective tool for propaganda and bolstering morale throughout World War II.

Early in the decade, increased censorship had led to a curbing of overt sexual references in films and promotional material, which is best evinced by Mae West's comedies before and after the introduction of the Motion Picture Production Code in Hollywood. Prior to Nazi rule, countries such as France and Germany were less controling.

There were significant changes to the trend regarding how movie posters were designed. Many 1920s designs featured a scene from a film, but in the 1930s the focus shifted onto the stars that appeared in the films or the characters they played. It wasn't unusual to see a floating head shot within a design. This was particularly effective on posters for the horror films produced by Universal throughout the decade. These artworks also emphasized much bolder typographic design, often in a font that helped reinforce the genre.

As Universal focused on horror movies, Warner Bros. became the official home of the gangster film. Although the tone of the designs differed, the posters still emphasized the studio's roster of "tough" stars, whose characters mostly existed on the wrong side of the law. The same was true of the posters featuring African American actors, who made a name for themselves in an arm of the film industry that catered specifically for black audiences, which existed outside of Hollywood. In addition, Jean Gabin became both a leading man and a romantic hero in France, thanks to the way in which his screen persona was developed over the course of the decade.

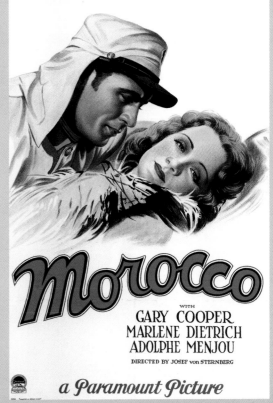

THE GOLDEN AGE OF HOLLYWOOD

In the 1930s, Hollywood entered its golden age, when it became the beacon of film production. At their best, Hollywood studios were capable of producing engaging, sophisticated cinema that delighted audiences. They employed playwrights, journalists, and novelists to pen scripts that could exude intelligence and wit. And there wasn't a genre that they didn't encompass in their quest for mass entertainment and box office success. The way in which the studios sold these films to audiences was often as smart and engaging as the films themselves.

When it comes to comedy, Hollywood in the 1930s has few equals. From knockabout slapstick and verbal sparring to social and romantic comedies, the studios excelled at making audiences laugh. The Marx Brothers provided first-class slapstick. Indeed, of all the comedy acts to graduate from music hall to Hollywood in the 1930s, the Marx Brothers were arguably the most ingenious. Their brand of zaniness, reflected in the frequently chaotic look of the posters that promoted their films, relied on physical and verbal dexterity. In addition, their artwork helped to define the brothers' individual personas, always with Groucho as the most savvy of the group. No less madcap, director Howard Hawks teamed up the normally debonair Cary Grant with a fast-talking Katharine Hepburn for *Bringing Up Baby* (1938). The film may have been unpopular with 1930s audiences, but it is now ranked as one of the greatest screwball comedies of all time. In 1990, the National Film Registry of the Library of Congress added it to its list of films to be preserved as "culturally, historically, or aesthetically significant."

The oddball romance that Hawks explored in *Bringing Up Baby* was perfected originally in *It Happened One Night* (1934), the first film to win the "Big Five" Academy Awards (Best Picture, Director, Leading Actress, Leading Actor, and Screenplay). It was directed by Frank Capra, whose work in the 1930s increasingly exhibited a social slant, culminating in *Mr. Smith Goes to Washington* (1939), starring James Stewart and Jean Arthur. Ernst Lubitsch also balanced comedy with a social edge, but as one of the finest filmmakers of the era his sleight of hand was extraordinarily subtle. Lubitsch had long wished to make a film with Greta Garbo, and his aim was finally realized

King Kong (1933)
This poster plays up the action climax of Merian C. Cooper and Ernest B. Schoedsack's monster epic. However, the artist features the Empire State Building in the background rather than under Kong.

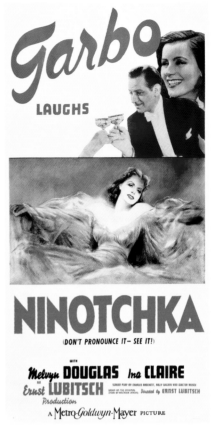

TOP LEFT

It Happened One Night (1934)
Gable and Colbert fall in love, and it is
a match made in the stars. This poster
doesn't suggest a comedy, but the film's
pairing of these two icons would have
been enough to attract audiences.

TOP RIGHT

Ninotchka (1939)
The painterly image suggests
sophistication, which is what audiences
came to expect from both the star and
the director. But the caption says it all:
"Garbo laughs."

ABOVE

Jezebel (1938)
William Wyler's costume melodrama
is a showcase for Bette Davis, and so
the poster needs nothing more than the
film's star wearing the dress that caused
so much outrage.

with *Ninotchka* (1939). This film took one of cinema's most beguiling screen sirens and transformed her into a comic actor, a change in gear so extraordinary that MGM's press department had a field day announcing to the world "Garbo laughs."

Drama in 1930s Hollywood was produced in various forms, none larger in scale than David O. Selznick's epic production of the historical romance *Gone with the Wind* (1939, see page 85). Not to be outdone, Warner Bros. speedily produced its own large-scale period drama, *Jezebel* (1938). Bette Davis' eponymous anti-heroine gave Vivien Leigh's Scarlett O'Hara a run for her money, as implied by Davis' appearance on the film's poster. At the opposite end of the scale, the quiet tragedy of working people's lives in Depression-era America was captured with grace and humility by Victor Moore and Beulah Bondi in Leo McCarey's *Make Way for Tomorrow* (1937).

For the most part, Hollywood was an industry characterized by escapism. As Warner Bros. indulged audiences with the wild lives of gangsters, MGM kept them entertained with upbeat musicals, Universal frightened them with its roll call of monsters, and RKO created the eighth wonder of the world in the form of the critically acclaimed *King Kong* (1933). Although this film was not the first monster movie, the tentative relationship between Fay Wray's Ann Darrow and the creature gave *King Kong* an emotional core that most other films of its ilk lacked. Not that the publicity for the film hinted at this. The audience wanted thrills, and that is what they were promised.

The arrival of color, through the implementation of Technicolor's three-strip process, might have proven challenging on technical and budgetary levels, but it offered audiences another form of escape. The first films made using this process were either animations or adventures and fantasies such as *The Adventures of Robin Hood* (1938) and *The Wizard of Oz* (1939). They showcased the level of creative innovation Hollywood had achieved over the course of the decade, both in vision and sound. *The Wizard of Oz* in particular arrived at the pinnacle of the studio system.

The year 1939 is regarded as the greatest twelve months in Hollywood's history. In addition to the films mentioned so far, 1939 saw the release of *Stagecoach*, *Goodbye, Mr. Chips*, *Of Mice and Men*, *Dark Victory,* and *Wuthering Heights*. All were nominated for the Academy Award for Best Picture, and *Gone with the Wind* won. These films capped a decade in which the star system churned out a roll call of stellar actors, writers provided some of the finest scripts, and directors and producers helped bring every component together to produce seamless entertainment.

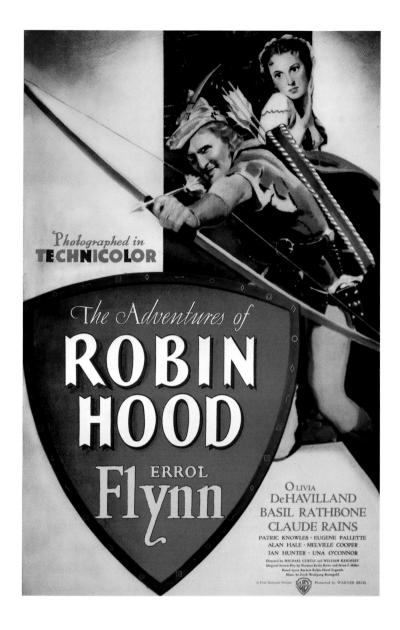

ABOVE

The Adventures of Robin Hood (1938)
All the most important attractions of Michael Curtiz's film are present in this poster: the star of the day Errol Flynn in action, the promise of thrills and adventure, and the allure of a Technicolor entertainment.

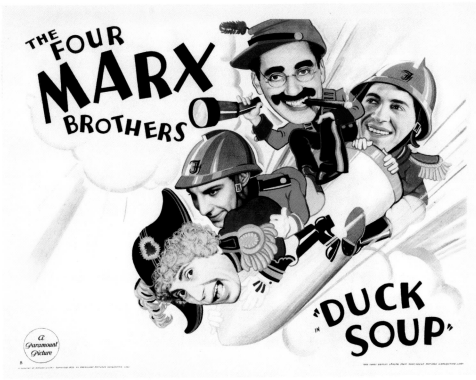

TOP LEFT

The Wizard of Oz (1939)

Victor Fleming's fantasy extravaganza was like nothing else in cinema history, and the publicity department at MGM was of the same opinion. The poster is a mishmash of ideas, all pointing toward something new.

TOP RIGHT

Bringing Up Baby (1938)

The artwork for Howard Hawks' screwball comedy promises two elements. The stills of Grant and Hepburn evince a dash of sophistication, but their cartoon selves suggest madcap comedy. And the title hints at a roller-coaster ride.

BOTTOM LEFT

Duck Soup (1933)

The Marx Brothers straddling a bomb and heading for oblivion is one way of suggesting that this is the ultimate comedy. Although the film was a box office failure, this artwork perfectly encapsulates the stars' madcap humor.

BOTTOM RIGHT

Make Way for Tomorrow (1937)

Leo McCarey was best known for his comedy shorts and features in the 1930s, so the weighty themes of his serious drama about the Depression era were leavened by the benevolent expressions of the characters.

The release and runaway success of D. W. Griffith's *The Birth of a Nation* (1915) raised the specter of racial prejudice in the United States. However, as early as the 1910s an alternative cinema, produced by and starring African Americans, had already established strong roots within black communities. Noble Johnson, who founded the Lincoln Motion Picture Company, was its first star and Oscar Micheaux its first auteur. Other small film companies appeared throughout the 1920s, and with the arrival of sound black film production increased.

Micheaux made the first all-black independently produced "talkie" in 1931, titled *The Exile*. What it lacked in technical expertise—Micheaux's films were notoriously rickety productions, made on extremely low budgets and rarely able to afford more than one take per shot—it made up for in the representation of peoples usually assigned marginal roles or forced to play lazy stereotypes. As the decade progressed, Micheaux continued to offer a positive racial spin on a Hollywood genre and to adapt his own novels. The emphasis was always on challenging crass representation, instead presenting black lives in the same way mainstream cinema represented a spectrum of white lives.

With sound came the musical, and African American filmmakers celebrated their rich cultural heritage. Bill "Bojangles" Robinson and Ethel Waters were just two singers to emerge as stars. The artwork for the films promised music and fun, tapping into the Jazz age as it was lived in Harlem. Filmmakers also adapted other genres for black audiences, with former Apollo Theater master of ceremonies Ralph Cooper overseeing the gangster dramas *Dark Manhattan* and *Bargain with Bullets* (both 1937). In the same year, Flournoy E. Miller wrote the Western musical *Harlem on the Prairie*. The posters for these films echoed the genre styles of the Hollywood mainstream, albeit with a black cast.

These films did not signal any significant change in US culture. They existed outside of the Hollywood machine and tended to be seen only in black communities. Some stars were so exasperated at being marginalized by the studios, or suffering the yolk of stereotyping, that they decided to leave the United States. Both Josephine Baker and Paul Robeson chose to relocate to Europe and carved out successful careers in France and Britain.

OPPOSITE

Princess Tam Tam (1935)
Josephine Baker was the star of three films. This was her last and she is promoted as its main attraction. Although the Hays Office refused to pass the film, it played to independent cinemas that catered to black audiences.

ABOVE

The Exile (1931)
The artwork for *The Exile* rails against the poverty of mainstream representations of African American life, while its subject matter, based on Micheaux's novel *The Conquest* (1913), would likely have shocked some white audiences.

DIETRICH AND VON STERNBERG

OPPOSITE
CLOCKWISE FROM LEFT

Blonde Venus (1932)
Alexandros of Antioch's
sculpture is the basis of
this poster. Dietrich wears
long black gloves and her
torso is provocatively
covered by a semi-
transparent top. Even
her name is stylized.

**The Devil Is a Woman
(1935)**
This more lurid design
is fitting for the final
collaboration between
Dietrich and von Sternberg.
The flames of hell behind
the couple hint at the
dangers of temptation.

Shanghai Express (1932)
Anna May Wong and Clive
Brook both appear in
this image, but Dietrich's
feathered dress takes all
the attention. The border
and title font add to the
sense of a journey to an
exotic world.

BELOW LEFT

The Blue Angel (1930)
This was Dietrich's first
collaboration with von
Sternberg. Here, she is
seen in one of her most
iconic costumes, replete
with a tilted top hat.

FAR RIGHT

Morocco (1930)
There are two versions
of this design. This one
focuses on the two stars,
with Dietrich engaging
directly with the viewer.
The other features an
archway, palm tree, and
dusky sky.

Rapidly graduating from the sublime to the surreal,
the cinematic collaboration between filmmaker Josef
von Sternberg and star Marlene Dietrich epitomized
the glamour and excess of early 1930s cinema. Their
partnership began in Germany, but Hollywood promised
a larger canvas for them to work upon.

Von Sternberg had already achieved some success
in Hollywood in the late 1920s with the crime film
Underworld (1927) and the drama *The Docks of New
York* (1928). After a few failures, his position there looked
precarious, so he accepted the offer to make *The Blue
Angel* (1930) in Germany. Dietrich had already played
the role of Lola on stage and was a natural choice to
star. The success of the film in Europe and the United
States transformed both their careers. Dietrich implicitly
followed von Sternberg's direction, and the filmmaker
helped shape her image. With each subsequent film
the pair made together, Dietrich's persona became
increasingly sophisticated.

Morocco (1930) was their first Hollywood project,
followed by *Dishonored* (1931). They both pushed at the
boundaries of what was morally acceptable on screen.
Sexuality was key to the way in which the films were sold
to audiences. If Greta Garbo was all mystique, Dietrich

was the provocateur personified. In *Morocco*'s artwork,
Dietrich looks directly at the audience as Gary Cooper
attempts to seduce her. Her expression is one of pleasure,
free of guilt. Posters for *Dishonored* play with gender
identity. Dietrich is a Mata Hari-like spy with clothes that
have a strong masculine look.

Shanghai Express and *Blonde Venus* (both 1932) were
the pair's most financially successful collaborations.
Von Sternberg described the former as "*Grand Hotel* on
wheels," but the film is far more exotic than Edmund
Goulding's static drama. Anna May Wong occasionally
appears on the posters for the film, but the majority
feature Dietrich alone or dominating a scene with her
impeccable taste in fashion. *Blonde Venus*, based on a
story conceived by Dietrich, is less a cohesive narrative
than a showcase for its star, as suggested by almost every
poster for the film, which run the gamut from featuring
her in a revealing posture to having her resemble the
Venus de Milo.

Although von Sternberg and Dietrich's final two films
were less popular, *The Scarlet Empress* (1934) and *The
Devil Is a Woman* (1935) approach the baroque in terms
of their style. Wildly excessive, they remain two of 1930s
Hollywood's most indulgent films.

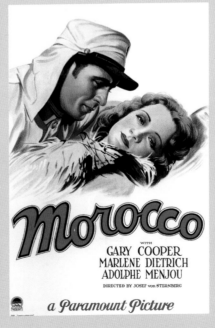

THE MUSICAL

The musical was the natural format for a medium that had successfully integrated sound. Although early experiments were little more than rudimentary, as parodied in *Singin' in the Rain* (1952), technology quickly developed. And if camera movement was still restricted in order to reduce unwelcome sound levels, what better way to explore the possibilities within the static frame than through dance? Various countries experimented with the musical, but none achieved the vertiginous heights of Hollywood. It released hundreds of musical productions, from adaptations of popular stage shows to original films featuring compositions by some of the greatest songwriters of the era.

Beyond the capabilities of the medium, the Hollywood musical gave audiences respite from the Great Depression that followed the Wall Street Crash of 1929. Musicals were the perfect escape, with audiences witnessing glamour on a magnificent scale. One of the earliest stars of the genre was the influential figure who created magical worlds through synchronized dance.

Busby Berkley choreographed or directed twenty-three films between 1930 and 1939. They featured a regular cast of actors such as Ruby Keeler, Joan Blondell, and Dick Powell. The stories were often paper thin, dialogue was at best perfunctory, and the acting occasionally flimsy. But audiences didn't flock to see high drama. Like the posters that advertised them, Berkley's films were all about spectacle. They could play to the fashions of the time and emphasize the exotic or outrageous. But with each film, Berkley was expected to outdo himself. Each installment of *The Gold Diggers* series, for example, which appeared in 1933, 1935, and 1936 (although billed as 1937), saw Berkley raising the bar. In addition, the posters for each film always promised something bigger and better.

Ginger Rogers and Fred Astaire first performed on screen together in *Flying Down to Rio* (1933). Although that film was a vehicle for Dolores del Rio, their appearance was electric and they were soon topping the bill in their own films. Unlike the actors in Busby Berkley's productions, who appeared secondary to the dance sequences, Rogers and Astaire were the main attraction. The posters for their films reflected this. Audiences knew they could dance, but Rogers and Astaire could also act and so were promoted like other major stars.

ABOVE

Top Hat (1935)
By Rogers and Astaire's fourth screen collaboration, there was no need to show them dancing. Instead, there is more detail to their faces than generally appears in film musical posters. It is their relationship that attracts audiences.

OPPOSITE

42nd Street (1933)
The first major Busby Berkley musical places the cast secondary to the lineup of dancers, setting the tone for subsequent film posters. The juxtaposition of the dancers and the Manhattan skyline also taps into the film's magical quality.

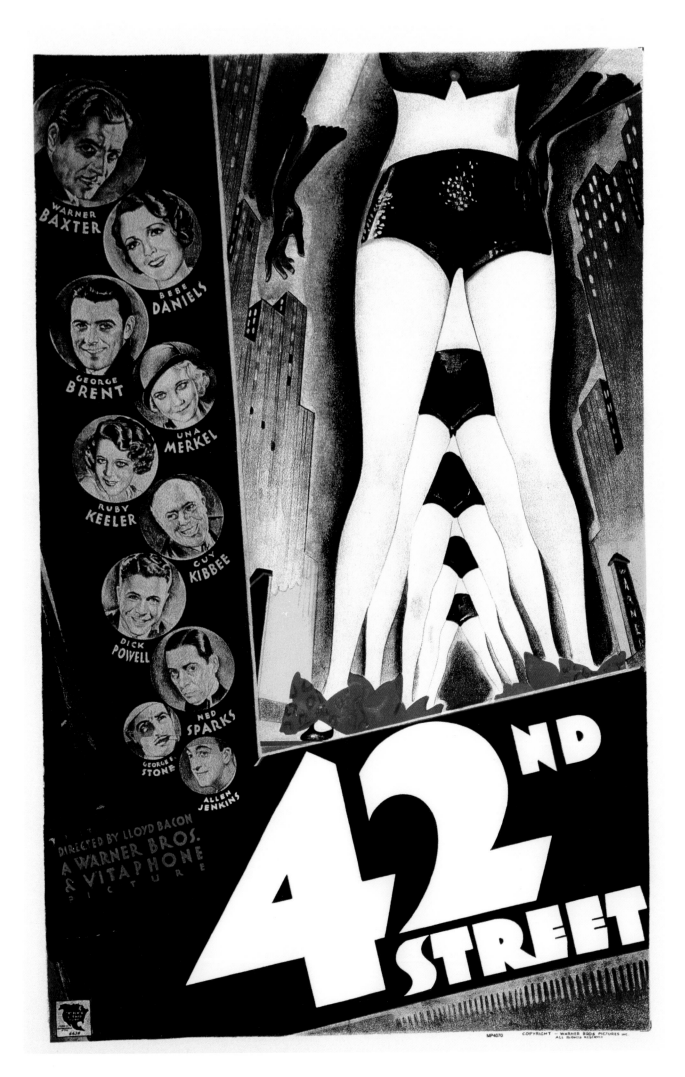

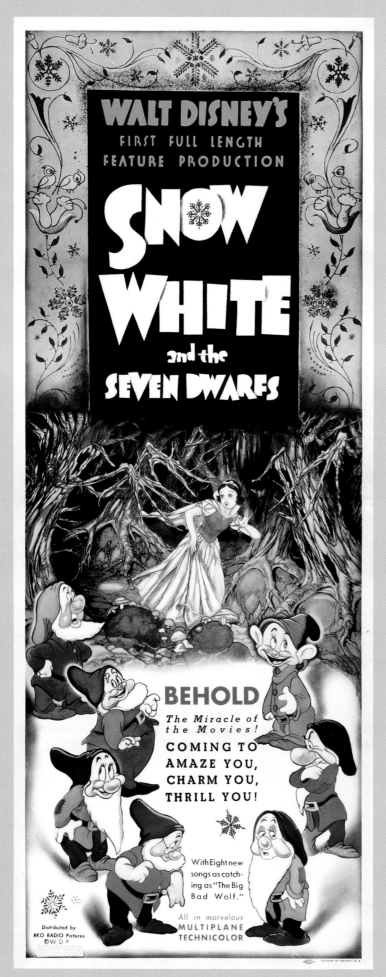

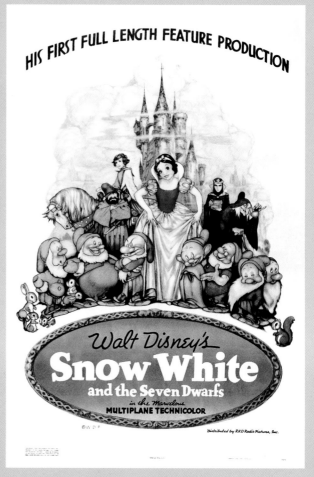

SNOW WHITE AND THE SEVEN DWARFS

OPPOSITE AND BELOW

The posters featured
here are examples of
the variety of designs
employed for the release
of the first official Disney
feature film. They vary in
tone in order to attract
the widest possible
audience. The film's
success saw subsequent
advertising campaigns
hone in on the key
audiences to whom the
studio wished to appeal.

Contrary to popular belief, Walt Disney's *Snow White and the Seven Dwarfs* (1937) wasn't the first animated feature ever made. There are at least seven known earlier films. However, these examples comprise cutout, silhouette, or stop-motion animation. The Disney film was the first to be completely hand-drawn. (The company's earlier *Academy Award Review of Walt Disney Cartoons*, 1937, doesn't quite count because it was an anthology film intended to promote *Snow White*.)

Snow White was also the first animated feature to have widespread distribution. By the late 1930s, audiences were used to seeing cartoons in some form or another, usually as a supporting short to a main feature, or as part of a children's program on a Saturday. But the idea that audiences would pay to see a full-length animated film was not only considered odd for an adult audience, but it also led to derisory caricatures of Disney during the film's three-year production period. Moreover, the production posed a severe financial risk. Having originally been budgeted at US$250,000, it ended up costing six times that amount. However, "Disney's Folly," as it was known, became an overnight success and inspired MGM to press ahead with its own fantasy, *The Wizard*

of Oz (1939). Furthermore, *Snow White was* re-released in 1944 and another seven times over the subsequent five decades, and established the Disney company as a major Hollywood studio.

Prior to *Snow White*'s successful premiere, Walt Disney created a campaign that he hoped would play to the film's strengths. It actually set the template for the next fifty years, until John Alvin's designs brought a revitalized "Mouse House" into the modern age with his artwork for the series of successful animated features released in the 1990s (see pages 268-269). It is easy to recognize the charm and allure of such films in an age when they are released on a regular basis, but tempting an audience who have only ever seen live action features was no small challenge.

The promotional artwork primarily focused on the uniqueness of *Snow White*, referring to the film as "The Miracle of the Movies." It connected the earlier popular shorts with the feature, implying more of what audiences had enjoyed previously. In addition, it emphasized the use of color, which was still in its infancy in mainstream cinema. Finally, it offered audiences fun—a period of pure escapism.

UNIVERSAL AND HORROR

In the 1930s, Universal became known as the home of horror. It didn't hold a monopoly over the genre, but of the seventy or so horror films made throughout the decade, almost one-third of them were produced and released by Universal. It also established itself as home to some of the most famous horror characters.

Universal's reign over the genre began in the 1920s. *The Hunchback of Notre Dame* (1923) and *The Phantom of the Opera* (1925) made a star of Lon Chaney (see page 28) and displayed the style of artwork that would come to dominate poster designs for the films over the next decade. *The Cat and the Canary* (1927) followed, blending photography—a terrified woman—with hand-drawn imagery. The artwork for *The Last Performance* (1929), which stars *The Cabinet of Dr. Caligari*'s Conrad Veidt, draws heavily on German expressionism. It features a disfigured hand and its exaggerated shadow edging toward the actor's sinister magician.

Universal's domination of horror in the 1930s began with *Dracula* (1931), Tod Browning's adaptation of Bram Stoker's novel, with Bela Lugosi as the eponymous vampire. It was a landmark film, and Universal's faith in its success prompted a Spanish version, with George Melford directing at night after Browning had stopped filming and Carlos Villarías in the lead role. The poster shows Dracula's head and hands trapped in a spider's web—a far less stylized image than the full-blooded artwork for the Lugosi version.

Frankenstein arrived toward the end of 1931 and made Boris Karloff the studio's most recognizable horror star. His face featured prominently in the artwork for *The Old Dark House* (1932), *The Black Cat* (1934), *The Raven* (1935), *The Invisible Ray* (1936), and *Night Key* (1937). He was also seen swathed in strips of cloth in the artwork for *The Mummy* (1932). Karloff's monster for *Frankenstein* became the model for subsequent versions of the story.

The posters for each of the Universal productions, some of which are extremely sought-after by collectors, emphasize the contrast between light and dark, are awash with color, and feature titles that are often inventively inserted into the design. For example, the title for *The Bride of Frankenstein* (1935), one of Universal's finest horror films, seems to have received an electric charge like the characters above it.

The Bride of Frankenstein (1935)
Karloff appears with the bolt in his neck in this poster for the popular sequel. But the draw is Elsa Lanchester's female monster, whose shock of hair, suggesting a wildness beyond control, dominates.

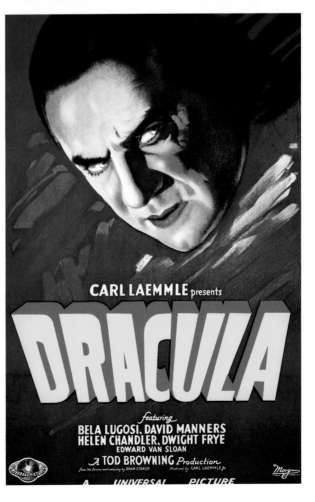

CLOCKWISE FROM TOP LEFT

Frankenstein (1931)
Karloff's appearance is toned down in this artwork, which also features the main characters. The real beauty of the poster is its expressive backdrop, hinting at raging fire and a wind of change.

Frankenstein (1931)
Karloff dominates here, as he did in many subsequent posters for horror films. Once again, an expressive backdrop—the use of red—plays up the sense of danger and excitement.

Dracula (1931)
The title is very imposing in this image, with the yellow and red contrasting wildly with the blue and white brushstrokes of the backdrop. Lugosi's eyes make this image all the more unsettling.

Dracula (1931)
One of the most sought-after posters by collectors, this image helped to establish Universal's brand. It is overwrought, almost to the point of parody.

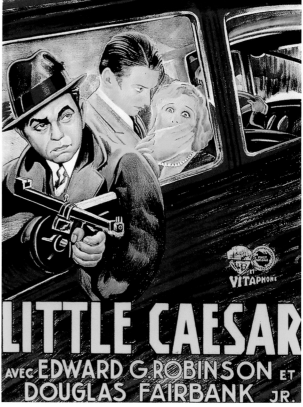

ABOVE

"G" Men (1935)
It is hard to distinguish what separates
the lawman James Cagney from his
previous gangster persona in the design
of this poster. The promise of violence
and thrills remains.

TOP RIGHT

The Public Enemy (1931)
This poster features the highs and lows
of the 1920s. People party together while
their vices support Tom Powers' rise. Jean
Harlow looks more like a partner in crime
here, while Cagney is all angst.

BOTTOM RIGHT

Little Caesar (1931)
Edward G. Robinson's Rico set the
template for the Warner Bros. gangster.
The "dame" in distress was a key motif,
and audiences of the time would have
known what the Tommy gun represented.

WARNER BROS. AND THE GANGSTER FILM

Prohibition, the rise of organized crime, the financial collapse of Wall Street in 1929, and a generation of military-trained men returning home from World War I only to find their career prospects diminished within a few short years resulted, by the early 1930s, in a volatile US society. Newspapers regularly reported on the rise of a new criminal elite, whose incendiary cocktail of violence and glamour was irresistible to a nascent Hollywood. The arrival of sound made the gangster film even more appealing, but it was the look of this world and the people who lived in it that attracted cinema audiences.

In the few short years between the arrival of sound and the introduction of the Hays Code, which censored sex, violence, and "immoral" behavior on the screen, the gangster film flourished. Nowhere was this more so than at Warner Bros., where the genre found its perfect home and whose roster of stars included such ideal gangster bosses as Edward G. Robinson, James Cagney, Paul Muni, and, latterly, Humphrey Bogart. Although Robinson fired the first shot in early 1931 with *Little Caesar*, it was Cagney's outrageous performance as Tom Powers later that year in *The Public Enemy* (1931) that truly caught the audience's imagination.

The artwork for these gangster films presents their protagonists as aggressive, the women accompanying them occasionally complicit, but more often shocked or fearful. Violence seeps out of the images, but rarely with such vigor as it does in the posters for Howard Hawks' *Scarface* (1932). Here, Muni is the raging id of a gang boss. By comparison, Cagney's Tom is the epitome of control.

These films offered the glamour of a high life that few were experiencing in the 1930s, and the artwork publicizing them promised adventure and escape. However, with the arrival of the Hays Code in 1935, films were forced to toe the line. The gangsters always met their end in the earlier releases, but audiences were no longer treated to such vicarious thrills. Cagney was promoted in the same way, as the perennial tough guy, but now he played a federal agent in *"G" Men* (1935)—a clever way to depict him being able to act violently but within moral boundaries—or a criminal with a conscience, in films such as *Angels with Dirty Faces* (1938).

ABOVE

Angels with Dirty Faces (1938)
Cagney's expression is, once again, tough. But the presence of Pat O'Brien's comforting priest softens that aggression, and the boys behind represent his conscience. Humphrey Bogart stands apart, as the film's real villain.

THE EARLY WESTERN

The Western found its perfect medium in cinema, with the genre dominating Hollywood from the 1920s to the 1960s. Charting the expansion of the frontier by peoples who originally arrived on the East Coast from Europe, the Western genre first gained popularity in fiction. However, the success of *The Great Train Robbery* (1903) cemented its association with the moving image, and its tales of crime, pursuit, retribution, and justice became staples of subsequent films.

The genre achieved real success in the 1930s, presenting audiences with a nostalgic image of the United States' recent past. As more and more people migrated to cities in search of work, the Western became one of their only points of reference to a world beyond the chaos of urban life. It is during this period that the genre split into identifiable sub-categories, which became immediately recognizable from the way each film was sold to audiences. Like any other genre, the Western featured classic archetypes and scenarios, tweaked in the best films to ensure a modicum of originality. *Stagecoach* (1939) cemented John Ford's position as the preeminent Western director—and John Wayne its perennial star—but the film is also recognized as the Western in its purest form. It honed and refined the elements that had seeped into the genre over the decade, which began with films such as Raoul Walsh's *The Big Trail* (1930) and Hamilton MacFadden's *Riders of the Purple Sage* (1931). The latter was based on the novel by popular Western writer Zane Grey and it made a significant impact on the narrative development of the genre.

The poster for the Walter Huston vehicle *Law and Order* (1932) underpins the genre's clearly defined moral code, with good fighting bad (and, until later revisions, always coming out on top), but *The Cisco Kid* (1931) and *Cimarron* (1931) both hint at the battles fought between men over a woman. Silent star Tom Mix retained his image as the flawless hero of the West in *Destry Rides Again* (1932), although his star waned as the genre developed. In George Marshall's 1939 version of the film, James Stewart plays another morally incorruptible hero, but the presence of Marlene Dietrich and a wickedly entertaining Brian Donlevy muddies the waters. In France, Dietrich's presence was deemed a greater draw for audiences, and she dominated the film's promotional artwork.

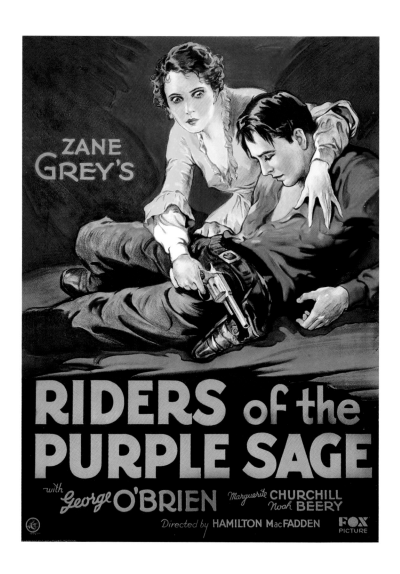

Riders of the Purple Sage (1931)
A key story in the development of the Western genre had already been a silent film (and would be remade in 1941). This image offers an enticing set-up to the tale of revenge.

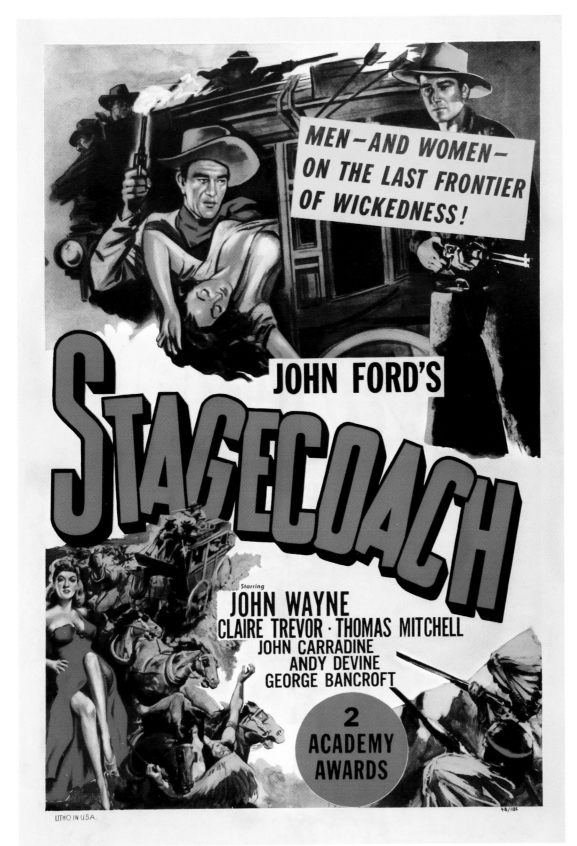

Stagecoach (1939)
Both the runaway coach and the title design hint at speed. Only the men atop the carriage identify the film as a Western, yet it is now seen as the archetype of the genre.

Law and Order (1932)
This could easily be a poster for one of the Warner Bros. gangster films. The set-up is the same. But whereas those films elevated the criminal to anti-hero status, here Walter Huston's lawman rules.

Destry Rides Again (1932)
There may be action and shooting, but Tom Mix's jovial face reassures audiences that all will be well. This represents the most wholesome type of Western, where the line between good and bad is clearly marked.

Destry Rides Again (1939)
A markedly different poster to the one for the earlier film, this is a star vehicle for Stewart and Dietrich. Stewart's character refuses to carry a gun for the majority of the film, yet he is seen holding one here.

LA DISTRIBUTION PARISIENNE DE FILMS présente

LA RÈGLE DU JEU
de JEAN RENOIR
avec

NORA GREGOR . PAULETTE DUBOST . MILA PARELY . DALIO
CARETTE . ROLAND TOUTAIN . GASTON MODOT . PIERRE MAGNIER

et

JEAN RENOIR

FRENCH POETIC REALISM

After a slump in the early 1930s, in part caused by major studios such as Pathé and Gaumont suffering financial difficulties, a group of French filmmakers—more a loose collection than a cohesive movement—emerged, whose work displayed a similar style in tone and look. Rather than seek to reflect the realities of daily life, they opted to portray a more expressive interpretation.

An early example of what became known as poetic realism was Jean Grémillon's *Little Lise* (1930). It looked ahead to the films that would dominate French cinema toward the end of the decade, which channeled the spirit of classic literature (in Grémillon's case, Victor Hugo's *Les Misérables,* 1862), focused attention on working-class life, and in their visual style tended toward the moody, thereby presaging the emergence of film noir in the 1940s.

Jean Vigo's *L'Atalante* (1934) was another step toward this new kind of cinema. The director's only feature before his early death from tuberculosis, the romantic tale of a pair of newlyweds living aboard the husband's barge is both rhapsodic and mournful. The posters for the film either feature the couple looking out from the bow of the barge as the sun is setting or focus on the array of working-class characters they encounter en route to Paris.

Pierre Chenal's *Street Without a Name* and Jacques Feyder's *Le grand jeu* (both 1934) developed the poetic realism style further, while Julien Duvivier's series of films in collaboration with Jean Gabin are regarded as the moment poetic realism came into its own (see overleaf). At the same time, Jean Renoir and Marcel Carné embodied the genre's key elements with works that rank among the best in French cinema.

The Crime of Monsieur Lange (1936), *La grande illusion* (1937), and *La bête humaine* (1938) revealed Renoir's compassion for his characters, but his finest film from the period was *The Rules of the Game* (1939), an account of the lives of the rich and their servants at a country retreat. Carné, meanwhile, located the action in more downbeat locales for *Port of Shadows* and *Hôtel du Nord* (both 1938). However, it is his crime drama *Le jour se lève* (1939) that best exemplifies the characteristics of poetic realism.

OPPOSITE

The Rules of the Game (1939)
Jean Renoir's 1930s masterpiece aims at so many targets that it is impossible to encapsulate them within one image. However, here an attempt has been made to set the scene in which his drama unfolds.

ABOVE

Port of Shadows (1938)
There is a noirish tone to this poster design, as the fiery orange backdrop hints at raging emotions. Jean Gabin is not completely visible, which is an indication of the moral ambivalence of his character.

JEAN GABIN

Jean Gabin embodied the best of French cinema and was one of the key figures of poetic realism. The quiet hero of Jean Renoir's anti-war treatise *La grande illusion* (1937), he went on to become one of cinema's most iconic gangsters. A stage actor and cabaret performer, Gabin entered cinema as sound arrived, and within the space of a decade was France's biggest screen star.

His screen career unfolded across three chapters. After he achieved stardom in the 1930s, his career took an uneven turn in the 1940s, before Jacques Becker's *Touchez pas au grisbi* (1954, see page 133) remade him as a tough gangster. His last two decades feature a string of successes up to his death in 1972.

Although Gabin's work with Julien Duvivier in Hollywood was less than stellar, his collaboration with the director a decade before in France helped to confirm his star status. They made five films together over the space of four years, and by the end of their collaboration Gabin had become the quintessential French screen icon. In 1934, the same year that he made an unremarkable

appearance in the Quebec-set *Maria Chapdelaine*, Gabin starred opposite Josephine Baker in *Zouzou*. However, it was his role in *La bandera* (1935) that attracted critical notices. He plays a killer who escapes to Spain, joins the Foreign Legion, and finds some kind of happiness in North Africa before his past catches up with him. The artwork for the film places Gabin alongside his costars Annabella and Robert Le Vigan.

Immediately after working with Jean Renoir on *The Lower Depths* (1936), Gabin returned to Duvivier and *La belle équipe* (1936). It is the tale of five friends who win the lottery and decide to invest in a property to transform it into a country cafe. Gabin's appearance on the poster is dominant, but it wasn't until his final 1930s film with Duvivier that his ascent was complete. *Pépé le moko* (1937) is a thrilling romantic crime drama set in the Casbah quarter of Algiers. Gabin plays the anti-hero, on the run from the police but who risks everything for love. It was perfect casting, and the film's posters show no hesitation in cementing Gabin's star status.

BELOW LEFT

La belle équipe (1936)
The jovial atmosphere of this image contrasts with the original cut of the film, which was amended following accusations that it was too bleak. Gabin stands out, but remains part of an ensemble.

BELOW RIGHT

Le jour se lève (1939)
Gabin is in archetypal mode here, playing a man trapped in a room surrounded by police who looks back on how his life fell apart. The dusky backdrop hints at the film's fatalism.

OPPOSITE

Pépé le moko (1937)
This film made Gabin a star, and his placement in the artwork suggests as much. The foreground characters contrast significantly in style with the backdrop, while Gabin's expression suggests a haunted, hunted man.

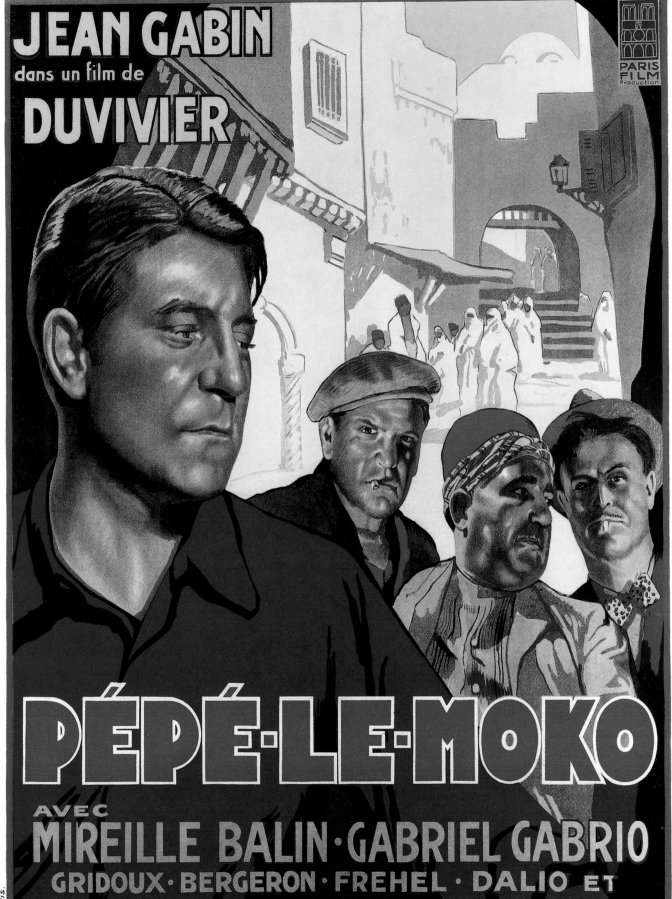

BRITISH CINEMA

British cinema in the 1930s was stymied by laws governing the mode of film production. The introduction of the Cinematograph Films Act of 1927 had a seismic impact. It was hoped that it would prevent British cinemas being flooded with US films, but instead it set unprecedented limitations on film production.

Producers were forced to acquiesce to rules that stipulated a film had to be made by a British or British-controlled company, three-quarters of all salaries must be paid to British subjects, either the screenwriter or the author of the work upon which the screenplay was based must be British, and all studio scenes had to be shot in Britain or somewhere in the British Empire. The resulting productions were either big-budget spectaculars that stood no chance of recouping costs domestically, or what became known as "quota quickies": low-budget features that drew from a pool of theater and music hall talent. The law was eventually changed a decade later and repealed completely in 1960.

A good example of the advertising for a quota quickie is the Bernard Vorhaus film *The Last Journey* (1936). It features a selection of scenes that cover bases from romance to thriller and drama—something for everyone. It is a contrast to the spectacular *The Private Life of Henry VIII* (1933), Alexander Korda's lavish period drama, which became the first British film to win the Academy Award for Best Picture. This film also benefits from the presence of stars, whose names and images dominate the poster. Another Korda production, *Things to Come* (1936), is busier, but it was sold to audiences on its concept, created by noted British science fiction writer H. G. Wells. His vision, realized by art director-turned-director William Cameron Menzies, is the film's main draw.

As the 1930s progressed, Alfred Hitchcock's star rose. A successful director in the silent era, whose career then floundered with a series of negligible films in the early sound era, Hitchcock firmly established his style with *The Man Who Knew Too Much* (1934). He then perfected it with *The 39 Steps* (1935), whose artwork perfectly summed up the attraction of a Hitchcock film. There was the promise of action or thrills, but never at the expense of character. It set the basic template for the more elaborate posters produced for Hitchcock's films following his move to Hollywood.

OPPOSITE

Things to Come (1936)
The type is futuristic, the images otherworldly, and H. G. Wells' name dominates. Various art movement styles converge in this image to create an imagined future that is both exciting and portends some danger.

ABOVE

The 39 Steps (1935)
Alfred Hitchcock had already had considerable success with the thriller genre, but this film set the template for his balance of thrills and romance, as evinced by this simply designed but effective poster.

ERIC ROHMAN

From the late 1970s onward, the Hollywood blockbuster developed into a global franchise and the marketing strategies that accompanied it differed very little from country to country. Today, a campaign for the latest *Marvel* adventure or Disney animation might take into account certain cultural or moral attitudes within a region, but the staple artwork rarely changes. Prior to this, designers in individual countries sometimes had the freedom to interpret a film. They still ensured that it appealed to audiences, but often in a way that spoke more locally, even drawing on contemporary trends.

Film releases in Sweden in the 1930s were accompanied by designs created by a group of gifted artists. One of the best was Eric Rohman. Born in 1891, he began working in design around 1915, first in Copenhagen, then in Sweden. He designed covers and illustrations for books, most notably *50 Poems* (1921) by Sweden's best-known poet Anna Maria Lenngren. Between the late 1910s and Rohman's death in 1949, film poster design dominated the artist's professional life. He claimed to have worked on more than 7,000 designs throughout his career, and was heavily influenced by art deco.

Key to Rohman's work, which was occasionally identified by the inclusion of his signature or printed name somewhere in the design, was his emphasis on the star of a given film. Two early designs for Roscoe "Fatty" Arbuckle's *Crazy to Marry* and *Brewster's Millions* (both 1921) refrain from detailing any aspect of the films' narratives, instead presenting two portraits of the popular comedian. Unlike the Hollywood poster for *The Life of Emile Zola* (1937), with Paul Muni looking dashing in the lead role, Rohman features him as an old man, dominating the frame, wizened and bespectacled. His poster for *La grande illusion* (1937), depicting the sober faces of Jean Gabin and Erich von Stroheim, is more conventional, but the design for *Frisco Kid* (1935) takes the studio's stock image of James Cagney and emphasizes his angst.

In the poster for *Gold Diggers of 1935* (1935), the dancers who usually feature so prominently in the artwork for Busby Berkley films are reduced to a solitary performer by Rohman, and an outline at that, lit up by a single spotlight. The emphasis in this design is more on the film's title, which appears in red, white, and gold.

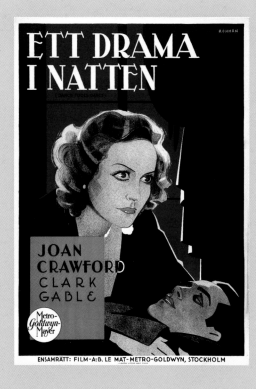

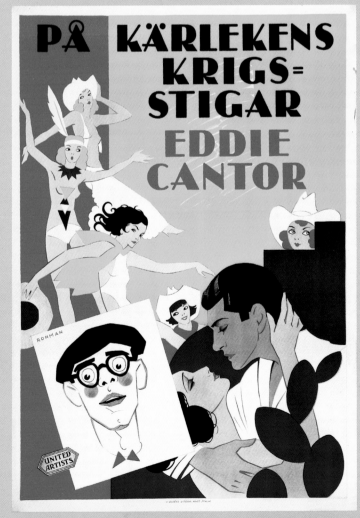

PROPAGANDA AND THE SPECTER OF WAR

While the Nazi regime used cinema to promote its message to the masses in Germany and beyond, in the United States, Hollywood was slower in its response to the rising tide of fascism. The government censured those who used film for propagandist purposes, although some studio heads persisted.

Joseph Goebbels oversaw the Nazi Party's propaganda machine. This included films that celebrated the *Übermensch*, or Nietzschean superman. Hitler's desire to promote the image of the Aryan super race found its perfect filmmaker in Leni Riefenstahl. Her documentary of the Nazi Party Congress at Nuremberg in 1934, *Triumph of the Will* (1935), was promoted as an exemplar of everything Nazi Germany represented. She followed it with *Olympia* (1938), a two-part account of the Summer Olympics held in Berlin in 1936. If the second section was more a record of sporting achievements, the first was more grounded in ideology. The artwork for both films expounded the myth of Aryan excellence.

The Nazi Party's propaganda films also decried the influence of Jews in German culture, business, and everyday life. Anti-Semitism increased after Kristallnacht in 1938 and culminated on film with the releases of the vile *Jud Süss* and *The Eternal Jew* (both 1940). The posters for each feature crude caricatures.

In the United States, there were a number of propagandist films prior to the bombing of Pearl Harbor in 1941, which prompted the country's entry into World War II. Although the released version of *The Road Back* (1937) was eventually watered down, *The Mortal Storm* (1940) was more direct in its critique of Nazism, with a poster that shows Sturmabteilung members beating people in the streets. British directors working in the United States also joined the fray. Alfred Hitchcock directed *Foreign Correspondent*, while Charles Chaplin lampooned Hitler with *The Great Dictator* (both 1940). The poster for the former resembles a conventional thriller—perhaps to avoid attracting controversy— but there is no doubting the target of Chaplin's satire.

However, the most powerful statement to come out of Hollywood in the late 1930s was Warner Bros.' *Confessions of a Nazi Spy* (1939). The studio was rabidly anti-Nazi, and the film, and its campaign, made no attempt to hide its hatred of Hitler's ideology.

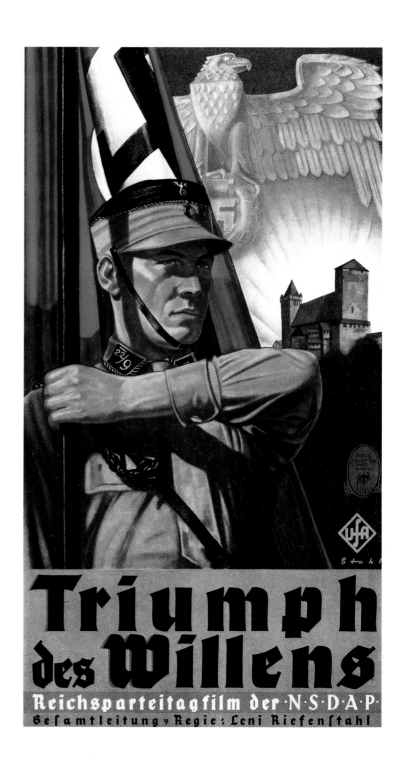

ABOVE

Triumph of the Will (1935)
A triumphant eagle rises above a Bavarian castle as a flag-wielding soldier marches by. There is no subtlety here, just the portrait of modern Germany with strong links to its past marching into its future.

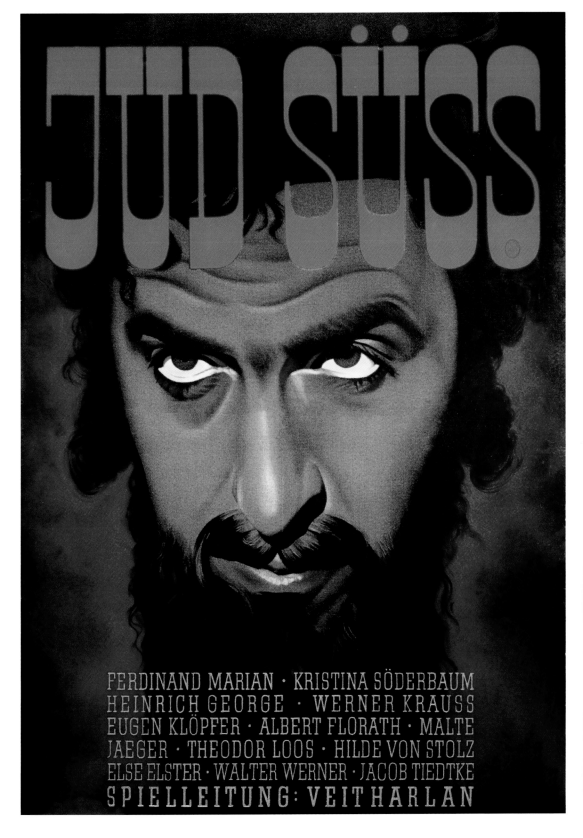

ABOVE

Jud Süss (1940)

Like the poster for *The Eternal Jew*, this artwork features a crude stereotype of a Jewish man. The green face and dark backdrop reinforce the message that this person is regarded as sub-human.

TOP RIGHT

Confessions of a Nazi Spy (1939)

This is a variation on Warner Bros.' posters for their gangster and "*G*" *Men* films. At the time, it was a bold statement for a studio in a country that still frowned upon anti-Nazi propaganda.

MIDDLE RIGHT

Olympia (1938)

The backdrop of Berlin's vast Olympic stadium is meant to conjure up images of the great ancient empires, sending the world an image of their strength. Unsurprisingly, the athlete is white.

BOTTOM RIGHT

The Eternal Jew (1940)

The Jew, according to this poster, is defined by the basest of caricatures and physical traits. The crudeness underpins the brutality that the Nazis employed in their anti-Semitic campaign.

JEAN GABIN
PIERRE FRESNAY
et
ERIC VON STROHEIM
dans

LA GRANDE
ILLUSION

adaptation et dialogues de
JEAN RENOIR et CHARLES SPAAK
Musique de KOSMA
avec DALIO

Un film de
JEAN RENOIR

ÉTAB? DELATTRE 18 RUE LE BUA PARIS (20e)

RAC
DISTRIBUTION

POSTERS OF THE DECADE

OPPOSITE

La grande illusion (1937)
Bernard Lancy's design
for the 1945 re-release
remains the most famous
poster for Renoir's film.
Drawing on art deco,
this image is a powerful
symbol of what has been
lost after so many years
of war.

BELOW LEFT

M (1931)
This simple yet powerful
image conjures up a sense
of horror. The "M" could
have been smeared in
blood as an indication of
the film's controversial
subject matter, which
deals with a child killer
and the public's response.

BELOW RIGHT

Gone with the Wind
(1939)
With subsequent re-issues
of the film, the famous
clinch between Rhett and
Scarlett would dominate
the promotional material.
But for the film's original
release, the focus was on
Vivien Leigh and the film's
epic scale.

Hollywood certainly experienced the beginning of its golden age in the 1930s, but it wasn't the only cinema to undergo a creative boon. Before the specter of fascism and the shadow of war descended, Europe produced numerous films of startling originality that pushed the envelope of the medium.

Alongside F. W. Murnau, Fritz Lang was one of the German filmmakers who dominated the country's cinematic landscape in the 1920s. By the end of that decade, Murnau had left for Hollywood, and Lang followed in 1934, escaping the growing influence of Nazism. But before he did, the filmmaker produced two masterpieces: *The Testament of Dr. Mabuse* (1933, see page 44) and *M* (1931). Lang's story of a child killer pursued on the streets of Berlin took the perspective of both the killer and his pursuers. The result was a profoundly unsettling film, with a startling performance by Peter Lorre as the killer. In promoting such controversial material, posters for the film shied away from engaging with the events depicted, instead adopting a more oblique approach employing the "M" motif.

French filmmaker Jean Renoir gradually built a reputation throughout the 1930s, with *La Chienne* (1931),

Boudou Saved from Drowning (1932), and *The Crime of Monsieur Lange* (1936), before embarking on his two masterpieces of that decade, *La grande illusion* (1937) and *The Rules of the Game* (1939). *La grande illusion* remains one of the great anti-war films and the perfect example of Renoir's humanist filmmaking. The 1945 re-release artwork best captures the film's themes.

Hollywood only occasionally produced a work as monumental as *Gone with the Wind* (1939). Producer David O. Selznick's long-cherished project was an adaptation of Margaret Mitchell's *bildungsroman* of 1936, which details the struggles faced by Scarlett O'Hara, the spoiled child of Atlanta landowners, in the lead up to and during the American Civil War. The story behind the making of the film and the search for the perfect actor to play Scarlett are almost as legendary as the film itself, which only fueled the publicity machine promoting the film. The romance between Vivien Leigh's Scarlett and Clark Gable's Rhett Butler was a key point of appeal for audiences, but the scale of the destruction wrought by the Civil War, filmed in epic proportions by Victor Fleming, was also essential to *Gone with the Wind's* promotion.

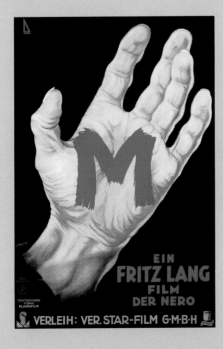

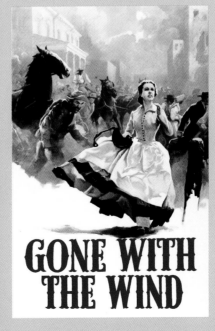

1940s

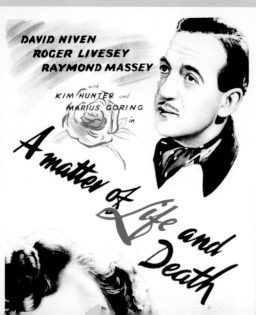

As the world emerged from World War II, a new film movement gathered momentum. Italian neorealism was founded by a small collection of filmmakers and writers with the common idea of shining a light on those who had suffered the horrors of fascism during the war and, subsequently, were affected by profound social inequality. They presented a different kind of filmmaking that pushed for a different kind of world. The neorealist movement may not have lasted much longer than a decade, but its influence was profound, shaping future film movements and highlighting cinema's importance as a social, cultural, and political barometer. If the posters that represented the films were conventional in the way they presented their subjects, they captured the passion of the filmmakers and their narratives.

Passion and lyricism motivated two filmmakers in particular, in France and England. Jean Cocteau had established himself as an artistic polymath by the time he made the beloved *La belle et la bête* in 1946. He had often used his own artwork for the posters that promoted his films, but for his sumptuous fairy tale,

starring Josette Day as Belle and Jean Marais as the Beast, the artwork made the most of the rococo period in which the story is set.

Michael Powell and his business partner Emeric Pressburger, who comprised the filmmaking team the Archers, produced rhapsodic color films that were a dream for any designer. Visually resplendent and swooningly romantic, they were the antithesis of most of the British films being made in the 1940s. In addition, the earthier Gainsborough Pictures costume dramas, made at its London studios, helped to promote James Mason as one of the era's great villains—all mood and rage.

Across the Atlantic, film noir drew heavily on German expressionism's extreme use of light and shade to create dark crime dramas. Simple notions of good and bad were replaced by shades of gray, in which the hero may well be as unlikable as the villain, the female lead could easily be a manipulative antagonist, and nothing is ever what it appears to be. The posters for the films reveled in this moral ambivalence, and designers had more freedom to play with stars' personas, transforming former good guys Dick Powell and Fred MacMurray into a tough private investigator and a killer.

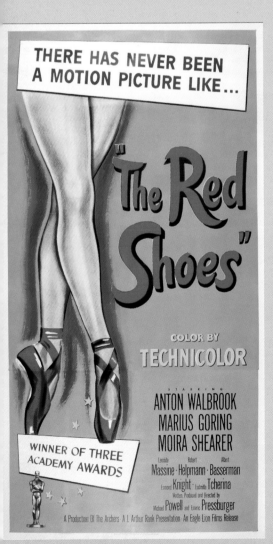

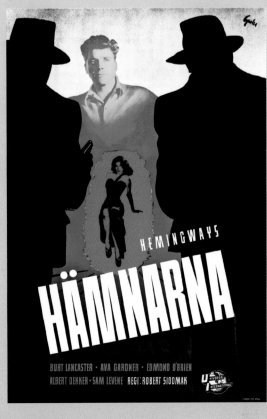

ITALIAN NEOREALISM

Italian neorealism was the first major film movement to emerge in the aftermath of World War II. A social realist cinema that engaged with the plight of ordinary people, it was a marked shift away from the bourgeois Telefoni Bianchi ("white telephone") films that dominated Italian cinema during Benito Mussolini's reign.

Neorealism comprised a collection of left-leaning writers and filmmakers that included Roberto Rossellini, Vittorio De Sica, Federico Fellini, Luchino Visconti, and Giuseppe De Santis. The guiding principles were laid out in a manifesto penned by Cesare Zavattini, who also wrote the screenplay for the key neorealist films *Shoeshine* (1946) and *Bicycle Thieves* (1948). They included an emphasis on real locations, working with non-professional actors wherever possible, and a focus on portraying the lives of those at the lower end of the economic and social spectrum of Italian society.

The artwork for many of the neorealist films didn't always distinguish them from other Italian films of the late 1940s. The majority of the locally produced posters were beautifully illustrated watercolors by artists such as Ercole Brini, who created the well-known image for *Bicycle Thieves*. Although that artwork skillfully manages to capture the tone of the film, other posters were less faithful to their themes, instead opting to make the films more commercially viable. One of the posters for De Sica's first neorealist film, *Shoeshine,* places a smiling boy in its foreground, standing in front of two boys behind bars. Like another poster for the film that depicts a group of boys in a gang, the image hardly represents the sense of despair that pervades the drama. Similarly, the main posters for Rossellini's *Rome, Open City* (1945), with Anna Magnani looking pensive, imply a conventional melodrama. However, another artwork, which features Aldo Fabrizi's priest confronting a silhouetted German soldier, is more in keeping with the film's tone. Although the Italian poster for Rossellini's *Paisan* (1946) is striking, it appears more euphoric than the film actually is. The face of an Allied soldier rises above two scenes from the film and a moment of domestic bliss. The best of these posters are beautifully illustrated, but unlike some of the international posters that were more direct in tapping into the films' portraits of Italian society, they don't always represent the ideals of the neorealist movement.

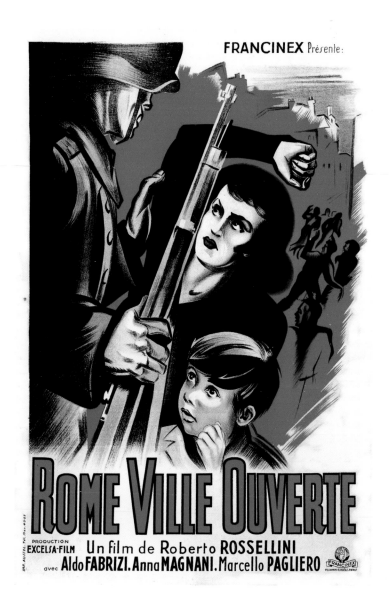

ABOVE

Rome, Open City (1945)
The French poster for Rossellini's film is direct in its portrayal of the brutality of Nazi rule, hinting at the film's climactic moment, featuring Anna Magnani, in which blood literally runs in the streets.

OPPOSITE

Bicycle Thieves (1948)
Ercole Brini captures the intensity of De Sica's celebrated film. His artwork subtly employs day and night as an emotional register of the man's mood and his son's angst over his father's growing despair.

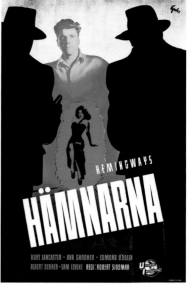

ABOVE

Out of the Past (1947)
This features all the classic elements of noir iconography. Robert Mitchum displays the hallmarks of the anti-hero, managing to appear laconic and suspicious as he looks toward Jane Greer's femme fatale.

TOP RIGHT

The Killers (1946)
The silhouetted assassins kill Burt Lancaster's character at the beginning of this thriller, hence Lancaster's spectral presence. Ava Gardner's appearance in red leaves no question as to why he is dead.

MIDDLE RIGHT

Kiss of Death (1947)
This Swedish poster taps into the visual elements that define film noir. The use of light creates a world of mood and dark desires, revealed in the way Victor Mature's face is half-shrouded in shadow.

BOTTOM RIGHT

Laura (1944)
Color is employed to startling effect here. Gene Tierney's eponymous victim appears as a ghostly presence in this unnatural light, while Dana Andrews' Det. Lt. Mark McPherson is a haunted figure.

FILM NOIR

An extension of the crime thriller, film noir took audiences into morally ambiguous terrain. It was a place where heroes were often indistinct from villains—or where the villains were simply more sadistic—where violence was a part of everyday life, and where the world was shrouded in shadow. Films that fall into this classification could originate from any country, but the archetypal film noir was American, urban, and contemporary. The most popular period ran from the early 1940s to the 1950s, but the influence of these films has continued to the present day, from their tone and their look to the way in which they are sold to audiences.

The term "film noir" was coined by French critics who, in the years after the end of World War II when a backlog of US features became readily available, identified certain similarities in prestige and B-movie thrillers. There has been much debate concerning which film started the trend, but in terms of the archetypal noir John Huston's *The Maltese Falcon* (1941) most perfectly fits the bill. Humphrey Bogart had spent much of the 1930s playing hardened criminals, which made him the ideal choice for the role of anti-hero detective Sam Spade.

Visually, classic film noir was seen to draw heavily on German expressionism, often emphasizing the contrast between light and dark, and creating worlds that were the physical projection of a character's psyche. In most cases, they were tortured, tormented, or compromised in some way. Billy Wilder's *Double Indemnity* (1944), widely acknowledged as one of the finest noirs, opens its flashback structure in broad daylight. But as Fred MacMurray's insurance salesman is drawn closer into the web of deceit woven by Barbara Stanwyck's adulterous schemer, both the film's tone and its physical world darken. The film's poster plays up these elements of desire and danger.

In addition, *Double Indemnity* sets out some of the key tropes of the film noir genre. Stanwyck is the classic femme fatale. Other noteworthy examples include Mary Astor in *The Maltese Falcon*, Rita Hayworth in *Gilda* (1946) and *The Lady from Shanghai* (1947), and both Cloris Leachman and Gaby Rodgers in *Kiss Me Deadly* (1955). Femme fatale characters tended to dominate promotional material for the films (in the case of *Gilda*,

ABOVE

The Maltese Falcon (1941)
Earlier in 1941, Humphrey Bogart played ruthless killer Roy Earle in *High Sierra*. He is playing anti-hero detective Sam Spade here, but Warner Bros. is still selling him as the gangster figure audiences love.

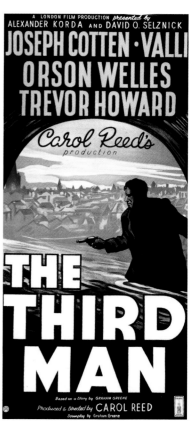

Touch of Evil (1958)
The pulpy image of Charlton Heston and Janet Leigh seems at odds with the image of the town and its occupants. But this clash of cultures and mind-sets is what makes Orson Welles' film so compelling.

Kiss Me Deadly (1955)
The title appearing on a pair of lips hints at the film's lurid tone. The captions are wildly over the top, while the central image does more than suggest desire: it smacks of undiluted lust.

Murder, My Sweet (1944)
In the 1930s, Dick Powell starred in Busby Berkley's musical extravaganzas. A decade later, he had transformed into a grizzled private eye with a cynical worldview, as evinced by his image here.

The Third Man (1949)
The Vienna backdrop here resembles the worlds depicted in the posters for the German expressionist films. It appears less as a city than a nightmare, with Orson Welles' character at the heart of it.

Hayworth in *that* dress *was* the reason to see the film), offering the sheen of glamour to the nefarious activities of cons and sleuths.

MacMurray's salesman in *Double Indemnity* is typical of the dupe—the guy who falls for the dame, but realizes far too late the mess she has gotten him into. A variation on this character was played by Orson Welles in *The Lady from Shanghai*, one of the more baroque noir thrillers. In addition to the dupe, another identifiable character is the investigator. Bogart's Sam Spade set the template in *The Maltese Falcon*, and it was then tweaked for different roles and actors, such as Dick Powell playing Philip Marlowe in *Murder, My Sweet* (1944) and Alan Ladd playing opposite Veronica Lake in *The Blue Dahlia* (1946). Robert Mitchum's character in *Out of the Past* (1947, aka *Build My Gallows High*) is a combination of the two. Fatally attracted to Jane Greer's schemer, he is both investigator and sucker. However, he occupies the moral high ground over Kirk Douglas' boss, who is one of the finest villains in film noir. Douglas appears suave, even benevolent, but a ruthless streak eventually emerges.

As film noir developed, it expanded outward, beyond the borders of the United States' urban centers. *The Night of the Hunter* (1955) travels to the Deep South, with director Charles Laughton making the most of a gothic atmosphere that chimes perfectly with noir's emphasis on chiaroscuro lighting. And Robert Mitchum's psychotic killer is a knowing look back to earlier noir roles.

Although the low-budget B-movie noirs may have lacked finesse, they certainly made up for it with style and shocks. Edgar G. Ulmer's impressive *Detour* (1945) is brief but taut. Its road trip flashback sequence is hinted at in one poster's use of chevrons as the border to a tableau of moments from the film, each playing to a specific trope of the genre. Robert Aldrich's independently produced *Kiss Me Deadly* went further. Arguably the finest—and one of the only—noirs to incorporate both science fiction and Cold War paranoia, Aldrich's adaptation of a Mickey Spillane Mike Hammer detective mystery is a lurid minor masterpiece. The poster for the story of a detective on the hunt for a suitcase that could bring about doomsday hints at the film's sensationalist tone.

Farther afield, Vienna provided the perfect backdrop for the finest European noir, with Orson Welles playing one of the genre's most iconic villains, Harry Lime, in *The Third Man* (1949). Welles returned to his directing role with *Touch of Evil* (1958), which traverses the US–Mexico border. In the film, he also plays one of the more memorable and perverse villains, Police Captain Hank Quinlan. The posters for all these films hint at their moody tone, which defines them as classic noir.

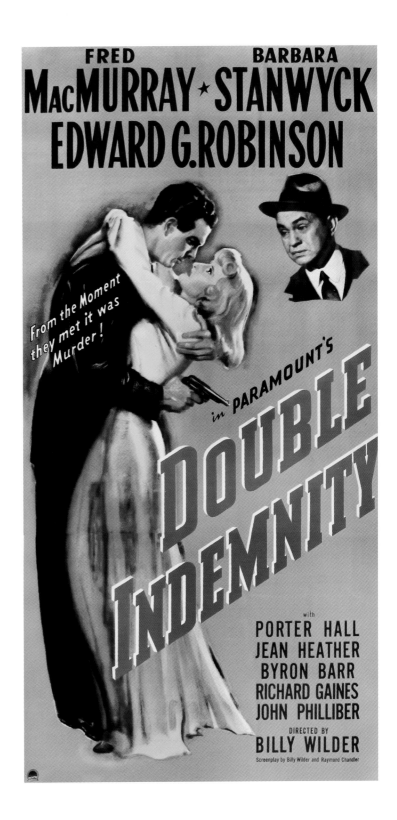

ABOVE

Double Indemnity (1944)
Take away the gun and Edward G. Robinson's insurance analyst and this could be a romantic drama. But the shadowy line surrounding Barbara Stanwyck and Fred MacMurray hints at something darker.

BILL GOLD

Across a career spanning eight decades, Bill Gold designed posters and campaigns for more than 200 films and collaborated with numerous high-profile directors and producers. His work reflected the times, from classical Hollywood in the 1940s and the changing face of US cinema in the 1960s to the emergence of the modern blockbuster. Many of his posters are key representations of their respective eras, and his work has made him one of the most influential designers in cinema.

A native New Yorker, Gold studied illustration and design at Brooklyn's Pratt Institute before gaining employment in the advertising department at Warner Bros. in 1941. Within six years, he was promoted to head of poster design. In 1959, the designer formed BG Charles with his brother Charlie, which focused on creating film trailers for studio productions. Then, in 1962, he set up Bill Gold Advertising. Although Gold retired in 2004, Clint Eastwood, who first worked with Gold in 1971, on the shattered glass poster for *Dirty Harry* (1971), convinced him to oversee the artwork for *J. Edgar* (2011), transposing a blue-tinted Leonardo DiCaprio over the vertical red and white stripes of the American flag.

Gold's first design defined his ability to convey a film's theme or narrative through striking visual representation. In his artwork for *Casablanca* (1942), he placed Humphrey Bogart's hero in the foreground, while behind him lay the images of characters who impact his life. Warner Bros. was apparently delighted with the result, but felt that the poster required some action, so Gold added a gun—an image taken from Bogart's previous Warner Bros. crime drama *High Sierra* (1941).

He followed it with a bombastic poster for the George M. Cohan biopic *Yankee Doodle Dandy* (1942). The design is a stark contrast to that of *Casablanca*—more a cacophony of images than a streamlined design, underpinning the wild life of its subject. His work on *The Big Sleep* (1946) highlighted the star power of Bogart and Lauren Bacall over the film's generic trappings.

Gold's subsequent work covered every genre, but with each of his designs, from *Casablanca*, *The Searchers* (1956), and *Bonnie and Clyde* (1967) to *Dirty Harry*, *Bird* (1988), and *Unforgiven* (1992), his brilliance lay in finding the kernel of an idea, a motif or a concept that would make audiences want to watch the film.

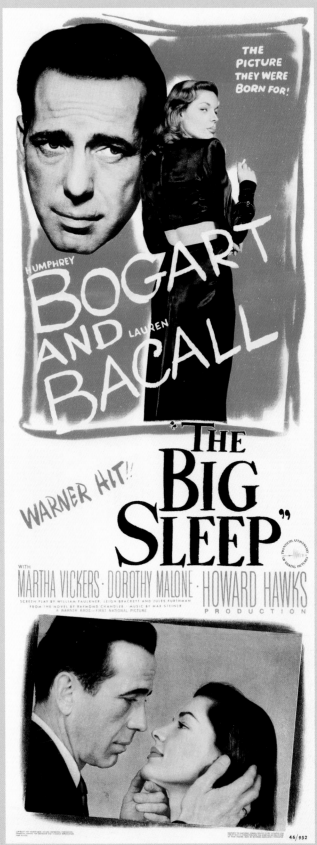

POWELL AND PRESSBURGER

Collectively known as the Archers, Michael Powell and Emeric Pressburger were the poet laureates of 1940s British cinema. Their key works were produced between 1939 and 1957, starting with *The Spy in Black* (1939, aka *U-Boat 29*) and ending with *Ill Met by Moonlight* (1957). Their films were marked by a lyricism and visual style that veered toward the expressive. Even their propaganda work often eschewed the conventions of realism. Although *The Small Back Room* (1949) can be seen as a chamber study of a bomb disposal expert struggling with alcoholism, it also features a moment of pent-up delirium that edges toward Dalí-like surrealism. As such, Powell and Pressburger were seen to be out of step with British cinema. It was not until the 1970s, after two major retrospectives, critical re-appraisal, and the championing of their work by directors such as Martin Scorsese and Francis Ford Coppola, that the duo were recognized as key figures in British film history.

The posters for Powell and Pressburger's films run from conventional artwork to bolder representations, reflecting the more radical nature of their later productions. Earlier work was rooted in propaganda and the war effort, and the posters for *Contraband* (1940) and *One of Our Aircraft is Missing* (1942) reflect this, rather than draw attention to the elements that set the filmmakers' work apart from other war films of the era. Even the satirical *The Life and Death of Colonel Blimp* (1943), a unique film for the period because it features a sympathetic German officer, was sold more on its romance than its political edge. It was the filmmakers' first color film (Powell had previously worked as one of the directors on Alexander Korda's 1940 fantasy *The Thief of Baghdad*), and their innovative use of color became increasingly prominent in each subsequent film's promotional artwork.

   By the end of the war, Powell and Pressburger were employing color as a means of exploring representation and expression. The romantic fantasy *A Matter of Life and Death* (1946) alternates between monochrome and color in its depiction of Heaven and Earth, while *Black Narcissus* (1947) uses color to heighten its melodrama and to suggest the exotic. The posters for these films, like those for *The Red Shoes* (1948) and *The Tales of Hoffmann* (1951), accentuate the uniqueness of these singular works.

A Matter of Life and Death (1946)
This poster for the Archers' wartime romance, featuring its US title, plays up the fantastical element of the film as well as the romance between David Niven's pilot and Kim Hunter's radio operator.

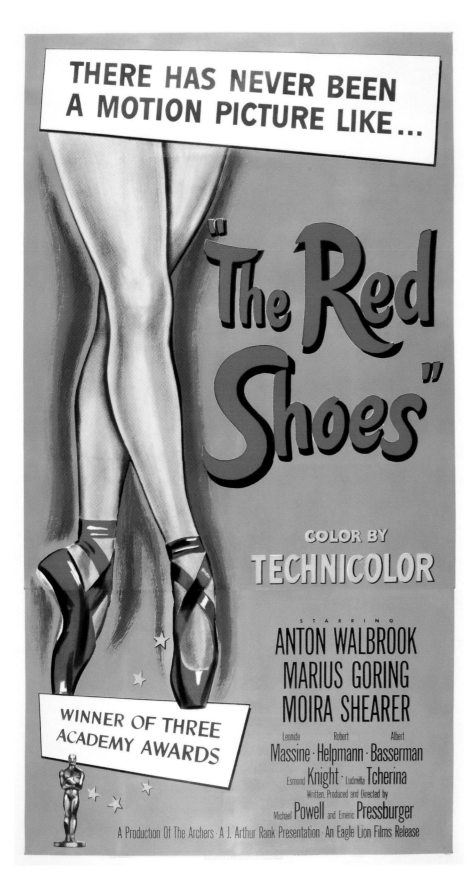

The Red Shoes (1948)
Some posters highlight the conflict
between Anton Walbrook's impresario
and Moira Shearer's ingénue. This artwork
plays to the film's prestigious credentials.

Black Narcissus (1947)
Exoticism is expressed through contrasting
colors and fabric design. There is no hint
that the narrative concerns a group of nuns,
which may have been a marketing ploy.

A Matter of Life and Death (1946)
This is one of the simpler designs. The
use of red highlights the film's ingenious
switch between color and black and white,
with the emphasis on life for Niven's pilot.

ANDRÉ PAULVÉ
PRÉSENTE

UN FILM DE

Jean Cocteau

JEAN MARAIS
JOSETTE DAY
dans

la BELLE et la BÊTE

HISTOIRE, PARÓLES, MISE EN SCÉNE DE **JEAN COCTEAU** D'APRÈS LE CONTE DE MADAME **LEPRINCE DE BEAUMONT**
illustré par
CHRISTIAN BÉRARD

avec
MILA PARELY, NANE GERMON, MICHEL AUCLAIR *et* **MARCEL ANDRÉ**
CONSEILLER TECHNIQUE: R. CLÉMENT   MUSIQUE DE **GEORGES AURIC**   DIRECT. DE PRODUCT. **ÉMILE DARBON**
UNE SUPERPRODUCTION ANDRÉ PAULVÉ

JEAN COCTEAU'S FANTASTIC WORLDS

OPPOSITE

La belle et la bête (1946)
In Jean-Denis Malclès' design, the Beast emerges from the darkness with only his head and mane visible. Likewise, Belle is bereft of a body. Her expression can be read as either pleading or desirous.

BELOW LEFT

Les enfants terribles (1950)
Cocteau's simple line drawing transforms into a Rorschach test in this poster for Jean-Pierre Melville's film. It is the perfect metaphor for the eponymous siblings and their tormented desires, which end up destroying them.

BELOW RIGHT

Orpheus (1950)
There is a formal beauty to the pyramid form of J. Harold's photomontage, featuring the three central characters from Cocteau's dream of a film. Death is ever present, while the statues hint at a tale that transcends time.

A unique presence in cinema, the writer, artist, playwright, and filmmaker Jean Cocteau produced a body of work that explores desire through dream-like imagery, conjuring up fantastical worlds where conventions of reality and normalcy have no place. He directed only a handful of films, but they all bear the hallmark of his unique vision. Some collaborations, such as *Les enfants terribles* (1950), which was written by Cocteau (based on his novel of 1929) and directed by Jean-Pierre Melville, also capture that spirit.

As a skilled designer and artist, Cocteau had a vision for his films that extended far beyond the remit of production. He also contributed poster ideas and artwork. Like those of Pablo Picasso, Cocteau's line drawings were exquisite, their delicacy conveying emotion in the subtlest of ways. This can be seen in the simple design for his film *Testament of Orpheus* (1960). The film title and director's credit are written, unfussily, in blue ink. Between them, a figure is seen in profile, drawn using one single brown line, with a few additional details making an eye and ear. Two haphazard green lines denote a laurel, a little orange some hair, and in the background is the

gold of a lyre. *Testament of Orpheus* was the final part of a trilogy Cocteau wrote and directed, which began with *The Blood of a Poet* (1932), followed by *Orpheus* (1950). Most of the posters for *The Blood of a Poet* feature a still from the film, depicting the moment when the Poet, played by Chilean actor Enrique Riveros, commits suicide. The artwork for *Orpheus* ranges from conventional posters, featuring stars Jean Marais and María Casares, to more daring explorations of the film's themes. Arguably the most successful is J. Harold's design, which uses photomontage to create a triangular image.

Cocteau's best-known and arguably most beloved film is his adaptation of Gabrielle-Suzanne Barbot de Villeneuve's fairy tale of 1740. A world in which inanimate objects don't so much come to life as take human form, Cocteau's resplendent *La belle et la bête* (1946) richly captures the contrast between innocence and darker undercurrents, while creating an erotic charge between the two. Most artwork for the film employs images of the two leads, but Jean-Denis Malclès' celebrated design is richly evocative in its interpretation of Cocteau's lush world.

THE EALING COMEDY

In the film industry, the name "Ealing" denotes a particular kind of comedy film that was produced in the late 1940s and 1950s. The films were promoted as portraying a quintessential Britishness through the prism of humor. In addition, the best of them became a document of the country in the period immediately following the end of World War II.

Ealing Studios were built in 1931, on a site where a film studio had existed since 1902. Comedies were produced there throughout the 1930s, featuring stars such as George Formby, Gracie Fields, and Will Hay. With the outbreak of war, the studio shifted gear and produced a number of propaganda-tinged features, such as *Went the Day Well?* (1942) and *Undercover* (1943), as well as the horror portmanteau *Dead of Night* (1945). The studio also produced crime films and the occasional period drama.

The success of *Hue and Cry* (1947), which tells the story of a criminal gang's plans being thwarted by a group of boys, was followed by a trilogy of Celtic-themed comedies: *Another Shore* (1948), *A Run for Your Money* (1949), and *Whisky Galore* (1949). This last film set the template for the studio's David versus Goliath narrative, in which an individual or small community would face up to elitism or bureaucracy. Furthermore, the poster for the film was the first for any Ealing production to play imaginatively with its themes.

In the same year, one of the studio's masterpieces was produced: *Kind Hearts and Coronets* (1949), a black comedy and social satire. The artwork for the film is a collage of photography and painting, which perfectly encapsulates the film's humor. A similar style was employed for *The Lavender Hill Mob* (1951), with a still of Alec Guinness and Stanley Holloway superimposed onto a tinted cartoon backdrop, while *The Man in the White Suit* (1951) plays up the physicality of Alec Guinness' enthusiastic protagonist.

For many, *The Ladykillers* (1955) remains the most beloved of the Ealing comedies, and its poster is also one of the most effective in conveying both the characteristics of the film's protagonists—criminal misfits planning a robbery—and the ethos of Ealing Studios. The studio passed its films off as playful slices of humor, but the best were also reflections upon postwar British life.

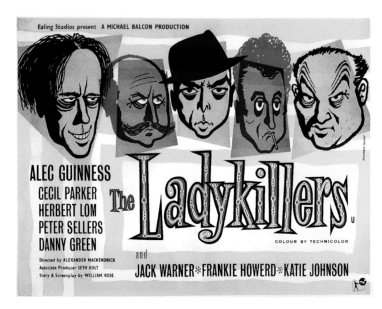

The Ladykillers (1955)
The most popular Ealing comedy is represented by caricatures of the five shady characters planning a robbery. The yellow lines resemble bars, suggesting luck may not be on their side.

ABOVE
A Run for Your Money (1949)
A more simple design hints at the knockabout, cartoonish caper of this early comedy from the studio's classic period. The use of red on white hints at a sense of urgency.

TOP

Whisky Galore (1949)
The playful use of Scottish
motifs underpins the
lightly satirical nature of
Alexander Mackendrick's
comedy, with the two
stars appearance on the
whisky bottle hinting
at the importance of
the drink to the small
community in which
they live.

BOTTOM

**Kind Hearts and Coronets
(1949)**
Like the poster for *The
Ladykillers*, the yellow and
white lines denote prison
bars. The design plays with
perspective and makes
clever use of stills and
hand-drawn imagery.

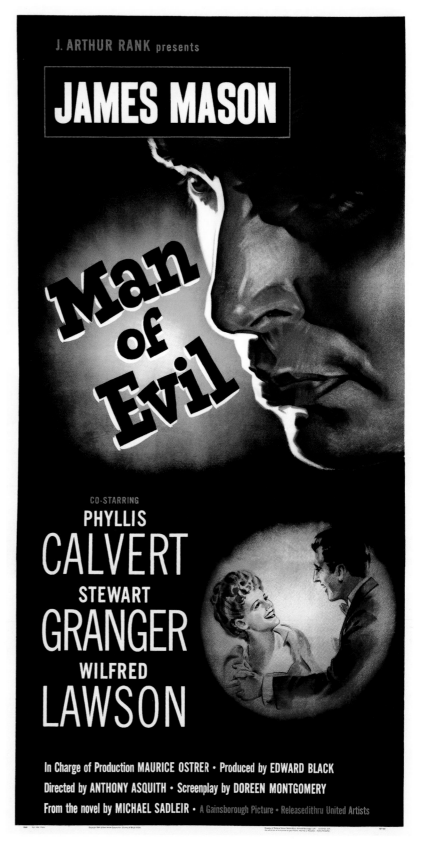

ABOVE LEFT

Madonna of the Seven Moons (1945)
The caption barely encompasses the plot
of Gainsborough's most bizarre film. But
by this point, audiences had some inkling
of what to expect: adventure, romance,
and more than an intimation of sex.

ABOVE RIGHT

Man of Evil (1944, aka Fanny by Gaslight)
James Mason is a dark, brooding presence
here. Like his role in the film, he exists at
one remove from Phyllis Calvert's heroine.
By this time, Mason was a bona fide star,
so his name appears above the US title.

GAINSBOROUGH MELODRAMAS

For two decades, Gainsborough Pictures was a significant presence in British cinema. Founded in 1924 by the producer Michael Balcon, the studio was known for producing B-movies alongside the superior productions of its sister company Gaumont British. The studio's logo, which precedes each production, is based on a portrait of the eighteenth-century tragedienne Sarah Siddons painted by Thomas Gainsborough.

Working out of a north London studio, before relocating to Gaumont British's studios in the west of the city during the war, Gainsborough Pictures became partly owned by the larger Rank Organisation in the late 1930s. This raised the studio's profile and resulted in its producing *Oh, Mr. Porter!* (1937), a vehicle for the popular British comedian Will Hay, and Alfred Hitchcock's *The Lady Vanishes* (1938). During the war, the studio produced a series of powerful dramas focusing on life in Britain, such as *Millions Like Us* (1943) and *Waterloo Road* (1945). However, Gainsborough was best known for its bodice-ripping costume dramas.

Beginning with *The Man in Grey* (1943), the Gainsborough melodramas were notable for their moral ambivalence and visual style. Most were based on recently published novels, many by female writers, and offered audiences the vicarious thrills of their characters' villainy. Good might win in the end, but the journey was often thrilling, if on occasion quite ludicrous. To accentuate the emotions and for dramatic effect, the films made the most of chiaroscuro lighting. And over the course of the disparate series, Gainsborough accrued a cast of regulars. If Patricia Roc and Phyllis Calvert mostly played innocents and Stewart Granger was the ruffian object of desire, Margaret Lockwood attracted controversy with her brazen sexuality, while James Mason appeared to revel in sadism.

Mason's trajectory over the course of the melodramas was captured in the posters that promoted them. *The Man in Grey* finds him at his splenetic worst, while *Man of Evil* (1944, aka *Fanny by Gaslight*) and *The Wicked Lady* (1945) vary the levels of his villainy. The artwork also highlights these films' aesthetics: their dark, brooding tones were a contrast to much of British cinema during the war years and remain singular in the history of British film.

ABOVE

The Man in Grey (1943)
Here, James Mason's villainy is a shadow looming large over the flashback story. Phyllis Calvert and Stewart Granger's contemporary characters are separated from him by both time and the title.

CITIZEN KANE

Citizen Kane (1941) generally tops the lists of the greatest films ever made. It was the feature debut of a theater and radio wunderkind—Orson Welles—and, in advance of its release, speculation and publicity hinted at something remarkable. Then news of the film's subject matter seeped out, and powerful businessman, politician, and publisher William Randolph Hearst used all his power to destroy the film.

Citizen Kane charts the early years, rise to power, and subsequent fall from grace of Charles Foster Kane. It is a tale of power and hubris. However, the story behind the making of the film is as compelling as its narrative. Central to it is Orson Welles. In an age when producers ruled in Hollywood and stars had to earn their way into the spotlight, it was unthinkable that a first-time director would cast himself in the lead role in a film, become the sole focus of all promotional material, and see his name emblazoned across every poster. Not since Chaplin had anyone so completely dominated a work. But Welles had spent years working his way up through the ranks of Keystone, Essanay, Mutual, and First National, developing a specific screen persona that audiences

would immediately recognize on any poster. Welles had only just arrived in Hollywood and appeared to expect star status, along with everything that came with it.

Herman J. Mankiewicz's screenplay, co-written with Welles, drew on various sources, but its overt reference to Hearst's life and his affair with silent star Marion Davies enraged the media magnate. Hearst's efforts likely dampened the box office returns, yet *Citizen Kane* remained one of the most garlanded films of the year.

Almost all the English-language posters used to promote the film steer clear of any details regarding the film's subject, instead emphasizing Welles' presence. Most feature the caption "It's Terrific!" with some adding "Everybody's talking about it." By contrast, other countries opted for more imaginative approaches to publicizing the film. While some emphasize Kane's primary occupation—a newspaperman—others accentuate his lust for power. Subsequent re-release artwork has also adopted a more inventive strategy. The artwork for the re-release in 1956, for example, could have easily been employed by Welles for his adaptation in 1962 of Franz Kafka's *The Trial* (1925).

BOTTOM LEFT

Nothing in this artwork hints at the radical experimentation of Welles' film. Kane's position on the poster hints at his power, while the images below him suggest little more than a conventional melodrama.

**OPPOSITE
CLOCKWISE FROM TOP LEFT**

Letters, like a swarm of bees, don't so much hover over Kane's face in this Italian poster as congregate to create it. This implies that Kane created his world—a history written as he wanted it to be read.

The use of print in this German poster constructs an entire city. In contrast to the Italian poster, it suggests that Kane has the power to create worlds. But those worlds can become larger than he is.

This Polish poster cleverly employs Kane's mid-career desire to enter politics. Adapted versions of his campaign poster appear in the background, with the film's credits—designed like billstickers—placed haphazardly over them.

The poster celebrating the film's re-release in 1956 is far more incisive than the studio's promotional campaign of 1941. Kane here is no giant, and his legacy is mixed, as evinced by the "K" covering his face.

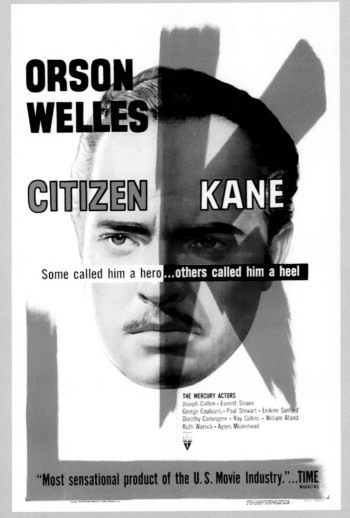

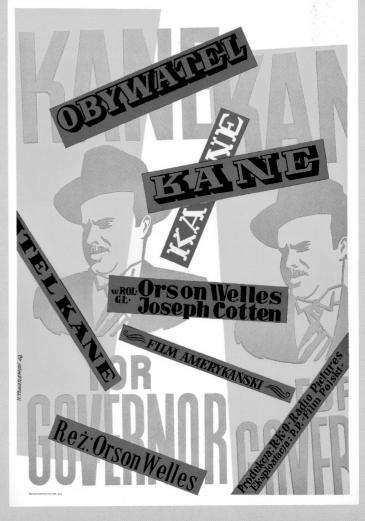

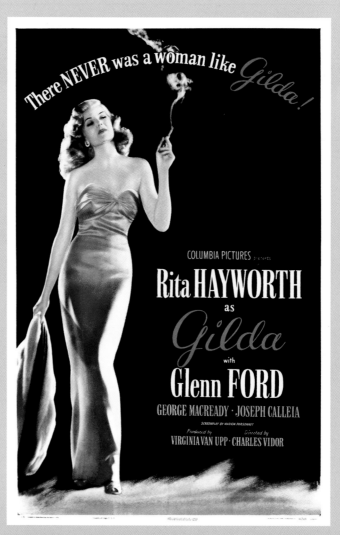

POSTERS OF THE DECADE

OPPOSITE
CLOCKWISE FROM TOP LEFT

Sullivan's Travels (1941)
This is an example of a star's box office power. Joel McCrea might be the lead actor in Preston Sturges' social comedy, but it is Veronica Lake and her platinum blond hair that are the draw here.

Cabin in the Sky (1943)
Hot jazz and big band tunes are given a Hollywood makeover. Vincente Minnelli's film is a rare example of a studio foregrounding black performers, and this poster plays up the film's devilish joy.

Gilda (1946)
Featured here is a variation on the dress that Rita Hayworth wears when she sings "Put the Blame on Mame" in Charles Vidor's noir classic. Along with the famous flick of the hair, it made her an icon.

Les enfants du paradis (1945)
Other posters capture the grace and elegance of Marcel Carné's exquisite feature, but this version throws us into a scene of high drama. It is presented as a poster from the era in which the film is set.

RIGHT

Adam's Rib (1949)
This is gender equality as a pitch battle between Spencer Tracy and Katharine Hepburn. MGM's art department devised the perfect visual metaphor to sell George Cukor's sparkling comedy of the sexes.

While Hollywood continued to produce films throughout World War II, many film industries were placed on hiatus until the defeat of Nazi Germany and its allies. As Europe emerged from the conflict, Italy led the way in cinema with the neorealist movement. France followed with a revolution in film a decade later, but first it produced one of its most beloved dramas.

Marcel Carné's *Les enfants du paradis* (1945) is an extraordinary accomplishment. Filming took place during the Nazi occupation, and extras on set were purported to have been a mix of Resistance members (using the production as cover for their activities) and Nazi sympathizers. Unfolding across the 1820s and 1830s, Carné's film is sumptuous, witty, and visually ravishing—and the artwork that accompanied its release is no less resplendent, capturing the tenor of that era.

Cabin in the Sky (1943) also centers on performance, albeit of a more fantastic kind, as Eddie "Rochester" Anderson's murdered gambler is given a second chance on Earth. Vincente Minnelli's musical was one of the few major studio features with an all-black cast, and its artwork makes the most of the jazz musicians that star in the film and the music they play. *Cabin in the Sky* was a popular and successful film, except in the southern US states that refused to show it.

Although Jane Russell perhaps attracted the most controversy of any female Hollywood star in the 1940s for her provocative appearance on the posters for Howard Hughes' Western *The Outlaw* (1943), she was not alone in making a memorable impression upon audiences. *I Wanted Wings* (1941) made Veronica Lake a star, developing her signature "peek-a-boo" look, with her hair falling over her right eye. *Sullivan's Travels* (1941) was released in the same year, and Paramount Pictures sold it on Lake's newly acquired stardom, and her hair. Rita Hayworth's hair and the dress she wears in a musical number are the main focus of the image used to attract audiences to *Gilda* (1946), in which Hayworth is a perfect femme fatale. By contrast, gender roles were up for grabs in *Adam's Rib* (1949), with Katharine Hepburn going her own way and defying Hollywood conventions as to what represents a female star.

1950s

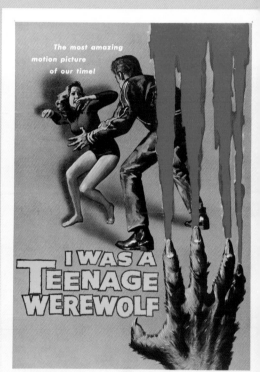

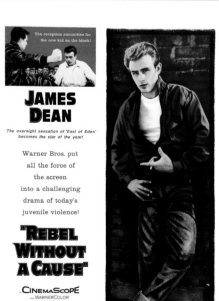

In 1947, the designer Paul Rand published a book titled *Thoughts on Design*. It made clear the relationship between design and art, but also set out the principles of what design should be. From his own career, which lasted fifty years, Rand defined the designer's role as one that "experiences, perceives, analyzes, organizes, symbolizes, and synthesizes."

Nowhere throughout the 1950s was the relationship between a film and its artwork more pronounced than in the posters of Saul Bass. His deceptively simple designs captured the essence of every film he worked on. They were rarely as esoteric as the posters of the Soviet constructivists, but they certainly moved away from the focus on stars being key to a film's promotional campaign. Bass' best work might seem simple—blocks of color and a silhouetted image, often disfigured or misshapen in some way—but his designs were always extraordinarily effective.

No less bold but often more surreal was a new generation of designers that emerged from Poland and then Czechoslovakia. Like Bass, they presented alternative interpretations of films. However, whereas his work was clearly defined by its lines, these artists presented a wild world with seemingly no rules or boundaries.

Being different was essential for cinema in the 1950s. For the first time in its existence, the medium was under threat. Television had become the favorite of the masses, supplying entertainment to its audiences every day and without the cost of having to leave home. So cinema had to offer something that television could not, and that was scale. For the first time since silent cinema, the epic was one of the main attractions. Science fiction also offered audiences the spectacle of Earth coming to an end, or occasionally suggested that the modern world faced a grave threat in the form of Communism. Both these genres allowed artists such as Reynold Brown to conjure up cartoon-like posters depicting eye-catching scenes from the films.

And difference defined the rise of the teenager. The term had been in existence only for a few years when the potential of a teenage market was recognized, and advertisers tapped into a deep well of revenue. Rebellion was key, but by the end of the decade youthful energy had been replaced by a sense of direction and a younger, more questioning cinema began to emerge.

THE AGE OF ADVERTISING

The years after World War II saw the West gradually emerge from the emotional, cultural, and economic impact of the conflict. The industries that had produced the weapons of war turned their attention to domestic life, from building affordable housing to the appliances that would populate them. At the same time, birth rates were increasing, a nascent middle class was accruing a sizable disposable income, and companies were looking for ways to encourage people to spend it. This was the age of advertising.

In the United States, the advertising executives based around Manhattan's Madison Avenue helped to drive the wave of consumer spending. They created a new image of the family. The Depression era was forgotten, and in its place came a vision of a bright future. The Jetsons were the family with everything (even the Flintstones were presented as a Stone Age family of means), and advertising executives and their art departments ensured that there was no such thing as enough.

"New and improved" appeared to be the mantra of the decade. The idea of making do with the old was replaced by ads that made everything seem affordable. In order to increase the success of a product, advertising firms offered companies the latest techniques in market research, which not only targeted specific social groups who had money to spend but also family members across generational divides. Children became potential consumers for the first time, and the emerging teenage culture was a lucrative demographic.

Leisure was key in this era. The car was no longer portrayed in purely functional terms. Elliott Erwitt's well-known photograph from 1955, of a couple seen kissing in the side view mirror of their car, is a romantic image involving three participants: the man, the woman, and the transport that brought them to this place. The right cigarettes, the right drink, and the right look were essential to achieve such an image of perfection.

Advertising for film was also in a state of flux, partly to keep up with changing tastes, but also because of a new threat: television. This medium dominated the decade, and cinema had to find ways of encouraging people to see the latest release. If new and improved didn't quite cut it—television was, after all, the new thing—bigger and better appeared to be the motto for Hollywood.

M-G-M presents The Comedy of The Year!

GREGORY PECK
LAUREN BACALL

IN

DESIGNING WOMAN

Co Starring DOLORES GRAY

ABOVE

Designing Woman (1957)
The artwork here gives the film an ultra-modern, cosmopolitan spin, reflecting the film's play with gender roles and representation. It was created by Jacques Kapralik, a Romanian emigré.

OPPOSITE

Will Success Spoil Rock Hunter? (1959)
Frank Tashlin's playful satire of Madison Avenue executive life features Jayne Mansfield in one of her most famous roles. The design underpins the madcap nature of Tashlin's world.

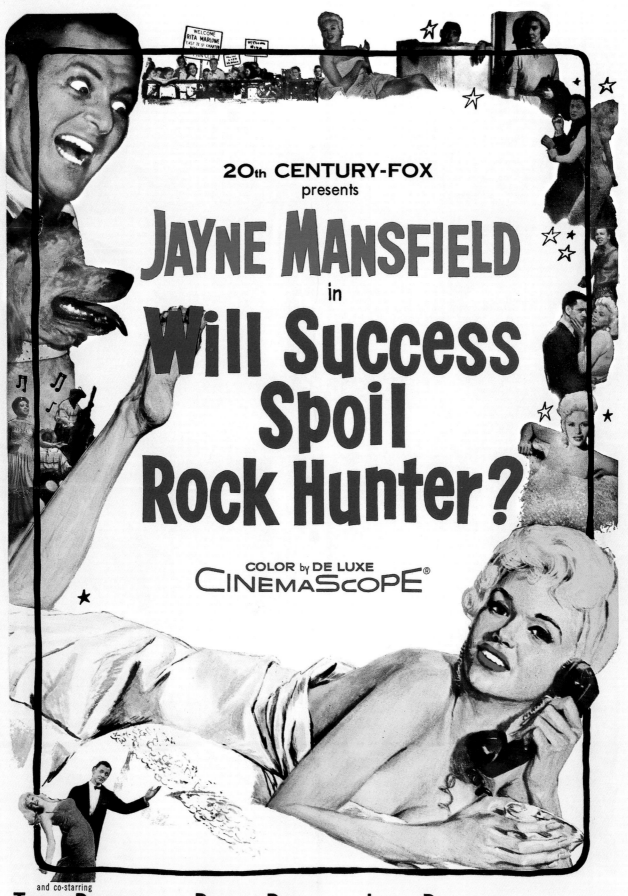

TEEN ANGST

In popular culture, the teenager didn't really exist until the 1950s. Prior to this time, it was as if children suddenly transformed into adults overnight, and the awkward, emotionally wrought, and sexually turbulent years in-between passed by without a hitch. Then the huge commercial potential of this young market was identified, and the teenager became a significant presence in everyday life.

In 1944, *Life* magazine published the photo-story "Teen-Age Girls: They Live in a Wonderful World of Their Own." Focusing on girls from a suburb of St. Louis, Missouri, it was the first article to address this "new" phenomenon. Within a decade, the term "teenager" had numerous connotations, few of which were positive. Cinema profited, in particular, from exploiting fears about teen rebellion and the moral vacuum that threatens to engulf teenagers. It was the perfect storm for producers: they could attract not only parents who wanted to see their worst fears reflected on the screen, but also teenagers who wished to enjoy the vicarious thrills of their peers. The clash between generations was perfectly represented in school dramas such as *Blackboard Jungle* (1955), which was the first mainstream US film to feature rock and roll music.

Marlon Brando was thirty years old when he played Johnny, a biker and gang leader, in *The Wild One* (1954). He was certainly no teen, but because of his attitude and the way he looked he became an anti-authoritarian icon. In posters, he is shown riding his motorbike or leaning on a bar, wearing his leather jacket and trademark cap. The text always appears as an exclamation, suggesting something shocking. In style, the design was no different to the moral outrage films of the 1930s, such as *Reefer Madness* (1936), and would be exacerbated in later films such as *The Flaming Teenage* (1956).

Hollywood's first teen icon star, who captured the angst of youths bristling against an older generation's mores, was James Dean. Even though he was twenty-four when *Rebel Without a Cause* (1955) was released, the pent-up rage he displayed was new for a mainstream Hollywood film. Whether depicting Dean leaning against a wall with his jacket undone and cigarette in hand, or captured in a moment of anger, the posters for the film made the actor cool, in the eyes of teenagers at least.

ABOVE

The Flaming Teenage (1956)
There is no subtlety to this poster for a film that purports to lift the lid on the life of a modern teenager. Originally, it was released as *Twice Convicted* in 1945, but its name change reflects the times.

OPPOSITE

Rebel Without a Cause (1955)
This is the defining look of the modern youth and the image that made James Dean a star and icon. It promises violence and romance, but the key image is one of coolness.

The reception committee for the new kid on the block!

JAMES DEAN

The overnight sensation of 'East of Eden' becomes the star of the year!

Warner Bros. put all the force of the screen into a challenging drama of today's juvenile violence!

"REBEL WITHOUT A CAUSE"

IN CINEMASCOPE
AND WARNERCOLOR

...and they both come from 'good' families!

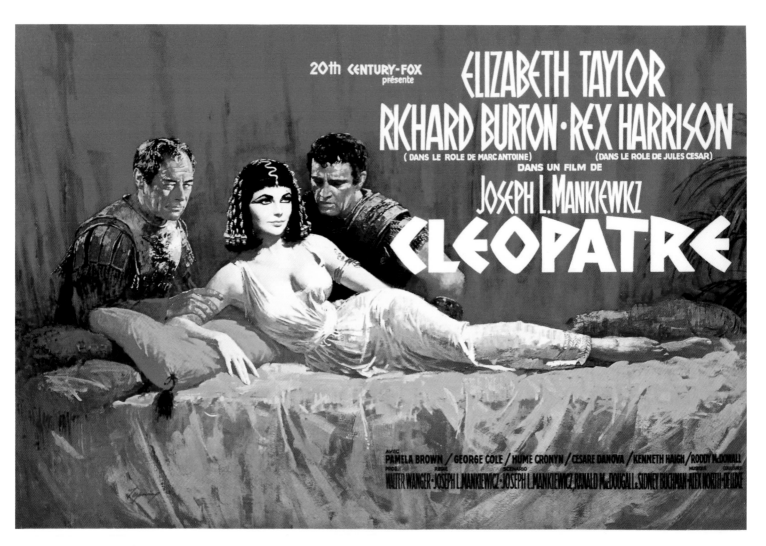

Cleopatra (1963)

The scene may be intimate but the sense of scale remains. The title suggests something grand, but it is Elizabeth Taylor's presence, her paleness contrasting with the backdrop, that gives the design its weight.

The Ten Commandments (1956)

This German design, like the majority of posters for Cecil B. DeMille's biblical epic, focuses on the rivalry between Charlton Heston and Yul Brynner's siblings, and the film's most famous scene.

THE RETURN OF EPIC CINEMA

From biblical tales to historical dynasties, Hollywood reached far and wide to sate audiences' appetites for one of the 1950s staple genres—the epic. It is a genre that didn't so much return from its heyday in the 1920s by choice as much as by necessity. Cinema faced a new and formidable competitor in the form of television. It therefore needed to offer audiences something that this new medium could not. And that thing was scale. The 1950s epics had to be seen on the big screen, and new formats were being created to maximize the impact of these films. For the most part, it didn't matter how fast and loose filmmakers were with the truth when it came to the story they were telling.

The genre, which ran the gamut from the respectable to the nonsensical, hadn't completely gone away since the 1920s, but its popularity surged once again with the release of Cecil B. DeMille's *Samson and Delilah* (1949). A Technicolor spectacle, it was the highest-grossing film of 1950. *Samson and Delilah* was promoted around the lustful romance between Hedy Lamarr and Victor Mature's titular characters, its destructive climax, and DeMille's name as Hollywood's master of the epic. He returned to a biblical theme in 1956 with a remake of his own epic *The Ten Commandments* (1923). Once again, the filmmaker's name loomed large, but this time the design mostly featured Charlton Heston as a bearded, aged Moses, along with a depiction of the parting of the Red Sea, which helped to emphasize the scale of the newly invented VistaVision format.

The poster for the earlier *The Robe* (1953), with the main cast and scenes from the film in one hectic tableau, made much of the fact that it was the first film to be shot in CinemaScope. As such, it was no different to MGM's *Quo Vadis* (1951), for which the artwork featured an Ionic column with the accurate but unsubtle caption, "This is the big one!"

Whereas the poster for the atypical Howard Hawks production *Land of the Pharaohs* (1955) unsuccessfully attempted to modernize the look of the epic by featuring Joan Collins in what appeared to be a bikini, *Cleopatra* (1963) was all about star power. By contrast, Reynold Brown's simple, powerful poster for *Ben-Hur* (1959, see page 140) exuded a sense of greatness.

Land of the Pharaohs (1955)
The poster for Howard Hawks' only epic set in the distant past is a mishmash of styles, particularly the inclusion of Joan Collins' far too contemporary princess. It failed to attract audiences.

THE GOLDEN AGE OF THE WESTERN

With John Ford's *Stagecoach* (1939), the classical Western reached its apotheosis. It was a box office success and, along with *Destry Rides Again*, *Dodge City*, and Ford's first color film, *Drums Along the Mohawk* (all 1939), it sparked a resurgence in the popularity of the genre, which made the subsequent two decades the golden age of the Western.

The 1940s witnessed Ford excel with *My Darling Clementine* (1946), *Fort Apache* (1948), and *She Wore a Yellow Ribbon* (1949). Howard Hughes introduced more than a modicum of sex with *The Outlaw* (1943), and William Wellman brought a conscience with *The Ox-Bow Incident* (1943). Then Howard Hawks hinted at the moral complexity that would develop in later Westerns—and certain roles played by the genre's most iconic actor, John Wayne—with *Red River* (1948).

This exploration of morality was taken further in James Stewart's collaboration with Anthony Mann across five Westerns in the early 1950s. *Winchester '73* (1950) is a tale of vengeance and the story of the eponymous rifle as it passes through the hands of various owners. Like Alfred Hitchcock's work with Stewart, Mann gave the actor a much darker screen persona. The film's artwork, like the posters for *Bend of the River* (1952), *The Naked Spur* (1953), *The Far Country* (1954), and *The Man from Laramie* (1955), emphasizes this tone as well as Stewart's toughness. His is a character that edges close to the boundaries of the law in seeking justice. This darker tone was also reflected in the films and accompanying artwork for B-movie Western directors such as Budd Boetticher, Delmer Daves, and André De Toth.

In the prestige productions *High Noon* (1952), directed by Fred Zinnemann, and *Shane* (1953), directed by George Stevens, the moral backbone of the main protagonists is never called into question, but the strength of the townsfolk and settlers is less rigid. Zinnemann's film is a real-time countdown to the arrival of the villains and Gary Cooper's impending gunfight with them. The climactic shoot-out was all the artwork needed to sell the movie. Like so many other Westerns, the big draw for *Shane* was the confrontation between the hero and the villain, but the relationship between Shane and the family he resides with adds more nuances, so this film's artwork details more than a shoot-out.

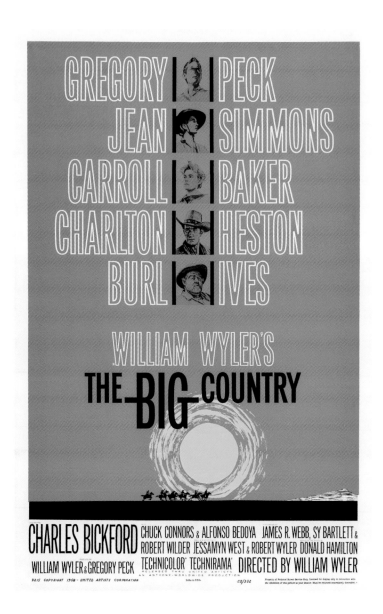

The Big Country (1958)
Saul Bass' design emphasizes the grueling heat of the sun over the vastness of the landscape. The protagonists are silhouetted, and their destination appears to be little more than a rocky outcrop.

The Searchers (1956)
The threat of turbulence in the sky above John Wayne and Jeffrey Hunter hints at the storms ahead for the men in John Ford's dark and troubling take on frontier life.

Rio Bravo (1959)
This poster is atypical for the genre, as there is no emphasis on any recognizable Western landscape or town. It hints at a different kind of Western.

Shane (1953)
The artwork sets up the conflict in the film. Alan Ladd's unwilling hero and Jack Palance's villainous gun for hire battle over the future of Van Heflin's rancher and his family.

John Ford's *Rio Grande* (1950) rounded off the "cavalry trilogy" that began with *Fort Apache* and continued with *She Wore a Yellow Ribbon*. In each, John Wayne plays the irascible but honorable officer, a variation of which crops up in Hawks' *Rio Bravo* (1959). Ford returned to the Western in 1956 with *The Searchers*. It is a significantly different vision of that world, paving the way for the various transformations the Western genre would undergo over the next two decades. It introduced ambivalence into Wayne's character, Ethan Edwards. The artwork for the film, presenting the richly resplendent backdrop of Monument Valley, features Wayne and Jeffrey Hunter in the foreground, side by side on their horses. However, the caption that accompanies the image hints at the obsession that would almost drive Edwards to madness.

In many Westerns, women play stereotypical roles, but *Johnny Guitar* (1954) and *Forty Guns* (1957) challenged this trend. The former, directed by Nicholas Ray, stars Joan Crawford as a hardened saloon keeper and features a climactic shoot-out between two women. Samuel Fuller's gothic Western stars Barbara Stanwyck as a ruthless landowner. On a lighter note, Doris Day entered the fray with her all-singing outlaw *Calamity Jane* (1953). The posters for each film feature their stars armed, with Joan Crawford's headstrong Vienna ready to draw.

Like the epic films produced in the 1950s, the Western was sold to audiences as "big" cinema, offering grand vistas of the US landscape when it was still "wild." Whereas most designers played upon the vast horizons of the West in their posters—featuring action, wagon trails, or lone cowboys against an open plain—Saul Bass' artwork for *The Big Country* (1958) accentuates height. Land is merely a black strip at the bottom of the artwork, with a group of riders crossing it. Behind them is a setting sun, lighting up an orange sky and upon which the names of the film's stars appear. Reynold Brown achieved a similar effect with his vertically designed poster for *How the West Was Won* (1962), but in the place of the stars' names are scenes from the film that show how the frontier gradually evolved into the modern age.

The Western also entered the modern age. George Stevens' *Giant* (1956) bears all the hallmarks of the genre, albeit with the presence of a very contemporary James Dean and the gunfights replaced by boardroom jousts. It nevertheless features the rivalry of frontier life and the setting certainly plays with genre elements. John Sturges' *Bad Day at Black Rock* (1955) features a central character similar to Shane, who is unwilling to fight at the first provocation, but who ultimately stands up against a gang just like the lone gunmen of old.

High Noon (1952)
An archetypal image of the Western, this poster captures the climactic scene from Fred Zinnemann's film, with Gary Cooper's lone sheriff pictured heroically from a low angle.

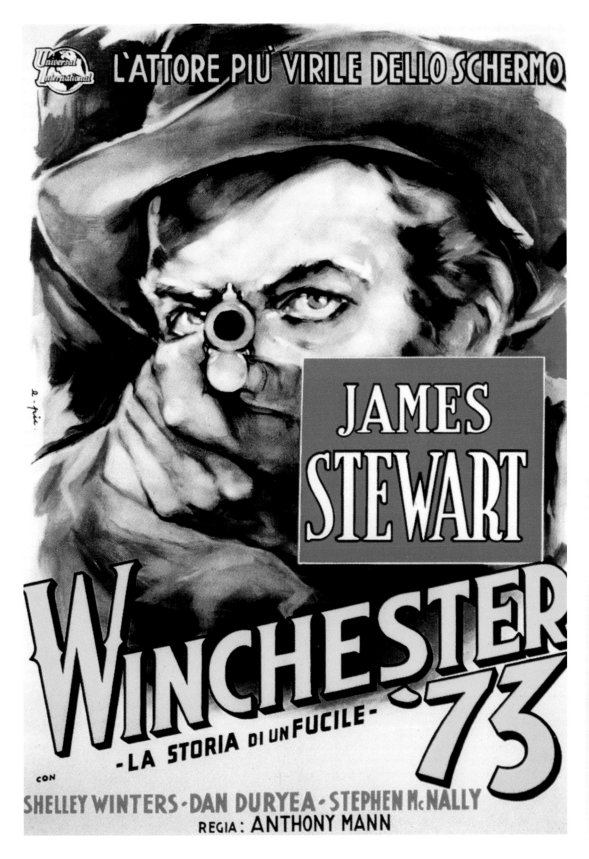

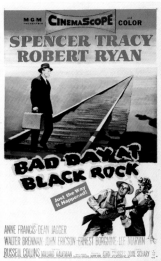

ABOVE

Winchester '73 (1950)
Not dissimilar to the artwork for Spaghetti Westerns, this Italian poster represents a more ambivalent screen persona for James Stewart. The style is more impressionistic than the US posters for the film.

TOP RIGHT

Giant (1956)
Like *The Big Country,* the vast location dominates, while the headshots hint at the film's more melodramatic style. This is a Western hybrid, updating elements of the genre to a modern world.

BOTTOM RIGHT

Bad Day at Black Rock (1955)
The two images seem to be from different eras. The smaller is a classic Western shot, while Spencer Tracy's character is from a more modern world. Only the familiar use of shadows hints at a showdown.

SAUL BASS

In the world of film poster and title design, there is Saul Bass and then there is everyone else. No single graphic designer made such an impression and became so well known, both within the industry and across the world at large. He earned the respect of some of Hollywood's greatest filmmakers, even stepping in occasionally to direct a sequence. Bass' poster designs adorned cinemas, and his title sequences became the stuff of legend. He also made a name for himself in the corporate world, just as big business was waking up to the potential of the ad man.

Bass began his career in Hollywood in the early 1940s, designing print advertisements for studio products. His work on Otto Preminger's *The Moon is Blue* (1953) began one of his most fruitful relationships with a filmmaker. After seeing Bass' work on the poster for *Carmen Jones* (1954), Preminger decided to commission him to create the opening title sequence for the film. Bass garnered the attention and respect of the industry for his groundbreaking poster artwork and credit title designs for *The Man with the Golden Arm* (1955) and *Anatomy of a Murder* (1959). They feature body parts, one

symbolizing drug addiction, and the other both the body of a victim and the film's deconstruction of the legal process. *Advise & Consent* (1962), which lifted the lid on Washington, was Bass' last great collaboration with Preminger.

The designer also enjoyed a successful collaboration with Alfred Hitchcock, creating the title sequences and posters for *Vertigo* (1958, see overleaf), *North by Northwest* (1959), and *Psycho* (1960). He added a modern twist to the tale of Stanley Kubrick's *Spartacus* (1960), and designed some of the film's scenes, too. Bass' work on *The Magnificent Seven* (1960) was so different from the traditional iconography of the Western—just seven red strokes of paint against a white background—that the studio never used it. If the artwork for *Ocean's 11* (1960) was all fizz, Bass hinted at the birth of a new kind of Hollywood musical for *West Side Story* (1961).

He entered the filmmaking fray as a director with *Phase IV* (1974), but his most notable late career work was a collaboration with Martin Scorsese on *Goodfellas* (1990), *Cape Fear* (1991), *The Age of Innocence* (1993), and *Casino* (1995).

BOTTOM LEFT

Advise & Consent (1962)
This is one of a number of designs that Saul Bass employed for Otto Preminger's film, each using the motif of Capitol Hill's dome opening up to reveal its secrets. The briefcases here intimate personal agendas.

OPPOSITE
CLOCKWISE FROM TOP LEFT

Bonjour Tristesse (1958)
What could have been a simple and affecting portrait of youth, with the simplest of Modigliani-style facial features, is transformed into something more ambivalent by a single black tear.

Anatomy of a Murder (1959)
The perfect distillation of Bass' "less is more approach" to poster design, this artwork for Preminger's taut courtroom thriller remains one of the designer's most iconic and influential creations.

The Man with the Golden Arm (1955)
This influential Bass design was one of his earliest to use the body as a motif. The mangled arm hints at the malaise of Frank Sinatra's jazz drummer, while the darker blocks of color add dramatic weight.

Grand Prix (1966)
John Frankenheimer's drama details the travails of life on and off the track for a group of Formula One drivers. Bass employs a series of lines to highlight the film's key selling point—speed.

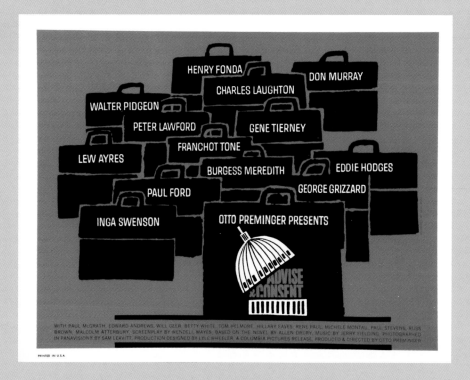

Otto Preminger Presents
DEBORAH KERR · DAVID NIVEN
JEAN SEBERG · MYLENE DEMONGEOT
GEOFFREY HORNE in
BONJOUR TRISTESSE
JULIETTE GRECO · WALTER CHIARI

with MARTITA HUNT · ROLAND CULVER · JEAN KENT · DAVID OXLEY · ELGA ANDERSEN · Screenplay by ARTHUR LAURENTS · Based on the novel by FRANCOISE SAGAN
MUSIC BY GEORGES AURIC · PRODUCED AND DIRECTED BY OTTO PREMINGER · CINEMASCOPE · TECHNICOLOR® · RELEASED BY COLUMBIA PICTURES

Last year's No. 1 best-seller...This year's No. 1 motion picture.

OTTO PREMINGER'S
ANATOMY OF A MURDER

STARRING
JAMES STEWART
LEE REMICK
BEN GAZZARA
ARTHUR O'CONNELL
EVE ARDEN
KATHRYN GRANT

and JOSEPH N. WELCH as Judge Weaver

GEORGE C. SCOTT/ORSON BEAN/RUSS BROWN/MURRAY HAMILTON/BROOKS WEST screenplay by WENDELL MAYES from
the best-seller by ROBERT TRAVER photography by SAM LEAVITT produced & directed by OTTO PREMINGER/a Columbia release
► music by Duke Ellington ◄

A JOHN FRANKENHEIMER FILM IN CINERAMA

GRAND PRIX

STARRING
JAMES GARNER · EVA MARIE SAINT · YVES MONTAND
TOSHIRO MIFUNE · BRIAN BEDFORD · JESSICA WALTERS
ANTONIO SABATO · FRANCOISE HARDY · ADOLFO CELI

Directed by John Frankenheimer · Produced by Edward Lewis

FRANK SINATRA · ELEANOR PARKER · KIM NOVAK

THE MAN WITH THE GOLDEN ARM

A FILM BY OTTO PREMINGER

With Arnold Stang, Darren McGavin, Robert Strauss, John Conte, Doro Merande, George E. Stone, George Mathews, Leonid Kinskey, Emile Meyer, Shorty Rogers, Shelly Manne,
Screenplay by Walter Newman & Lewis Meltzer. From the novel by Nelson Algren. Music by Elmer Bernstein. Produced & Directed by Otto Preminger. Released by United Artists.

WORKING WITH HITCHCOCK

Of all Saul Bass' designs, his *Vertigo* (1958) poster remains one of his most famous. He took a single image from the opening credits and made it the central theme of the film's artwork. Although *Vertigo* fared less well at the box office, the promotional campaign perfectly distilled its themes and Bass embarked on a short collaboration with the filmmaker.

Over a period of three years, Bass worked with Alfred Hitchcock on *Vertigo*, *North by Northwest* (1959), and *Psycho* (1960). Unlike their first film together and so many of the features for which Bass was commissioned to design the titles, the posters for *North by Northwest* and *Psycho* differ greatly from the opening credit sequences. For *North by Northwest*, Bass has a grid of lines intersect against a green backdrop, resembling a map, with credits moving quickly, like vehicles, across it. Bernard Herrmann's furious score adds to the sense of movement. The screen then dissolves into a network of glass panes on a Manhattan skyscraper. The poster has Cary Grant's Roger O. Thornhill free-falling backward, seemingly through a series of square and rectangular frames. The central one is a block of black and red, with Eva Marie Saint's character firing a gun at him.

The *Psycho* title sequence is more abstract. As Herrmann's staccato music jolts, gray lines slice the screen horizontally and diagonally, dissecting each credit that flashes across the screen. The main credits are also divided into sections, hinting at the damaged psyche of the film's antagonist. The artwork for the film (see page 177) employs the rough-edged blocks of color and features three of the main characters.

For *Vertigo*'s credit sequence, Bass opens with a close-up on a woman's face—her lips and then her right eye, from which the film's title and then a spiral appear. The screen fades to black and is dominated by a series of spirals that hint at the psychological complexity of the film's narrative, before returning to the shot of the eye and Hitchcock's director credit. The posters designed for the film are a variation on this theme with James Stewart's Scottie lost in them, trapped in a maze of his own psychoses and obsessions from which there appears to be no escape.

SCIENCE FICTION AND THE ATOMIC AGE

The atomic explosions over Japan in August 1945 brought the world into the atomic age. Science, it was believed, had been harnessed by humanity. Its power was in our control and it could be put to good use. But for all the optimism of the postwar world, the West had a new threat: Communism. Furthermore, the concern raised by Russia's increasing prominence on the world stage resulted in a state of paranoia, particularly in the United States. There were fears that the country might already be riddled with spies. No wonder so many filmmakers saw science fiction as the perfect genre with which to exploit these fears.

Like much genre cinema, the majority of science fiction films were low-budget productions—early incarnations of the exploitation film, whose sole intention was to thrill. Larger studio productions were less common, but some Hollywood entrepreneurs saw the box office potential in films that showcased Hollywood's nascent special effects departments. George Pal produced *When Worlds Collide* (1951), in which an intrepid group of scientists embark on a mission to save humanity as a species by building a rocket to a new world after it is discovered that a planet is hurtling toward Earth. But it was Pal's modern update of H. G. Wells' *The War of the Worlds* (1953) that attracted the most attention. The artwork for both films uses vibrant colors and images of destruction to attract audiences.

The image of an invading force, even one from another planet, became the perfect metaphor for what was believed to be the very real Communist threat within the United States' borders. In *The Day the Earth Stood Still* (1951), another sizable studio production, a spaceship lands in Washington and although its occupants claim they are there to restore world order as a result of nuclear testing, it can also be read as an incursion by an unwelcome force. *Invaders from Mars* (1953) and *Them!* (1954) take this theme further—even their artwork spells out the imminent danger of invasion.

Invasion of the Body Snatchers (1956) offers a more complex scenario, albeit with similarly styled artwork. It suggests that the danger is already present, but is more ambiguous as to whether it is referring to Communist sleepers or to the threat to democracy that Senator McCarthy and his acolytes pose.

Invaders from Mars (1953)
The use of red in the text plays up the fact that the film is shot in color, but also taps into Cold War paranoia about the "Red" threat. Elsewhere, the artwork highlights popular sci-fi tropes of the era.

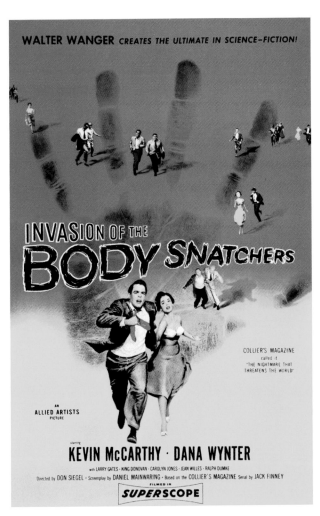

REYNOLD BROWN

The posters for science fiction and monster movies in the 1950s were wildly imagined creations. They exaggerated their subjects in order to appeal to an audience with a hunger for journeys into outer space or for witnessing Earth under attack. They had to balance a sense of terror with the assurance that audiences would also have a great time. Few artists performed this remit as comprehensively as Reynold Brown.

In the late 1930s, Brown became an apprentice to cartoonist Hal Forrest, who hired him to ink his comic strip series *Tailspin Tommy* (1928–1942). However, an encounter with respected *The Saturday Evening Post* illustrator Norman Rockwell encouraged Brown to study art at college. After serving as a technical artist at North American Aviation during World War II, Brown began to work freelance, producing illustrations and advertisements for periodicals such as *Illustrated Argosy*, *Popular Aviation*, *Flying Magazine*, *Boy's Life*, *Outdoor Life*, and *The Saturday Evening Post*. He not only created evocative images with cinematic flair, but he was also commissioned to illustrate pulp novels and was soon employed by Hollywood.

Although best known for his science fiction and horror posters, Brown showed imaginative flair within any genre. He captured the intensity of emotions running high in Douglas Sirk's *Written on the Wind* (1956) and *Imitation of Life* (1959), as well as in Richard Brooks' adaptations of Tennessee Williams' *Cat on a Hot Tin Roof* (1958) and *Sweet Bird of Youth* (1962). Early posters for the Westerns *The Big Sky* (1952) and *Quantez* (1957) play to genre tropes, but his artwork for *How the West Was Won* (1963), with its vast tableau representing frontier life, perfectly encapsulates the ambitions of the film. And if he channeled the absurdity of the biblical epic spin-offs *Goliath and the Sins of Babylon* (1963) and *Goliath and the Vampires* (1961) with his comic-style approach, he brought gravitas to his artwork for *Ben-Hur* (1959).

However, it is posters such as *Creature From the Black Lagoon* (1954), *This Island Earth* (1955), *The Incredible Shrinking Man*, *I Was a Teenage Werewolf* (both 1957), *Attack of the 50 Foot Woman* (1958), and *The Time Machine* (1960) for which Brown is most fondly remembered. They delight in their absurdity, play up their B-movie thrills, and promise audiences a fun night out.

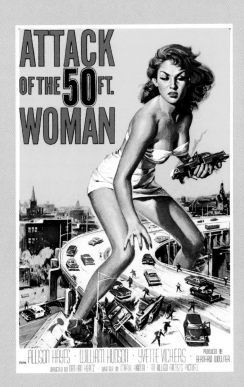

TOP LEFT

Look Back in Anger (1959)
The bold typography, the use of the color red, and Richard Burton's stance all suggest a sense of urgency. The presence of the bed also points to a more frank attitude to sex.

BOTTOM LEFT

The Loneliness of the Long Distance Runner (1962)
The target superimposed onto Tom Courtenay's face taps into the film's approach, revealing the world through the thoughts of the main character.

RIGHT

Room at the Top (1959)
The repetition of the image in this poster reflects the line spoken by Simone Signoret's character, but also highlights her desperation. It was a daring image to use at the time.

THE BRITISH NEW WAVE

Unlike its French counterpart, the British New Wave was less interested in challenging the grammar of film than it was in addressing the rigid class structures that existed in British society in the 1950s. Previously, the working class had been represented by comic roles or included to add "color" to a scene. But a new generation of filmmakers set about changing this.

The shift began in theater and with the Free Cinema movement that appeared in the mid 1950s. Among the playwrights, John Osborne led the charge. In 1959, Tony Richardson, who had codirected the Free Cinema documentary *Momma Don't Allow* (1956), brought his stage version of Osborne's searing debut *Look Back in Anger* (1959) to the screen. It was the first of this new kind of drama, with Richard Burton reprising his stage performance as Jimmy Porter, a rage-fueled man revolting against society. He is the focus of the poster, which depicts him as a rebel. Like *Room at the Top* (1959), which immediately followed it, *Look Back in Anger* focuses on the clash between middle- and working-class characters. Later films, such as *Saturday Night and Sunday Morning* (1960) and *This Sporting Life* (1963)— the artwork for both emphasizes the protagonist's masculinity—unfold solely within the working class.

Alongside the shift in the way class was represented, gender roles began to be questioned. Richardson was at the vanguard once again, directing in 1961 the screen version of Shelagh Delaney's play *A Taste of Honey* (1958). Rita Tushingham plays Jo, a teenager who leaves home when she discovers she is pregnant. Although the film was beautifully shot, expressively capturing the British industrial landscape, the film's posters mainly focus on Tushingham, her wry smile perfectly conveying Jo's character and the tone of the film. *The L-Shaped Room* (1962) also concentrates on a young pregnant woman, but its poster implies more engagement with the wider social issues raised by the film.

Richardson's third New Wave film was *The Loneliness of the Long Distance Runner* (1962), an adaptation of Alan Sillitoe's short story of 1959. Featuring, arguably, the most stylized artwork of any British New Wave film, it is one of the movement's most impressionistic films as it captures the life and thoughts of a young man attempting to break free from the shackles of borstal life.

THE RANK ORGANISATION presents
A JULIAN WINTLE—LESLIE PARKYN PRODUCTION

'BEST ACTOR' AWARD TO RICHARD HARRIS
XVI CANNES FILM FESTIVAL

CRITICS PRIZE
(F.I.P.R.E.S.C.I.)
XVI CANNES FILM FESTIVAL

THIS SPORTING LIFE

ABOVE

This Sporting Life (1963)
In this more naturalistic portrait, the focus is on Richard Harris' protagonist. Rachel Roberts' lover blends into the background, thus highlighting her relationship with the self-centered rugby player.

JAPANESE CINEMA

The 1950s was the golden age of Japanese cinema. Although the films produced achieved commercial and critical success domestically, they also began to make a significant mark at major festivals and with international audiences.

Akira Kurosawa's *Rashomon* (1950) was a watershed film in Japanese cinema. Its unique structure—presenting one incident from multiple perspectives—and the charisma of its star, Toshiro Mifune, made it Japan's first international success. The winner of the Golden Lion at the Venice Film Festival, the film established the director as one of the key filmmakers of the era. Action and a kinetic forward momentum drove Kurosawa's *Seven Samurai* (1954), one of the most popular international successes of the decade. This film also starred Mifune, thus cementing one of cinema's most celebrated actor–director collaborations. *Seven Samurai* upped the ante and scale of Kurosawa's work, while *Throne of Blood* (1957) and *The Hidden Fortress* (1958) delivered set pieces whose directorial ingenuity and flair outstripped Hollywood. The posters for these films emphasize the thrill of the expertly choreographed action scenes.

On a larger scale, and with more than a dose of silliness, Ishiro Honda's *Godzilla* (1954) introduced the *kaiju* (strange beast) genre. Although the film revels in B-movie thrills, as evinced by its promotional artwork, the inspiration for its creation was the A-bomb attacks on Hiroshima and Nagasaki.

Yasujiro Ozu and Kenji Mizoguchi, two of the most respected filmmakers of the era, achieved a quieter but no less powerful note. Both had been making films since the silent era, but their work in the 1950s reached an extraordinary level of sophistication. Ozu was known for the stateliness of his carefully composed static shots, his favorite camera angle allowing audiences into the center of his family drama. His Noriko trilogy in particular, comprised of *Late Spring* (1949), *Early Summer* (1951), and *Tokyo Story* (1953), was promoted for the films' intimacy and quietness. Mizoguchi, by contrast, was the master of movement. His camera prowled through rooms and open spaces. His greatest works of the 1950s—*The Life of Oharu* (1952), *Ugetsu Monogatari* (1953), and *Sansho the Bailiff* (1954)—were driven by their intensity in detailing the plight of women in Japanese society.

ABOVE

Early Spring (1956)
Yasujiro Ozu's penultimate film shot in black and white centers on infidelity in the workplace. The image, like so many for the director's films, only hints at the state of unease as the drama progresses.

ABOVE LEFT

Rashomon (1950)

An act of violence makes up the central thread of this multi-perspective drama, as evinced by Toshiro Mifune's posture and drawn sword. This became one of the defining images of the actor.

ABOVE RIGHT

Ugetsu Monogatari (1953)

The role of women in society is subtly suggested in this poster for one of Kenji Mizoguchi's most acclaimed dramas. Its importance as a film is underpinned by the inclusion of its two awards.

LE SAMOURAÏ

PRODIS présente

ALAIN DELON

LE SAMOURAÏ

avec

FRANÇOIS PERIER

et

NATHALIE DELON

production
FILMEL · FILMS BORDERIE · T.C.P.
FIDA CINÉMATOGRAFICA

Producteur délegué EUGÈNE LEPICIER

Photo de HENRI DECAE

un film de
JEAN-PIERRE MELVILLE

ABOVE

Le samouraï (1967)
The grainy image of an inexpressive Alain Delon underpins the existential nature of Melville's thriller. Delon's character is a blank canvas, detached from the world and with only his job to live for.

TOP RIGHT

Bob le flambeur (1956)
Roger Duchesne's character holds the ace in this image, which underpins the noirish tone of Melville's taut drama. It is a more classic image than the film itself, which edges closer to the French New Wave.

MIDDLE RIGHT

Rififi (1955)
Every element of this poster smacks of classic-era film noir. There is the cool anti-hero, the brains behind the heist, an intimation of simmering passions, and the red backdrop suggesting imminent danger.

BOTTOM RIGHT

Elevator to the Gallows (1958)
The fragmented elements of Louis Malle's thriller are represented in this poster by the circle of torn photographs, which includes Jeanne Moreau's lover–accomplice and the gun that kills her husband.

THE FRENCH CRIME THRILLER

The French crime film has been a staple of cinematic output for as long as the medium has existed. Louis Feuillade created the earliest memorable criminal mastermind in his crime serial *Fantômas* (1913–14). Jean Gabin added machismo and swooning romanticism in the 1930s, playing the titular anti-hero in *Pépé le Moko* (1937, see page 77). Later, it was Gabin who resurfaced as the supreme criminal icon when the genre had its heyday in the 1950s and 1960s.

The actor's comeback role was as the gangster Max in Jacques Becker's *Touchez pas au Grisbi* (1954). A tough crime drama, it finds a gangster pulling off a major heist only to have his success thwarted by the actions of other criminals. Becker's handling of the material imbues the film with a realistic edge, reflected in the film's poster, which presents the heist as though it has been ripped from the headlines.

Gabin played a key role in French crime films, working on both sides of the law, over the course of twenty years, before his death in 1976. He was an effective Jules Maigret, Georges Simenon's popular fictional detective, giving the role an air of world-weariness. His vice inspector in Gilles Grangier's *The Night Affair* (1958) appears as the intersection between two women in the film's stylish poster, while the artwork for heist thriller *The Upper Hand* (1966) portrays him as a seasoned veteran of the Parisian underworld. Gabin appears at his most hardboiled, flanked by Alain Delon and Lino Ventura, on the poster for *The Sicilian Clan* (1969), one of his best roles after *Touchez pas au Grisbi*.

In 1955, blacklisted US director Jules Dassin directed one of the classic crime films of the decade, *Rififi* (1955). It also involves a heist, but this time the crime is the centerpiece of the film, detailing every moment of a skilled gang's robbery of a jeweler. Although it has the same rough edge as Becker's thriller, *Rififi* was sold more in the style of a classic noir. Similarly, the poster for Jean-Pierre Melville's *Bob le flambeur* (1956) evinced a noirish edge. Roger Duchesne plays the eponymous anti-hero. He's an ex-con and gambler who, down on his luck, decides to rob the casino where he works. However, the film's style is more modern than the poster lets on—its hand-held camera work and jump cuts presaging the work of the French New Wave.

ABOVE

Band of Outsiders (1964)
Jean-Luc Godard employs stills to play with the iconography of the crime movie. His film is less a thriller than a knowing play with genre tropes—a deconstruction of the genre.

ABOVE RIGHT

Plein soleil (1960)
Tom Ripley is part sociopath, part social climber. His indifference to those around him as he achieves his ambitions is visible in the expression the artist has given Alain Delon's character in this image.

ABOVE LEFT

Touchez pas au Grisbi (1954)
This poster suggests that Jacques Becker's film isn't so much a crime drama as a record of a crime that could have come straight out of the headlines of a daily newspaper.

Melville was one of the French directors beloved by the New Wave. His tough crime films were a huge influence on the early work of Jean-Luc Godard and François Truffaut. He even played a cameo role in Godard's *Breathless* (1960). In the early 1950s, Melville worked with Jean Cocteau (see page 99), but it was as a director of crime films that he reigned supreme from the mid 1950s to his last film, *Un Flic* (1972). His classic gangster dramas, which include *Le doulos* (1963), *Le deuxième souffle* (1966), *Le samouraï* (1967), and *Le cercle rouge* (1970), all feature images of men toughened by their lifestyles, almost always photographed in austere black and white and with the film's title appearing in red, as if sealing their fate. The images become bleaker with each film, hinting at an existential crisis. This is nowhere more apparent than in the image of Alain Delon on the poster for *Le samouraï*, Melville's tale of a solitary hit man who begins to question his profession.

Delon's collaboration with Melville led to roles in crime films throughout his career. However, one of his most iconic appearances came early in the 1960s, playing Patricia Highsmith's sociopathic anti-hero Tom Ripley in René Clément's rapturous thriller *Plein soleil* (1960). In contrast to the bleakness of the posters for Melville's films, the star here appears to resemble a matinee idol; however, on closer inspection his expression suggests otherwise.

In the same year in which *Breathless* was released, Truffaut became the second New Wave director to enter the criminal fray with his stylish thriller *Shoot the Piano Player* (1960). Two years previously, Louis Malle had made the chamber crime drama *Elevator to the Gallows* (1958). Both films took the tropes of the crime film and gave them a modern spin that reflected the changing times in which they were set. The poster for Malle's film uses a series of stills to hint at its tone, whereas the artwork for Truffaut's drama focuses on Charles Aznavour's pianist, emphasizing the danger he is in.

Godard returned to crime with *Band of Outsiders* (1964). The characters begin as fans of the crime film, but soon indulge their passions with a real-life robbery. Like *Elevator to the Gallows*, the promotional poster uses stills from the film, but they are more formal in their presentation, standing out against the blood-red backdrop. The following year, Godard took the crime movie into the future with *Alphaville* (1965). Starring Eddie Constantine as detective Lemmy Caution, everything about the film, including its artwork, is a futuristic spin on classic noir tropes. Its bleakness presaged the way in which the genre would progress into the late 1960s, moving from the thrill of a heist to a bleaker, more world-weary tone.

THE FRENCH NEW WAVE

The films of the French New Wave, or La Nouvelle Vague, sent a seismic shock through world cinema. They didn't only challenge film form, they threw down the gauntlet to the whole culture of filmmaking: how films were made, how they looked, and how they were presented to audiences. The ideas that resonated from the filmmakers corralled into this movement were forged when they themselves were audience members in the late 1940s and early 1950s. They thrived on film and would eventually take it in a new direction.

US cinema hadn't been screened in France since before the outbreak of World War II, so these young French enthusiasts gorged themselves on the works of John Ford, Howard Hawks, Alfred Hitchcock, and others. What they saw impacted them in two ways. The signature style of certain directors defined for them the notion of the auteur, or author of a work whose vision and style shone through almost everything they produced. However, these films also contrasted sharply with French cinema of the time, which prompted this new generation to pick up a camera.

Inspired by André Bazin, the cofounder of the respected film journal *Cahiers du cinéma*, and Henri Langlois, the cofounder of the Cinémathèque Française, this group initially became a new generation of critics. François Truffaut's article "A Certain Tendency of the French Cinema" (1954), a declaration of war by a younger generation on the French filmmaking establishment, was their manifesto.

This group's transformation from critics into filmmakers began gradually in the late 1950s. Both Jacques Rivette and Eric Rohmer began making short films in the 1950s, while Jean-Luc Godard and Truffaut moved from criticism to directing in 1955. The latter's *Les Mistons* (1957) presaged his feature debut. By the early 1960s, their influence had spread across the globe, ranging from the new wave of filmmakers in Japan to the political radicals of Central and South America.

A different kind of cinema was already beginning to appear by the time the group's first film, Claude Chabrol's *Le beau Serge*, was premiered in 1958. The Rive Gauche, or Left Bank, was a group of filmmakers, artists, writers, and intellectuals that included Agnès

The 400 Blows (1959)
This impressionistic artwork gives little indication of the direction Truffaut was heading, but it does capture the troubled spirit of Jean-Pierre Léaud's Antoine Doinel in the film's ambiguous final moments.

Le beau Serge (1958)
The love triangle at the heart of Claude Chabrol's feature debut is the focus of the film's poster. The use of red is more a reflection of the times than a part of the movie's moral compass.

Varda, Louis Malle, and Alain Resnais. Varda had directed *La pointe courte* in 1955, and her carefree style and preference for real locations presaged the approach the New Wave would take. *Cleo from 5 to 7* (1962) was a New Wave film in all but name, albeit with Varda's own take on gender. Likewise, Malle and Resnais hinted at the arrival of a new kind of cinema with *Elevator to the Gallows* (1958) and *Hiroshima Mon Amour* (1959), respectively.

If Chabrol lit the fuse for the New Wave, Truffaut and Jean-Luc Godard created the fire. *The 400 Blows* (1959) is a semi-autobiographical account of Truffaut's youth and the first in a series of films that feature the character Antoine Doinel, played by Jean-Pierre Léaud. The poster, like that for Chabrol's film, wasn't radically different, but in capturing Doinel's last moments from the film, on the beach at Honfleur in Normandy, it exudes a certain freshness. Truffaut followed it with the stylish crime drama *Shoot the Piano Player* (1960, see page 135) and *Jules et Jim* (1962). The latter became one of the most popular French New Wave films, whose style reflected the carefree nature of the best of the early New Wave.

Arguably, it was Godard's *Breathless* (1960) that defined the lengths to which the New Wave filmmakers were prepared to challenge the cinematic establishment. At its core, it is a crime film. Jean-Paul Belmondo is a small-time crook modeling himself on Humphrey Bogart's screen gangster persona. Jean Seberg is his moll. But with its radical editing—eschewing the many conventions of classical Hollywood style—philosophical digressions, half-heard conversations, and rough camera work, Godard was changing the rules and producing cinema that was thrilling, intelligent, and provocative. The artwork for the film is more playful.

Like Truffaut's later *Jules et Jim*, Godard employed a ménage à trois scenario with his next film, *A Woman Is a Woman* (1961), which features his muse and partner at the time, Anna Karina. She also appeared in *My Life to Live* (1962), sporting a Louise Brooks-style bob that was once again made iconic through the film's artwork, and *Le petit soldat* (1963). The latter is Godard's most overtly political film to date, and its poster more austere than those for his previous films.

The artwork for *Le mépris* (1963), featuring Brigitte Bardot, appears more conventional, classical even, but it works because the whole film is a deconstruction of cinema and what it represents. It was at this point that Godard began to break away from the movement he helped create, although the artwork for *Pierrot le Fou* (1965) and *Two or Three Things I Know About Her* (1967) still echoes the style that helped define the French New Wave.

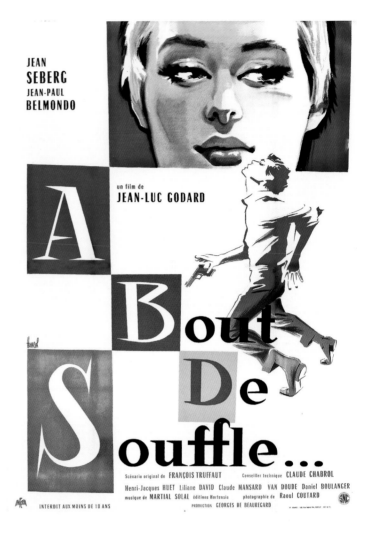

ABOVE

Breathless (1960)
Jean-Luc Godard said that all you need to make a movie is a guy, a girl, and a gun. They are the only components in this poster, but its design hints at something different.

ABOVE

Le mépris (1963)
This artwork resembles the Italian posters of the 1940s and 1950s. Godard is playing with the very form of cinema and the filmmaking process, including the deconstruction of Bardot's star persona.

TOP RIGHT

Pierrot le Fou (1965)
As the 1960s progressed, Godard moved away from the earlier playfulness of the French New Wave to a more politically radical style of filmmaking. This film appeared at a mid-point between the two.

MIDDLE RIGHT

My Life to Live (1962)
Anna Karina's character leaves her husband in search of her own place in the world. The poster depicts the various roles she inhabits. Her black bob recalls that of Louise Brooks in *Pandora's Box* (1929).

BOTTOM RIGHT

Two or Three Things I Know About Her (1967)
Godard's essayistic approach to contemporary life—played out in seemingly random order—is reflected in the collage design of the film's artwork.

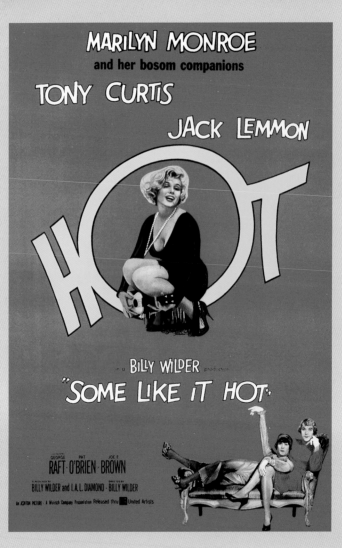

POSTERS OF THE DECADE

Alongside the iconic designs of Saul Bass, the 1950s
witnessed a creative boom in the way Hollywood films
were promoted. At a time when television was a notable
threat to the future of the medium, posters emphasized
scale. But they were also nuanced in their representation
of US life.

The 1950s proved to be the greatest decade for
Nicholas Ray. He directed one of the finest film noirs and
Hollywood insider films with *In a Lonely Place* (1950),
played with the conventions of the Western with *Johnny
Guitar* (1954), and introduced the ultimate teenage icon—
James Dean—in *Rebel Without a Cause* (1955). He also
looked beneath the veneer of the United States' rapidly
expanding suburbia with the controversial *Bigger Than
Life* (1956). One of the first films to deal with prescription
drug addiction, it stars James Mason as a teacher whose
consumption of cortisone dramatically alters his mood
and behavior. It received a mixed reception upon first
release but has since been hailed as one of the finest
US films of the decade. The artwork for *Bigger Than Life*
employed a simple design to convey the protagonist's
mental state.

With a huge budget and large sets, *Ben-Hur* (1959)
dwarfed even Cecil B. DeMille's *The Ten Commandments*
(1956) as the grandest epic of its era. Unlike most other
poster designs, Reynold Brown's simple use of the film
title as a monolithic structure was enough to emphasize
the scale of William Wyler's biblical-themed adventure.

Sidney Lumet's feature debut *12 Angry Men* (1957)
is the polar opposite of Wyler's epic. Unfolding almost
entirely in one room, where a jury of men has retired
following the end of a court trial, the drama is a
microcosm of US attitudes toward politics, race, culture,
and class. One of the main pieces of evidence is a knife,
which features as the key design element in many of the
film's posters.

Billy Wilder began the decade with a death and ended
on a laugh. *Sunset Boulevard* (1950) is a bleak appraisal
of Tinseltown's voraciousness, whereas *Some Like It Hot*
(1959) is a knowing blend of genres that makes the most
of Marilyn Monroe, Tony Curtis, and Jack Lemmon's comic
skills to achieve one of the most perfect comedies. Both
films' posters employ the same colors in their design, but
whereas one is threatening, the other is joyous.

1960s

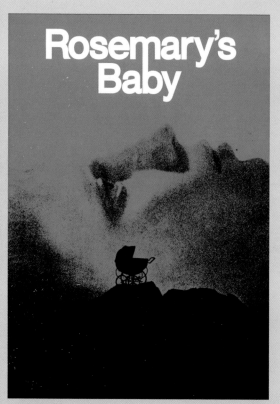

Rosemary's Baby

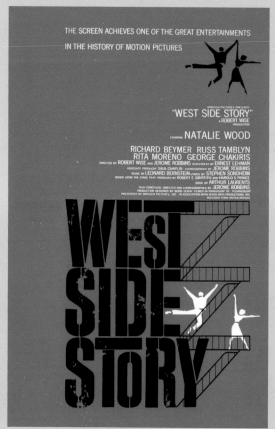

THE SCREEN ACHIEVES ONE OF THE GREAT ENTERTAINMENTS
IN THE HISTORY OF MOTION PICTURES

MIRISCH PICTURES PRESENTS
"WEST SIDE STORY"
A ROBERT WISE PRODUCTION

STARRING NATALIE WOOD

RICHARD BEYMER · RUSS TAMBLYN
RITA MORENO · GEORGE CHAKIRIS
DIRECTED BY ROBERT WISE AND JEROME ROBBINS · SCREENPLAY BY ERNEST LEHMAN
ASSOCIATE PRODUCER SAUL CHAPLIN · CHOREOGRAPHED BY JEROME ROBBINS
MUSIC BY LEONARD BERNSTEIN · LYRICS BY STEPHEN SONDHEIM
BASED UPON THE STAGE PLAY PRODUCED BY ROBERT E. GRIFFITH AND HAROLD S. PRINCE
BOOK BY ARTHUR LAURENTS

PLAY CONCEIVED, DIRECTED AND CHOREOGRAPHED BY JEROME ROBBINS
PRODUCTION DESIGNED BY BORIS LEVEN · FILMED IN PANAVISION 70 · IN TECHNICOLOR®
PRESENTED BY MIRISCH PICTURES, INC. · IN ASSOCIATION WITH SEVEN ARTS PRODUCTIONS, INC.
RELEASED THRU UNITED ARTISTS

WEST SIDE STORY

Joseph E. Levine presents
FEDERICO FELLINI'S

8½

This film talks about you...about your life...about your family...
about your work...about your doubts...about your dreams...
You will see yourself in the leading role as though you
were looking in a mirror...This is your film—

Federico Fellini

MARCELLO MASTROIANNI · CLAUDIA CARDINALE · ANOUK AIMÉE · SANDRA MILO · ROSSELLA FALK · BARBARA STEELE

Look deep into "THE EVIL EYE"
to the twilight world of the
Supernatural!

AMERICAN INTERNATIONAL
presents

JOHN SAXON
AND LETICIA ROMAN
STARRING IN

THE

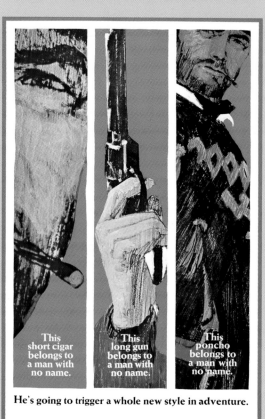

This
short cigar
belongs to
a man with
no name.

This
long gun
belongs to
a man with
no name.

This
poncho
belongs to
a man with
no name.

He's going to trigger a whole new style in adventure.

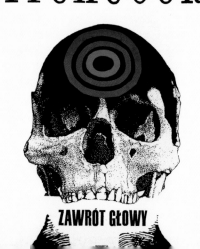

KIM NOVAK W PODWÓJNEJ ROLI | JAMES STEWART
BARBARA DEL GEDDES W MROŻĄCYM KREW W ŻYŁACH BARWNYM FILMIE

HITCHCOCKA

ZAWRÓT GŁOWY

More than any other decade in film, the 1960s can be seen as the bridge between an older world and an emerging one. Some radical film movements had already established themselves by the start of the decade, but they continued to grow—sometimes splintering into other groups—and to influence other filmmaking communities.

Radical change hit Hollywood in the late 1960s, but before that the studio system that had dominated for four decades began to collapse. And like a house of cards, the effect traveled out to other countries. As the Hollywood majors lost their monopoly over distribution and exhibition, smaller film production companies and independent producers saw their chance to weigh in. Variety became key, and cinemas that might previously have shown only Hollywood fare began to offer audiences all manner of films.

At the same time, the profiles of international directors rose. It was a golden age for Italian cinema. Federico Fellini, Michelangelo Antonioni, Luchino Visconti, and Pier Paolo Pasolini became regular fixtures with art

house crowds. Sophia Loren cemented the dominant position of her country's cinema by winning the Best Actress in a Leading Role Academy Award for *Two Women* (1960), a first for a role not performed in the English language. In northern Europe, Ingmar Bergman was unsettling audiences with his stark explorations into the human psyche, culminating in *Persona* (1966). That film features a character discussing with extraordinary frankness a sexual encounter she experienced. Such encounters appeared on screen elsewhere, transgressing moral boundaries and breaking taboos.

As each year of the decade passed, films were made that confronted censorship guidelines. Explicit sex, violence, and language began to appear, forcing censors to enforce rules that hadn't changed for decades, to create a new system of guidelines, or to assess films on an individual basis. Many chose this last option initially, which meant that permissible content shifted with each release. By the late 1960s, the floodgates had opened and the gradual move to a new kind of cinema became a runaway train. By the end of the decade, the world on and off the screen was a very different place.

THE END OF CLASSICAL HOLLYWOOD

Hollywood had had to contend with the arrival of both television and nascent teenage culture in the 1950s, but the 1960s turned the US filmmaking establishment on its head. The dismantling of the system that had allowed the studios to dominate the means of production, distribution, and exhibition not only allowed for more democracy in the industry, but also fueled the growth of independent production companies and cinema chains. This reflected a shift in a culture—not only in the United States—that railed against the hegemony of mainstream entertainment.

Although society was changing, a studio's control over what could be seen and heard on the screen or in a film's promotional material remained in the hands of the Motion Picture Association of America (MPAA) and a production code drawn up in the early 1930s. However, films such as *The Pawnbroker* (1964), which featured partial female nudity, and *Who's Afraid of Virginia Woolf* (1966), which included sexually suggestive language, pushed the envelope of what was approved for public viewing. This erosion of the code, which started around 1963, had by 1966 made the guidelines irrelevant, and they were ultimately abandoned. Their replacement, a ratings system introduced in 1968, has remained in place ever since.

As the films changed, so too did the way in which they were promoted. Sexuality became increasingly present in the marketplace. The poster for *The Graduate* (1967), for example, offers the promise of the illicit through the juxtaposition of a woman's leg and Dustin Hoffman's student. Meanwhile, the crime genre was turned on its head. If Lee Marvin, a stoic presence in classical Hollywood productions, is enmeshed in a world he can barely recognize in *Point Blank* (1967), Steve McQueen exudes a characteristic cool and anti-authoritarian expression in posters promoting *Bullitt* (1968).

The men who feature in the main image of the poster for *The Wild Bunch* (1969) are faceless, hinting at the moral ambivalence that permeates the film, and its excessive violence is explicit in the stills that appear beneath them. By contrast, a different kind of cowboy dominates the image used to promote *Midnight Cowboy* (1969). His demeanor and surroundings are out of keeping with what would have been expected of such a man from the West.

Midnight Cowboy (1969)
The poster for John Schlesinger's Oscar-winning film suggests a bleak New York, with Jon Voight the antithesis of the Western hero and Dustin Hoffman a world away from his preppy role in *The Graduate*.

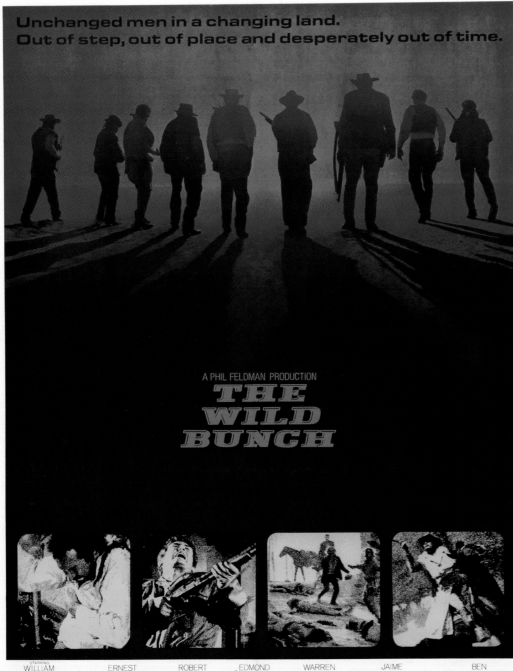

Unchanged men in a changing land.
Out of step, out of place and desperately out of time.

A PHIL FELDMAN PRODUCTION

THE WILD BUNCH

STARRING
WILLIAM HOLDEN · ERNEST BORGNINE · ROBERT RYAN · EDMOND O'BRIEN · WARREN OATES · JAIME SANCHEZ · BEN JOHNSON

ALSO STARRING
EMILIO FERNANDEZ · STROTHER MARTIN · L Q JONES · Screenplay by WALON GREEN and SAM PECKINPAH · Music by Jerry Fielding · Story by Walon Green and Roy N. Sickner
Produced by PHIL FELDMAN · Directed by SAM PECKINPAH · TECHNICOLOR® PANAVISION® FROM WARNER BROS.-SEVEN ARTS

69/168

STEVE McQUEEN IST 'BULLITT'

ROBERT VAUGHN

LEE MARVIN "POINT BLANK"

There are two kinds of people in his up-tight world:
his victims and his women. And sometimes you can't tell them apart.

ANGIE DICKINSON

ABOVE

The Wild Bunch (1969)
Sam Peckinpah's motley crew eschew the classic image of Western heroes. Instead, they appear to have embarked on a road to nowhere, the violence of which is borne out in the four images above the credits.

TOP RIGHT

Bullitt (1968)
Bill Gold's design posits an ordinary-looking cop in negative. Steve McQueen's role bucks the establishment image of law enforcement, suggesting a character who lives by their own moral code.

MIDDLE RIGHT

The Graduate (1967)
Like the film still of this image, which was also used in the film's promotion, the effectiveness of the poster for The Graduate lies in the suggestion of sex, not the presence of it.

BOTTOM RIGHT

Point Blank (1967)
Nelson Lyon's design skillfully keeps intact Lee Marvin's tough guy image while transposing him onto the psychedelic world of the late 1960s. The trippy backdrop also serves as a target.

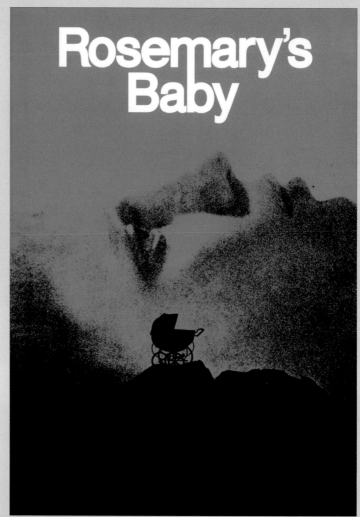

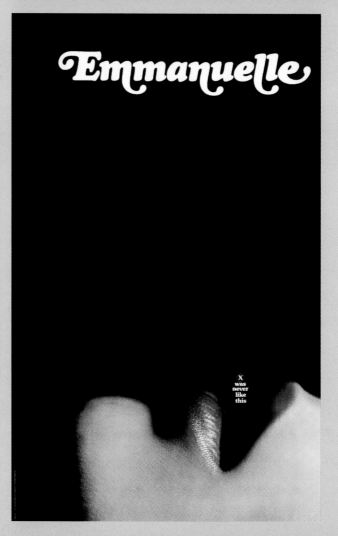

STEPHEN FRANKFURT

Stephen Frankfurt had been out of college for a year when he joined the New York-based advertising agency Young & Rubicam in 1957. His subsequent rapid ascent to company president was aided by a sharp eye for detail, a whip-smart ear for a catchy pitch (he came up with the well-known tagline "In space no one can hear you scream" for *Alien* [1979]), and being acutely attuned to cultural change, all of which made him the archetypal Mad Man. However, in addition to his commercial projects for television, print, and billboards, Frankfurt helped to orchestrate a different approach to the way in which films were promoted. He even had a hand in the construction of a number of films.

Frankfurt frequently oversaw the entirety of a film campaign, and was sometimes commissioned to design a credit or opening sequence, too. For example, he was responsible for the memorable opening title sequence of *To Kill a Mockingbird* (1962). In the late 1960s, he certainly took advantage of the crumbling censorship system, although his work tended toward suggestion and inference rather than explicitness. It held the promise of something more, even if the artwork designed to promote a film was marked by its restraint. The iconic

image for the *Alien* campaign (see page 187) shies away from the brutality of the film's indulgence of slasher movie gore, instead producing an abstract object in an otherworldly environment that makes sense only with a viewing of the film.

It was the idea of selling the concept of a film to its potential audience that made Frankfurt such hot property in Hollywood. In 1968, shortly after he was made president of Young & Rubicam, he was famously approached by producer Robert Evans, who had realized that no one in Paramount's marketing department could come up with a constructive idea for how to promote *Rosemary's Baby* (1968). Frankfurt told Evans, "I'm going to tell it you straight; it's not an easy picture to sell and I'm not going to take one dime from you. But if you buy what I give you, I want one hundred thousand dollars." Frankfurt's innovative advertising campaign made the film a huge success, redefined what could be done with the horror genre, and gave Frankfurt and his collaborators (including key designer Philip Gips) an intimate style that they employed successfully in various modes over the next two decades.

ABOVE

The Manchurian Candidate (1962)
The blocks of color reference the flag of the United States, but the inclusion of black at the top of the poster for *The Manchurian Candidate* denotes a malign presence in American life. The actors' expressions and accompanying drawings only add to the sense of unease.

TOP RIGHT

The Ipcress File (1965)
The artwork for *The Ipcress File* presents the staples of the spy genre: secrecy, officialdom, and danger. The gun's position suggests that Michael Caine's Harry Palmer may be as much the target of the narrative's conspiracy as he is the man investigating it.

BOTTOM RIGHT

The Spy Who Came in From the Cold (1965)
John Le Carré's novel was already an international success so there was no need to identify the genre to which it belonged. However, the film hints at a world far removed from the glamour of Bond and its imitators.

THE SPY FILM

The growing crisis between East and West, and in particular between Russia and the United States, in the early 1960s was reflected in the prominence of espionage thrillers. But whereas 1950s spy films often presented little more than simplistic Manichaean battles between good (capitalism) and bad (anything socialist or to the left of it), the more serious 1960s entries evinced a distrust in government and its institutions.

Although the increasingly outrageous adventures of Ian Fleming's 007 dominated the box office that decade, the spy genre also offered up far more nuanced and low-key examples of an era entering a period of political, social, and cultural uncertainty. The archetypal spy was no longer just a hero playing by the establishment's rules; he sometimes had to exceed his remit to get the job done, which included breaking rank.

The Manchurian Candidate (1962) was one of the first serious spy films of the decade. It is a world away from the exoticism of *Dr. No*, which appeared in the same year, and was sold to audiences as a serious drama—the unsmiling expressions of Frank Sinatra, Laurence Harvey, and Janet Leigh in the film's poster denoting the gravity of the film's intent. Three years later, John Le Carré's low-key spy novel *The Spy Who Came in From the Cold* (1965) reached the screen. It is tense and claustrophobic, yet the film draws as much from late 1950s British kitchen sink drama as it does from the legacy of earlier spy thrillers. It is espionage as an exercise in austerity. Likewise, *The Ipcress File* (1965), based on Len Deighton's novel, is very much rooted in its milieu: 1960s London. It offers a combination of postwar drabness with a sprinkling of the fashionable. *The Ipcress File* also promises mystery in its understated promotion.

The flip side of these dour worlds was the arrival of increasingly absurd spy franchises that reveled in explosions of color and glamour, as well as in a fetishization of the male protagonist's attraction to women. If *The Man From U.N.C.L.E.* series (1964) is palpably silly, James Coburn's turn as Derek Flint in *Our Man Flint* (1966) approaches the surreal. A parody of excessive proportions, it ultimately took the spy genre into a creative cul-de-sac where all logic and seriousness were lost to absurdity.

ABOVE

Our Man Flint (1966)
Like his artwork for *Modesty Blaise* (1966) and *The Spy Who Loved Me* (1977), Bob Peak's design for *Our Man Flint* veers toward the camp. A clear parody of Bond posters, it combines sex, action, and an unimpeachable cool on the part of its hero.

DEFINING BOND

The James Bond franchise dominated 1960s cinema. Although the productions increased in scale with each adventure, the staple elements of their allure remained constant. Naturally, the films' promotion highlighted the successful combination of glamour, danger, action, and thrills. Mitchell Hooks' designs for the first entry, *Dr. No* (1962), hint at the spy's sardonic nature, which contrasts markedly with the way the villain is presented. And women appear as playthings for Bond. In the artwork for *From Russia with Love* (1963) and *Goldfinger* (1964), sex and action are given equal prominence. However, it was with the fourth entry in the series, *Thunderball* (1965), and Robert E. McGinnis' appointment as designer—alongside Frank McCarthy—that the archetypal approach to Bond's image began to take shape.

In the late 1950s, McGinnis made a name for himself as a designer of pulp novel covers, particularly for the US publisher Dell, where his artwork was much sought after. His specialty was representations of women, in which he emphasized their attitude and sex appeal. He was responsible for the campaign that created Audrey Hepburn's look in *Breakfast at Tiffany's* (1961, see page 163) and later designed the artwork for the science

fiction film *Barbarella* (1968, see page 167), which redefined Jane Fonda's screen persona.

McGinnis' artwork for *Thunderball* accentuates Bond's enviable sex appeal and action status. Notably, it is more kinetic than that for previous films in the franchise. *You Only Live Twice* (1967) followed suit, although Sean Connery was so closely identified with the character by that time that the artwork emphasizes his name as much as Bond's. When Connery departed from the series for the first time, his replacement—George Lazenby—was relegated to being a mere name in the credits. However, the staple elements remained. Connery's return in *Diamonds Are Forever* (1971) features a minimal design; after all, audiences knew what to expect by that point. A more chaotic design developed with Roger Moore being cast in the role. McGinnis remained on board with the Bond franchise until the mid 1970s.

In a footnote to McGinnis' long career, in 2004 Pixar director Brad Bird, who had long been a fan of the artist's designs, commissioned the seventy-eight-year-old to draw on his experience with Bond for part of the artwork promoting the animated spy caper *The Incredibles* (2004). It was a perfect match.

BELOW LEFT
You Only Live Twice (1967)
The artwork makes the most of Ken Adam's vast sets, particularly the villain's lair. It also highlights the film's aerial action sequence.

BELOW RIGHT
On Her Majesty's Secret Service (1969)
The emphasis is on reassuring audiences that they can expect the same from the new Bond, Lazenby. Once again, the film's main action set piece dominates.

OPPOSITE
CLOCKWISE FROM TOP LEFT
Diamonds Are Forever (1971)
Connery's return to the role prompted a shift to a less frenzied look, compared to previous Bond poster designs. There is a single image, with no overlay of action scenes.

The Man with the Golden Gun (1974)
This is Bond on overload. Moore's second outing as the super spy saw an increase in gadgets, while the action became more outrageous. This is reflected in one of McGinnis' busiest designs.

Casino Royale (1967)
McGinnis' use of color is bold, but the design opts for a minimal approach.

Thunderball (1965)
McGinnis and McCarthy's design set in stone the elements that were key to the Bond franchise. This look was so successful that it remained, mostly unchanged, until the 1980s.

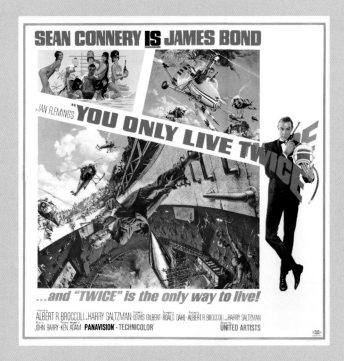

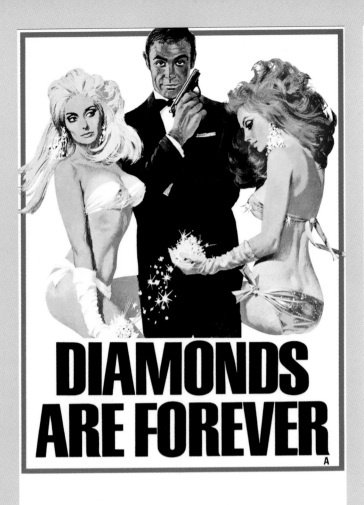

A NEW KIND OF WESTERN

The Westerns of the 1960s offered arguably the clearest example of how cinema was shifting in tandem with developing cultural tastes. The early part of the decade witnessed more traditional fare, such as *The Alamo* (1960) and *How the West Was Won* (1962), but in a genre that was always splintered by various accounts of frontier life, race, politics, gender, and geography soon began to play an increasingly significant role as revisionism and Native American history were incorporated into Western narratives.

John Ford's *The Searchers* (1956) and *The Man Who Shot Liberty Valance* (1962) had already begun to question the role of heroes and the myth of the West, but *Cheyenne Autumn* (1964) laid bare the director's acknowledgment that earlier representations of Native American culture were, at best, factually incorrect. The film's poster maps a trail through one such example of injustice. Later films, such as *Little Big Man* and *Soldier Blue* (both 1970), offer more graphic appraisals of Western expansionism in the late nineteenth century.

Arguably, the most notable shift in the genre as the decade progressed was the appearance of Westerns that weren't even American. The Spaghetti Western was a more brutal variant of life on the frontier. Moreover, it was one populated by all manner of nationalities, like its makers. Italian director Sergio Leone was its bright star, and his border town drama *A Fistful of Dollars* (1964) set the template for the new mode of Western. This reached its apotheosis with Leone's *Once Upon a Time in the West* (1968), a film that German filmmaker Wim Wenders regarded as the deconstruction of everything for which the classic Western stood. Politics intermingle with the genre in Leone's lesser—and morally questionable—*A Fistful of Dynamite* (1971, aka *Duck, You Sucker*), and similar films such as Damiano Damiani's *A Bullet for the General* (1967) dabble in the revolutionary politics of the era.

The Western genre even branched out into other worlds, most notably embracing science fiction in Michael Crichton's *Westworld* (1973). The film recasts Chris Adams, the gunslinger played by Yul Brynner in *The Magnificent Seven* (1960), as an out-of-control cyborg cowboy.

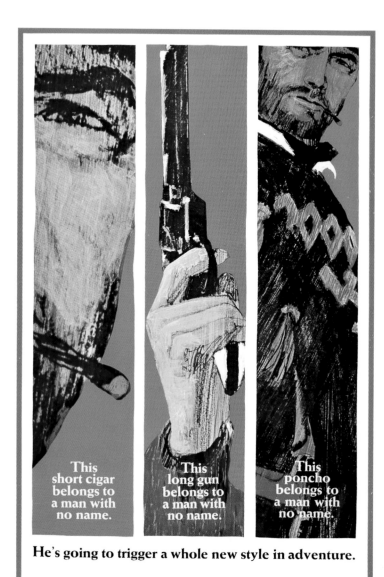

Dollars Trilogy (1964–1966)
The artwork for Leone and Clint Eastwood's first collaboration differed from country to country. Of particular note is the emphasis on the characteristics of the Man with No Name rather than the actor playing him.

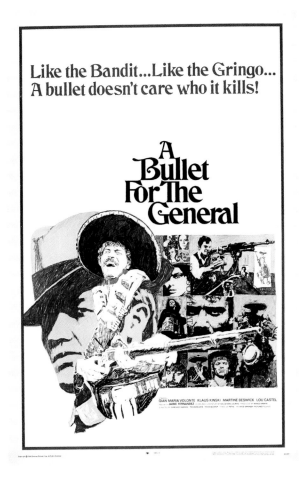

CLOCKWISE FROM TOP LEFT

**A Bullet for
the General (1967)**
A Bullet for the General
features elements of the
genre, but the character to
the left and the presence
of a machine gun suggest
more modern times. This
was a world away from
the Hollywood West.

Westworld (1973)
If Yul Brynner's detached
face weren't enough
to suggest a revision
of Western tropes, the
appearance of a frontier
town and the images of
two cowboys on computer
screens highlight Michael
Crichton's melding of
two worlds.

Cheyenne Autumn (1964)
In contrast to the
stark simplicity of most
earlier John Ford Western
posters, the journey
highlighted in the artwork
for *Cheyenne Autumn*
underpins the complex
issues surrounding the
development of the
American Frontier,
which the film attempts
to tackle.

**Once Upon a Time
in the West (1968)**
There is something
of the operatic in the
image inspired by the
opening shoot-out of
*Once Upon a Time in the
West*, which dominates
the bottom half of this
poster. The appearance of
Sergio Leone's name also
suggests a different kind
of Western.

A NEW KIND OF WESTERN 153

CLINT EASTWOOD

As the Western genre transformed, its perennial hero John Wayne was usurped by Clint Eastwood, playing grittier characters. The moral ambivalence these characters exuded was not only key to Eastwood's appeal but also a reflection of the times. After five years playing an upstanding drover, Rowdy Yates, in the television series *Rawhide* (1959–1965), Eastwood made the transition to Sergio Leone's corrupt worlds with ease. Culminating in *The Good, the Bad and the Ugly* (1966), Eastwood's characters in the *Dollars Trilogy* only seemed concerned with making money. However, beneath the cynicism lay a recognizable code of honor.

If Eastwood couldn't—and didn't want to—play Western characters permanently, his star persona needed a bridge that would have audiences accept him in modern times. It came with *Coogan's Bluff* (1968), which fitted the trappings of the Western genre in every respect except location. The film opens with a shoot-out on a hill, but the wilderness of Arizona is soon replaced by New York City. However, the shoot-outs and bar room brawls that are commonplace in Westerns remain. Furthermore, the promotional materials confirmed that audiences were watching a Western, just one that was set in the heart of a city. Don Siegel's *Dirty Harry* (1971) followed, and Eastwood's transformation into a contemporary cowboy was complete.

Although Eastwood returned to the old West regularly, he played around with the genre. The various artworks for *The Beguiled* (1971) underpin the film's ethereal atmosphere and ambiguous story, perhaps opening a variation of the Western to an audience resistant to the genre. *High Plains Drifter* (1973) is a ghost story of sorts, but Eastwood's posture in Bill Gold's artwork emphasizes his iconic status. Only the fiery backdrop hints at malevolence beyond the battle between gunfighters.

From *High Plains Drifter* to *J. Edgar* (2011), Bill Gold designed almost all the artwork campaigns for Eastwood's films. He brought the style of classical Hollywood to modern film, emphasizing star persona but within the context of a given narrative. Eastwood's image dominates Gold's artwork for both *The Outlaw Josey Wales* (1976) and *Unforgiven* (1992), but their tones could not be more different. Although both posters play to Western archetypes, the former is wild and untrammeled, whereas *Unforgiven* is stately and quiet, yet hinting at an approaching storm.

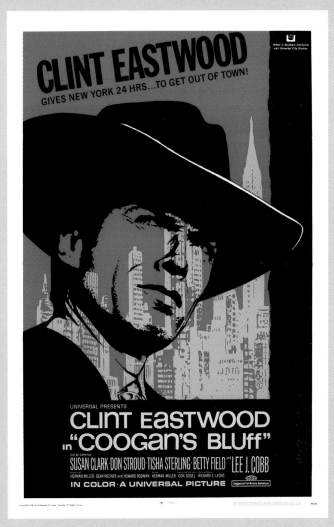

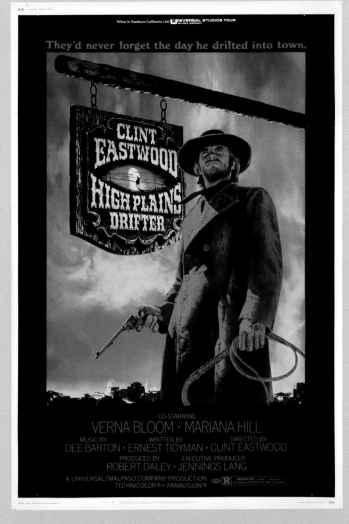

A NEW ITALIAN CINEMA

Italian cinema returned in some style to the world stage in 1960. Although directors such as Federico Fellini, Michelangelo Antonioni, Luchino Visconti, and Vittorio De Sica had been a significant presence since the postwar period, they all reached an artistic apotheosis in the early 1960s, which helped transform Italy's cinematic fortunes for the next decade. The radical shift began at the Cannes Film Festival in 1960, where Fellini's *La Dolce Vita* (1960) was awarded the Palme d'Or and Antonioni's *L'Avventura* (1960) the Jury Prize. Three months later, Visconti's *Rocco and His Brothers* (1960) was one of the sensations at the Venice Film Festival. De Sica's *Two Women* (1960) continued the winning streak; it won a Golden Globe for Best Foreign Language Film, and its star, Sophia Loren, became the first non-English actress to win an Academy Award for Best Actress in a Leading Role.

Each of these films presented a specific take on life in Italy. *Rocco and His Brothers* might have borne some resemblance to Visconti's earlier experiments with neorealism, but it was marked by an intensity and a charged sexual environment. The film was promoted as a multi-stranded melodrama, because it employs certain tropes of that genre, but it was a notable shift from Visconti's previous film, *Le Notti Bianche* (1957), and the two opulent costume dramas that bookend these works: *Senso* (1954) and the magisterial *The Leopard* (1963).

De Sica also came from the neorealist tradition, and *Two Women* was marketed as a melodrama. However, the film's promotional machine understood the star power of Sophia Loren and made the most of her presence. De Sica's later *Marriage Italian Style* (1964) is a more complex account of modern relationships, and its semi-comic tone underscores an exploration of gender roles in contemporary Italy. Likewise, the marketing of the film exuded a more sophisticated aesthetic.

The two Cannes winners were more radical in style, although the posters promoting them hardly appear to suggest anything new. Fellini's *La Dolce Vita* offers a vision of contemporary Rome, as seen through the eyes of Marcello Mastroianni's paparazzi reporter Marcello Rubini. He is in pursuit of Anita Ekberg's celebrity du jour, but as the film progresses the narrative becomes an expansive critique of the disparity between the wealthy

ABOVE

La Dolce Vita (1960)
The look is everything. Desire, or the expression of desire, drives the protagonist. Here, though, unconnected in space or time, the combination of two characters highlights the hedonism of Rome.

ABOVE

8 ½ (1963)
Save for the three film stills, this poster for *8 ½* is an exercise in minimalist design. Neither the visuals nor Fellini's statement reveal anything about the film, but that mystery makes it all the more enticing.

TOP RIGHT

Two Women (1960)
This artwork suggests a potboiler that the film is most definitely not. The disparity between a promotional poster and the content of a film can sometimes be at odds, but it is rarely this extreme.

MIDDLE RIGHT

Rocco and His Brothers (1960)
This poster underpins the fragmented narrative, but also suggests the combination of a neorealist-inspired aesthetic with a more contemporary approach to the story of one family's disintegration.

BOTTOM RIGHT

L'Avventura (1960)
An accurate representation of the existential angst in *L'Avventura* might have put audiences off. Instead, two contrasting images portray a troubled soul and a more conventional romantic relationship.

elite and the struggling working class in Italian society. As the artwork suggests, this is all carried off with an élan that gives the film's most celebrated moments their sheen.

Antonioni's *L'Avventura* divided audiences more than any other significant Italian release of 1960. It delves deeper into the lives of the beau monde who populated the bars and restaurants of Fellini's film, but suggests that such lives are empty—lacking any genuine affection or human contact. If the artwork once again implies a conventional melodrama, it also touches upon existential angst and a torrent of unexpressed feeling lying beneath the surface of a seemingly content bourgeois veneer.

That angst becomes more apparent with Antonioni's radical use of color in *Red Desert* (1964). Monica Vitti once again stars, albeit bereft of the blond hair she sported in both *L'Avventura* and *L'Eclisse* (1962, see page 164), the third film in Antonioni's loose trilogy. Her character's angst is palpable. Gone is the pretence at happiness, replaced instead by solitude. Audiences would have been familiar with Antonioni's style by this point, so any attempt to sell his films as anything but the pinnacle of rarefied 1960s European art house cinema would have been unlikely to succeed.

In 1963 Fellini released one of his most personal films, *8½*. Inspired by a bout of creative stagnation, the film is a fevered dream and as such a difficult proposition for any designer wishing to capture its shift between high drama, comedy, and moments of hallucinatory chaos. The US poster plays up the relationship between Marcello Mastroianni's troubled director and the women in his life.

Fellini's earlier films gave designers much to work with, but his wildly imagined features after *8½* saw the promotional posters engage with his films' playful, carnivalesque explosions of color and ribald humor. While *Fellini Satyricon* (1969) channels the world of first-century Rome and the artwork for *Roma* (1972) ranges from cartoon images of deities to a statue of a three-breasted woman on a pedestal, *Amarcord* (1973) presents a more muted image of life under Mussolini's regime. The posters helped define Fellini's unique style of cinema.

Pier Paolo Pasolini was the youngest of the group and became a director after achieving success as a poet and screenwriter. His early style echoed the neorealists, but by the time he made *Theorem* (1968) he was a singular force in Italian cinema. His was a provocative, sexually charged, and politically radical cinema. His tale of a stranger, played by Terence Stamp, entering a middle-class household and seducing each of its members was one of the seismic shifts in cinematic language that reflected the turbulence of the late 1960s. It also pointed to the kind of cinema that would come out of Europe in the 1970s.

The Leopard (1963)
The US poster for Visconti's *The Leopard* shies away from a more conventional design, instead sketching moments from the film and portraying Burt Lancaster's patriarch with dignity.

MICHELANGELO
ANTONIONI

DESERTO ROSSO

MONICA VITTI · RICHARD HARRIS
CARLO CHIONETTI · XENIA VALDERI
RITA RENOIR · ALDO GROTTI
PRODOTTO DA ANTONIO CERVI PER LA FILM DUEMILA, Roma · FRANCORIZ DISTRIBUTION, Parigi
TECHNICOLOR

TOP LEFT

Marriage Italian Style (1964)
The poster design for De Sica's *Marriage Italian Style* could be the cover of a book and in it lies the suggestion that the film is a guide to navigating modern relationships.

BOTTOM LEFT

Theorem (1968)
Terence Stamp exudes malevolence in the artwork here, but the main image also emphasizes desire and sex. The typography, usually seen in science fiction, suggests a world out of the ordinary.

ABOVE

Red Desert (1964)
Antonioni's first film shot in color was a radical experiment. The main still emphasizes the use of contrast, but the black-and-white inset confirms that Antonioni's intense filmmaking remains the same.

GIALLO FILMS

Alongside the internationally popular Spaghetti Western and a growing number of violent gangster thrillers, genre cinema in Italy was dominated by the Giallo film, a particular brand of stylized horror movie that featured macabre and often ingeniously constructed death sequences. Meaning "yellow" in English, Giallo derived its name from a series of pulpy paperback books, the covers of which featured a trademark yellow background. They tended to be mystery and suspense novels penned by various British and US authors.

The Giallo film genre was firmly established in the early 1960s with the appearance of Mario Bava's *The Girl Who Knew Too Much* (1963). It introduced the template for films that feature a protagonist—more often than not a woman—who witnesses a crime or something horrific, fails to convince the authorities of what they saw or believe, and thus places their own life in danger as they attempt to uncover the crime. Bava's film was re-edited in the United States and retitled *The Evil Eye*. His subsequent works of the decade, including *Blood and Black Lace* (1964) and *Kill, Baby … Kill!* (1966), helped to define the Giallo genre and to cement his position as a master of horror. His style became increasingly baroque as the genre developed, culminating in *A Bay of Blood* (1971), whose killings by assailants unknown until the film's climax become ever more extravagant.

The other important Giallo director is Dario Argento. His breakthrough came in 1970 with his directorial debut, *The Bird with the Crystal Plumage*, regarded as a landmark horror film and one that set Argento's course as the dominant director of the genre throughout the 1970s. It was the first in his *Animal Trilogy*, followed by *The Cat o' Nine Tails* (1971) and *Four Flies on Grey Velvet* (1972). Whereas these films followed the traditional whodunit narrative, *Deep Red* (1975) pushed Argento toward a more abstract style that embraced the supernatural—although the claims of its promotional material perhaps overstate the film's virtues as a first-class thriller. By *Suspiria* (1977), narrative lucidity had taken a back seat to atmosphere and complex Grand Guignol set pieces. That film has remained one of the artistic high points of the Giallo genre.

ABOVE

The Bird with the Crystal Plumage (1970)
Without the knife and the drops of blood, it would be difficult to place this film in the horror genre. But the knife and nude subject suggest something erotic, while the presence of the bird adds mystery.

Look deep into "THE EVIL EYE" to the twilight world of the Supernatural!

AMERICAN INTERNATIONAL
presents

JOHN SAXON
AND LETICIA ROMAN
STARRING IN

THE Evil EYE

What does it want...what will satisfy its cravings??
...only the dead know
and those they choose to tell!

The Only Thing More Terrifying
Than The Last 12 Minutes Of This Film
Are The First 92.

SUSPIRIA

Once You've Seen It
You Will Never Again Feel Safe In The Dark

RELEASED BY INTERNATIONAL CLASSICS INC.

BAHIA DE SANGRE

ABOVE

The Evil Eye (1963)

As the poster for a thriller, *The Evil Eye* is just too strange. The missing eye, the dangling woman, and the couple caught between a struggle and a dance all point toward something unconventional.

TOP RIGHT

Suspiria (1977)

For all its visual style, this artwork promotes sheer terror. The use of bold color against a black background is unsettling, while the caption promises the cinematic equivalent of a thrill ride.

MIDDLE RIGHT

A Bay of Blood (1971)

As this poster suggests, Bava's *A Bay of Blood* flows red. His previous work indulged in murder mystery but the culprits running amok in this slasher thriller employ simpler methods to do away with their victims.

BOTTOM RIGHT

Deep Red (1975)

This poster for *Deep Red* makes effective use of two contrasting images, both of which are barely suggestive of the film's narrative. However, they successfully convey mood and the hint of terror.

EUROPEAN FEMALE STARS

Alongside new approaches to film production, radical film movements, and a breakdown of moral codes that had been in place for decades, the representation of women in cinema was also changing throughout the 1960s. During the previous decade, Brigitte Bardot's performance in ... *And God Created Woman* (1956) tackled taboos regarding sexuality. By 1963, however, that representation had become more complex, and Jean-Luc Godard's *Le mépris* (1963, see page 139) offered a deconstruction of Bardot's star persona while at the same time acknowledging the power of her screen presence.

Jeanne Moreau became a star as a result of her two early collaborations with Louis Malle, *Elevator to the Gallows* and *The Lovers* (both 1958). Her position as an icon of European cinema was cemented through her work with Michelangelo Antonioni in *La Notte* (1961), François Truffaut's *Jules et Jim* (1962), and Luis Buñuel's *Diary of a Chambermaid* (1964). By 1965, she was an international star and worked with Malle again, alongside Bardot, on *Viva Maria!* (1965). Although hardly a success—commercially or creatively—the film nevertheless highlighted both actresses' status on the international stage and also played with gender roles by having two strong females as the main characters.

The other key French actress of the era was Catherine Deneuve. She became a star through her performance in Jacques Demy's everyday musical *The Umbrellas of Cherbourg* (1964), but her heft as a dramatic actor was confirmed by her performance as a woman edging toward insanity in Roman Polanski's claustrophobic *Repulsion* (1965). However, it was her starring role in Buñuel's *Belle de jour* (1967) that made Deneuve one of the screen icons of the 1960s.

Two female stars dominated Italian cinema in the 1960s. Sophia Loren and Monica Vitti were the simmering brunette and the cool blond. Whereas one was passionate in her performances, the other exuded nonchalance, even when playing a legendary comic book hero. Loren moved quickly from being a popular actress in Italy to being an international star, thanks to a multi-picture deal with Paramount Pictures. Over the next decade, she alternated between working in Hollywood and appearing in Italian productions, and it was her performance in

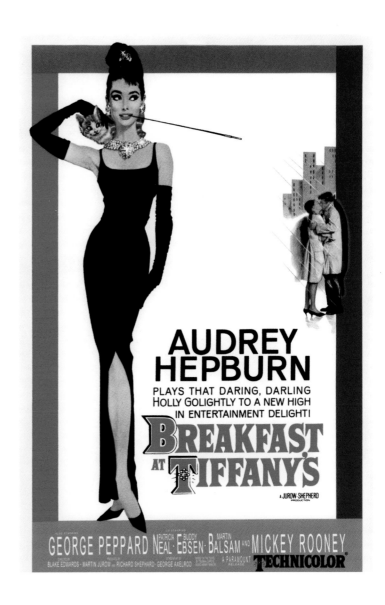

OPPOSITE
Isadora (1968)
Karel Reisz's film places the well-known ballet dancer in the context of history, but Reynold Brown's poster design ensures that the woman, and not the events that unfold around her, is the most important element.

ABOVE
Breakfast at Tiffany's (1961)
Robert E. McGinnis' design recalls his earlier work as a pulp fiction cover artist, particularly the scene with the couple. The main image, with Audrey Hepburn in an iconic pose, contrasts with the bold blocks of color that border the artwork.

Brigitte Bardot Jeanne Moreau
in
VIVA MARIA !

ein Film von
Louis Malle
mit Paulette Dubost Gregor von Rezzori Poldo Bendandi Claudio Brook
Carlos Lopez Moctezuma Jonathan Eden und
George Hamilton
Original Drehbuch: Louis Malle und Jean-Claude Carriere
Kamera: Henri Decae
Regie: Louis Malle Produktion: Oscar Dancigers und Louis Malle
aufgenommen in Panavision® Technicolor®

ROBERT et RAYMOND HAKIM —— CATHERINE DENEUVE
JEAN SOREL
MICHEL PICCOLI

un film de *Luis Buñuel*
BELLE DE JOUR

d'après le roman de JOSEPH KESSEL

GENEVIÈVE PAGE • PIERRE CLÉMENTI • FRANCISCO RABAL
FRANÇOISE FABIAN • MACHA MERIL
MARIA LATOUR • MUNI
...GEORGES MARCHAL ...FRANCIS BLANCHE EASTMANCOLOR

ROBERT et RAYMOND HAKIM

20th
Century-Fox
Presents
Modesty Blaise.

COLOUR by **TECHNICOLOR**®

**The World's deadliest
and most dazzling
female agent**

STARRING
MONICA VITTI   TERENCE STAMP
DIRK BOGARDE
HARRY ANDREWS · CLIVE REVILL
CO-STARRING
AND MICHAEL CRAIG · A JOSEPH JANNI PRODUCTION · DIRECTED BY JOSEPH LOSEY · SCREENPLAY BY EVAN JONES · MUSIC BY JOHN DANKWORTH

TOP LEFT

L'Eclisse (1962)
Her second credit notwithstanding, Vitti is this film's star and central to the artwork. The design reflects the stripped-down nature of Antonioni's film, particularly in the use of a single block of color.

TOP MIDDLE

Viva Maria! (1965)
Provocative and confrontational, Bardot and Moreau are the selling points. Their sex appeal is offset by the gun, which Bardot points directly at the audience, while Moreau hints at the film's humor.

TOP RIGHT

Belle de jour (1967)
René Ferracci's evocative design adopts a painterly aesthetic, with the background resembling an artist's canvas. It highlights the film as a work of art and by extension Buñuel as an artist.

ABOVE

Modesty Blaise (1966)
Bob Peak's *Modesty Blaise* poster revels in camp excess. Clearly a nod to the outrageous spy capers of the early 1960s, it also exudes a more offbeat appeal, capturing the anarchic spirit of the era.

Vittorio De Sica's melodrama *Two Women* (1960, see page 157) that won her an Academy Award for Best Actress in a Leading Role.

Loren made her Hollywood debut in the inauspicious *Boy on a Dolphin* (1957); however, it was the period epic *The Pride and the Passion* (1957), in which she starred opposite Cary Grant and Frank Sinatra, that saw her star rise. After *Two Women*, she appeared opposite Charlton Heston in *El Cid* (1961) and then in a range of films that included *The Fall of the Roman Empire* (1964), *Lady L* (1965), and *Judith* (1966). The posters for all these films portray Loren as exotic. Although she starred in epic period dramas and comedies, the role that truly tapped into the era was her turn in Stanley Donen's *Arabesque* (1966). The film and the posters that promoted it play on the vogue for espionage thrillers, and like Donen's earlier *Charade* (1963), they hint at glamour and adventure.

A number of high-profile international features notwithstanding, Vitti remained a very Italian star. Her breakthrough came with her performance in Antonioni's *L'Avventura* (1960, see page 157), which began a fruitful collaboration with the filmmaker. She took a back seat to Jeanne Moreau in *La Notte,* but returned to a leading role in *L'Eclisse* (1962). Like the artwork for her subsequent Antonioni collaboration, *The Red Desert* (1964), the posters for *L'Eclisse* feature Vitti most prominently. She was the filmmaker's star and muse, and also often the bridge by which audiences could access Antonioni's deceptively complex worlds. It was Vitti's coolness that won her the lead in Joseph Losey's *Modesty Blaise* (1966).

Although Audrey Hepburn was regarded as a bona fide US star by the time she appeared in *Breakfast at Tiffany's* (1961), there remained something quintessentially European about her. She was, after all, the princess from *Roman Holiday* (1953), the chauffeur's daughter who matures into a woman thanks to a European education in *Sabrina* (1954), and the book shop clerk-turned-model who desires nothing more than to study in Europe in *Funny Face* (1957). However, her role as Holly Golightly created one of the decade's most enduring style icons.

Vanessa Redgrave had already starred in the era-defining *Blow-Up* (1966) by the time she played the iconic 1920s ballet dancer Isadora Duncan in Karel Reisz's *Isadora* (1968). If the artwork suggests a more conventional period drama in its re-creation of moments from the film, the dominant image of Redgrave's fiery hair and unreadable expression hint at something new. Redgrave was a star because of her talent, but her interests always appeared less in the trappings of celebrity than in something more complex, perhaps reflecting a new kind of star, who melded the personal and the political.

Arabesque (1966)
McGinnis' artwork once again betrays his background in book cover design. It is more pared down than that for his Bond posters, but Sophia Loren wouldn't look out of place alongside Sean Connery.

JANE FONDA

In the space of a decade, Jane Fonda transformed from Hollywood starlet to outspoken activist, whose activities beyond the screen often attracted more attention than her film roles. Furthermore, this move away from conventional Hollywood stardom was reflected in her choice of roles between 1965 and 1972.

Fonda's appearance in the comedy Western *Cat Ballou* (1965), playing a schoolmarm-turned-outlaw, provided her first breakthrough role. *Barefoot in the Park* (1967) followed and quickly cemented her star status. She appeared alongside Robert Redford as a newly married wife who dreams of the perfect life in New York City. Like the Neil Simon play on which it is based, the film is bright and breezy, with the central relationship offering a light commentary on the shifting power between genders in personal relationships.

A year later, Fonda starred as the intergalactic hero of Roger Vadim's *Barbarella* (1968). Like Brigitte Bardot before her, Fonda was transformed by Vadim into the sex symbol of her generation. The artwork hints at the movie's kitsch, camp style—there couldn't have been another space film released that year that contrasted so wildly with Stanley Kubrick's *2001: A Space Odyssey* (1968). And *Barbarella* added yet another dimension to Fonda's rapidly changing persona.

The various international posters for *They Shoot Horses, Don't They?* (1969) tap not only into the film's bleak tone but also into Fonda's raw performance as a young woman who is desperate to win the prize money at a non-stop dance competition during the Great Depression. Of the many designs, few come as close to capturing the film's bitter irony as the US poster, which features a distraught Fonda and Red Buttons framed in a glitter ball.

Fonda's next two films sealed her status as one of the significant actors of a new generation. In *Klute* (1971), directed by Alan J. Pakula, she plays a prostitute at the center of a missing persons investigation and the potential target of a killer. And in Jean-Luc Godard and Jean-Pierre Gorin's *Tout va bien* (1972), she is a politicized journalist at the heart of a French industrial dispute. The line between acting and real life became blurred, and Fonda remained a politically incendiary figure throughout the turbulence of the 1970s, before transforming herself again in the 1980s into a fitness guru.

jane fonda · donald sutherland
in an alan j. pakula production
'klute'

One man is missing.
Two call girls lie dead.

...it starts with the jangle of a phone.

original soundtrack available on warner bros. records

an alan j. pakula production starring jane fonda · donald sutherland in "klute" co-starring charles cioffi · nathan george · dorothy tristan · roy r. scheider · rita gam · music by michael small · written by andy and dave lewis · co-produced by david lange · produced and directed by alan j. pakula / panavision® technicolor® · from warner bros...a kinney leisure service

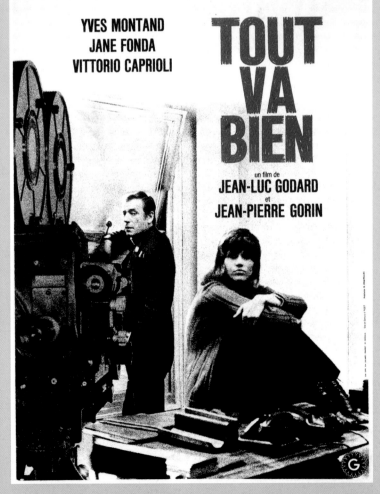

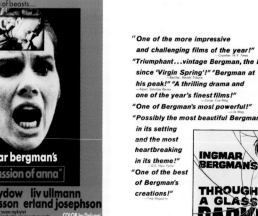

TOP LEFT

Hour of the Wolf (1968)
An exploration into the gray area between dreams and the conscious mind, the image in this design resembles a nightmare. The sense of unease is exacerbated by the use of color.

TOP MIDDLE

The Passion of Anna (1969)
Through a Glass Darkly (1961)
Both designs accentuate angst. While the object of pain for one woman appears as an image over her mind, for the other her life is shattered like a pane of glass.

TOP RIGHT

The Devil's Eye (1960)
This design suggests Bergman has embraced some levity, confirmed by the reviews on the poster. At this point, most audiences were familiar with his denser dramas, so perhaps some notice was necessary.

ABOVE

Persona (1966)
The grainy image of the actors and the outline of a puzzle piece suggest that the two women's psyches are interconnected. But the use of red highlights the danger inherent in their relationship.

THE FILMS OF INGMAR BERGMAN

By the late 1950s, after the successes of *Summer with Monika* (1953), *The Seventh Seal*, and *Wild Strawberries* (both 1957), Ingmar Bergman had established himself as one of contemporary cinema's finest filmmakers. *The Devil's Eye* (1960), in which Satan decides to bring Don Juan back to life in order to corrupt the innocent daughter of a vicar, began the 1960s on a lighter note, but as the decade progressed Bergman's work took on darker hues, offering probing examinations of the human psyche and personal relationships. His next film, *Through a Glass Darkly* (1961), explored the pain of a woman tortured by her faith. Although the posters for both films feature lengthy critical notices, the radical shift in tone between them is clear.

Persona (1966), arguably Bergman's defining film of the decade, features artwork that plays heavily on the drama's central relationship between Liv Ullmann's acclaimed actress, who appears to have lost the ability to speak, and Bibi Andersson's nurse. Alone together on a remote island, the two women engage in a power game, with their identities merging and repelling as the film progresses. A similar question of identity is proposed in Bergman's *Face to Face* (1976), which was intended to be a four-part television mini-series but was eventually released as a feature. This time, Ullmann is a psychiatrist who is experiencing a breakdown. The film's poster—a stylized, suggestive version of a Rorschach test—portrays Ullmann's character divided in two. That both of the films' artwork references psychological undercurrents highlighted what most audiences already knew: a Bergman film is a challenging but often rewarding work of art.

    Hour of the Wolf (1968) and *The Passion of Anna* (1969), along with *Shame* (1968), make up a loose trilogy. But unlike that for *Persona*, the artwork for these films hints at something closer to horror. The relationship at the heart of *The Passion of Anna*, between two grief-stricken individuals whose sense of loss transforms into rage, becomes increasingly tortured, while *Hour of the Wolf* resembles a waking nightmare whose passages of surreal imagery make it one of the decade's more disturbing excursions into psychological horror. That horror may be more imagined than real, reflecting the outward projection of the main character's emotional turmoil, but its impact is no less unsettling.

POLISH FILM POSTERS

In contrast to the propagandist work of the great Soviet poster designers, the Polish School of Posters represented a movement that railed against the system. Although part of the Eastern Bloc and expected to produce work that reinforced the ideological stand of a government closely aligned with its Soviet masters, the designers who made up this movement and whose work spanned from the 1950s to the 1980s were defined by their subtle attempt to critique authority. That they were successful is a testament to their creativity and ingenuity. Their designs made a lasting impact on the international development of graphic design in poster art and the blurring of the lines between the roles of designer and artist.

There were two main institutions responsible for commissioning poster designs during Soviet rule: Film Polski and Centrala Wynajmu Filmów. Although state-run, they showed little interest in each poster's content and tended to prefer employing artists. Because many artists found work scarce in an environment that abhorred individualism, working on film posters not only allowed them the opportunity to exercise their craft, but also gave them a surprising amount of freedom. Polish School artwork is known for its vivid colors resonant of folk art, and its painterly gesture, humor, and fantasy.

International films were represented in a way that was very different from the posters that sold these films on their domestic release. Waldemar Swierzy's design for *Sunset Boulevard* (1950), Maciej Hibner's for *Rififi* (1955), and Roman Cieslewicz's for *Vertigo* (1958), for example, offer radical interpretations of the films they represent. With the arrival of a new generation of Polish filmmakers, spearheaded by Andrzej Wajda, these artists found their freedom aligned with politicized filmmaking and produced works that began to question the state of the country. Over the course of the next decade, they drew heavily on surrealism and the fantastic, balanced with a studied, intellectual engagement with each film, its themes, and how it could best be represented.

The 1970s saw even more extreme interpretations of films. But beyond form, there is an anarchy at work in many of the posters, which ensures that they remain as fresh and occasionally shocking as they did when they first appeared.

ABOVE

Rebel Without a Cause (1955/1970)
Ryszard Kiwerski's design taps into the role played by the automobile in the 1950s, as an emblem of freedom for teenagers. But with its black backdrop and mangled chassis, it also hints at James Dean's fate.

OPPOSITE

Vertigo (1958/1963)
Roman Cieslewicz's poster for Hitchcock's thriller is a world away from Saul Bass' designs. Yet there remains a link, both in the circular target at the front of the skull and in the swirls of the fingerprints.

KIM NOVAK W PODWÓJNEJ ROLI | JAMES STEWART
BARBARA DEL GEDDES W MROŻĄCYM KREW W ŻYŁACH ☛ BARWNYM FILMIE
HITCHCOCKA

ZAWRÓT GŁOWY

PRODUKCJA
Paramount

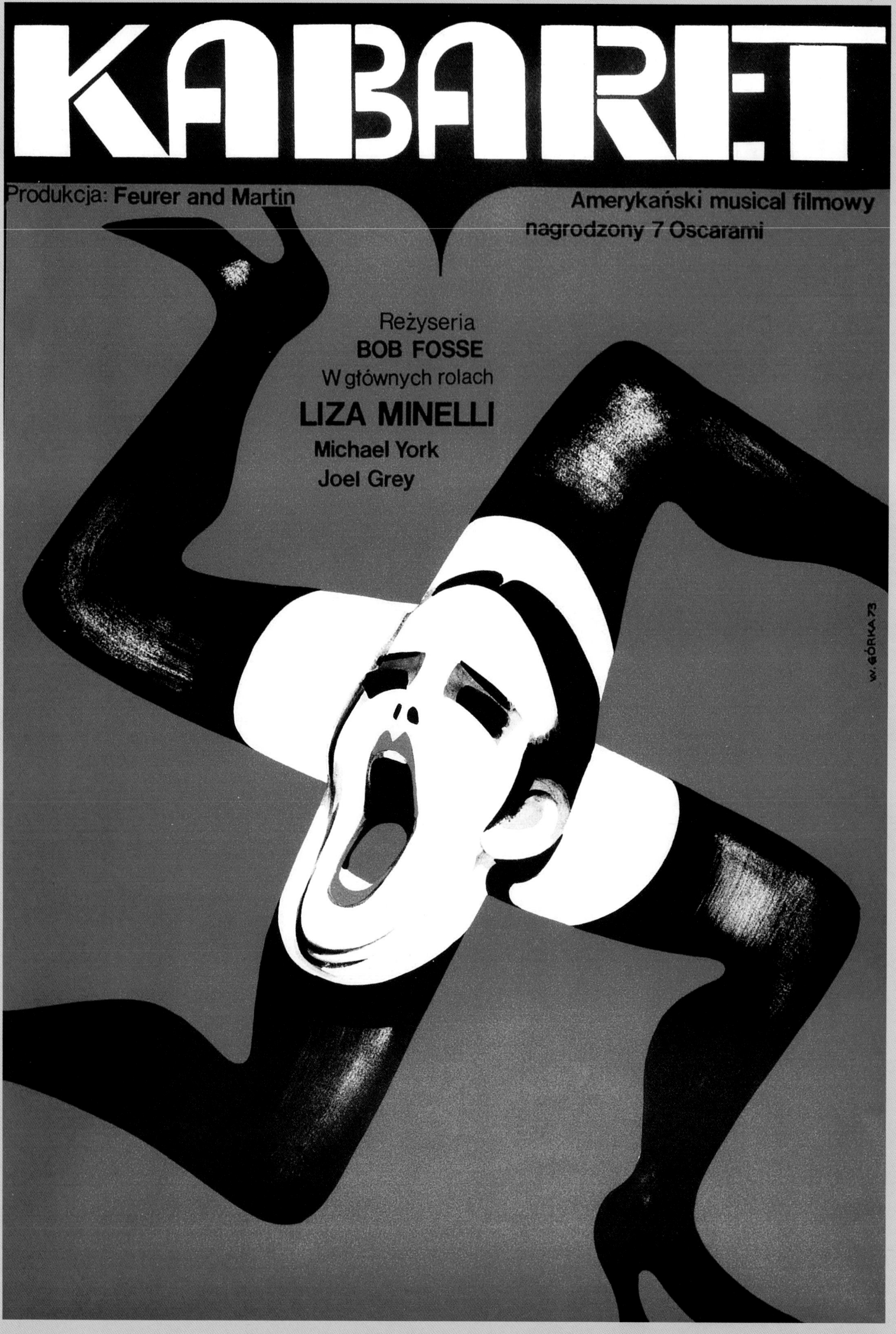
KABARET
Produkcja: Feurer and Martin
Amerykański musical filmowy
nagrodzony 7 Oscarami
Reżyseria
BOB FOSSE
W głównych rolach
LIZA MINELLI
Michael York
Joel Grey
W. GÓRKA 73

WIKTOR GÓRKA

Wiktor Górka was part of the second generation of Polish poster designers, who were born in the 1920s and 1930s, and came to prominence during the 1950s and 1960s. He graduated with a degree in graphic design from the Academy of Fine Arts in Krakow in 1952, although he had already gained recognition by being awarded second place in a national design competition in 1949. It was the first of countless accolades he received throughout his career. Following his graduation, he went to work for the country's leading publishers and film companies. He remained in Poland until 1970, when he was invited to teach in Havana, Cuba. From there, Górka traveled to Mexico where he taught until the mid 1990s, before returning to Warsaw. In 2000, at the 6th International Poster Biennale in Mexico, he received the top award for his contribution to the development of graphic arts in Mexico.

Górka was the cofounder of what became known as the Polish School of Posters. They collectively believed in clarity of design and simplicity of purpose, as well as the use of concise symbols and poetic metaphor in order to convey meaning. His peers included Roman Cieslewicz, Hubert Hilscher, Tadeusz Jodlowski, Jan Mlodozeniec, Marian Stachurski, Waldemar Swierzy, and Maciej Urbaniec, as well as Jan Lenica, who is arguably the most famous and acclaimed designer alongside Górka.

While working in Poland, Górka designed nearly 300 film posters, along with book and magazine covers. In addition to his film work, he gained recognition for his Cyrk, or circus, posters, which were popular throughout the 1960s. He drew on various styles for each new poster, whose subjects ranged from acrobatics to various performing animals. His 1964 design of three acrobats balancing against a red backdrop remains one of the best known of the thousands produced.

However, it is for his work on film posters that Górka is best known today. His 1973 design for *Cabaret* (1972) remains one of the most famous Polish posters of that era, while many earlier works are no less striking. His designs do not represent a film so much as reinterpret it. And like the work of his colleagues, the results are often wildly imaginative and audacious.

CZECH POSTER DESIGN

Like those from the earlier Polish School of Posters, the group of Czech poster designers who emerged in the late 1950s and 1960s were not a collective with a single artistic vision. They are better described as a generation who found that they had the freedom to be creative. These artists soaked up the spirit of change, like the filmmakers who represented the Czech *New Wave* in the 1960s.

The Central Film Distribution Center had not relinquished its control completely, but alongside the strict censorship of films produced for the masses there was a relaxation of the rules when it came to more peripheral areas of film production, such as animation and film promotion. It was dangerous to be overtly political, but artists found it easier to be more playful or adventurous with their work.

A key moment for this new movement happened in 1954, when an exhibition at Dům uměleckého průmyslu, Prague's House of Applied Arts, featured posters by Polish designers. Although Czech designers would often play with form and materials, the way in which the Polish artists had freed themselves from the shackles of Soviet control was a major inspiration.

One of the most important artists of this era was Zdeněk Ziegler. He took on various design jobs while studying architecture in the late 1950s, but his first film commission was for Jaromil Jireš' feature debut *The Cry* (1964). He subsequently worked with other acclaimed Czech filmmakers, including František Vláčil, Karel Zeman, Karel Kachyňa, and Jiří Menzel, as well as on international productions.

Other key artists from this period include Karel Teissig, Bedřich Dlouhý, and Jiří Balcar. They all found themselves in high demand, not only because they were creatively inventive, but also because, like in any country behind the Iron Curtain, shipping costs and political issues meant that commissioning locally produced posters was far easier. More remarkably, although the artists most likely knew what the films were about, it is unlikely that they would actually have seen them before working on the designs. This might account for why an artwork such as Jan Vyletal's poster for Alfred Hitchcock's *The Birds* (1963), featuring fantasy birds and female nudes levitating over a purple and yellow landscape, is quite so bizarre.

ABOVE

100 Rifles (1969/1971)
Zdeněk Ziegler employs the torn colors of the Mexican flag to hint at the revolt that unfolds in Tom Gries' action drama. A statuesque Raquel Welch features prominently as one of the film's main draws.

OPPOSITE

Closely Watched Trains (1966)
A key title of the Czech New Wave, Jiří Menzel's film tells the story of a young station guard at a country outpost in World War II. František Zálešák's design hints at the travails he faces.

ostře
sledované
vlaky
Filmový přepis novely Bohumila Hrabala
Scénář: Bohumil Hrabal a Jiří Menzel
Režie: JIŘÍ MENZEL
Kamera: Jaromír Šofr
Hudba: Jiří Šust
V hlavní roli:
VÁCLAV
NECKÁŘ
© ZALEŠÁK 66 F08*60378 OTK 23

POSTERS OF THE DECADE

Michael Powell's *Peeping Tom* and Alfred Hitchcock's *Psycho* (both 1960) forever changed the horror genre. They were both shocking, graphic nightmares on the screen. Previously, audiences and critics hadn't quite been ready for Powell's brilliant study in psychosis, *The Red Shoes* (1948)—a film no less fascinated by obsession but whose protagonist causes harm only to herself. Reviews were scathing and deeply personal toward the director, while audiences mostly stayed away. In more recent decades, *Peeping Tom*'s reputation has grown considerably. It might not attract as much praise as *Psycho*, but it has become a defining film of the 1960s. Hitchcock's shocker, meanwhile, brought horror into the modern age, introduced the slasher genre to a mainstream audience, and provided one of cinema's greatest surprises with *that* shower scene. Although out of step with the director's other productions from that period—studio-produced, big budget color releases—*Psycho* remains arguably Hitchcock's most influential film.

A year later, *West Side Story* (1961) gave audiences a very modern vision of New York City. It presents the everyday life of the city's working-class population, albeit in the form of a musical. The opening sequence, an aerial shot over the city—played out to Leonard Bernstein's "Prologue"—marks out the film's terrain, both thematically and aesthetically. This was a long way from the popular musical theater offerings of Rodgers and Hammerstein.

Arthur Penn's gangster drama *Bonnie and Clyde* (1967) has come to be seen as the production that sealed the fate of the studio system. It actually took more than one film, but *Bonnie and Clyde*'s approach to morality, its black humor, and the visceral punch of the climactic shoot-out signaled a new age and direction for mainstream cinema.

If Penn's film burned the house down, *Easy Rider* (1969) was the phoenix that rose out of it. The runaway success of Dennis Hopper and Peter Fonda's road movie marked a new era in US filmmaking. It also became emblematic of a shift toward independent productions in cinemas across the world. That *Easy Rider* ends on a bleak note only made the film prophetic about what was to come, in both cinema and society.

They're young... they're in love

...and they kill people.

MICHAEL J. POLLARD · GENE HACKMAN · ESTELLE PARSONS

Written by DAVID NEWMAN and ROBERT BENTON·Music by Charles Strouse·Produced by WARREN BEATTY·Directed by ARTHUR PENN

TECHNICOLOR® FROM WARNER BROS.-SEVEN ARTS

THE SCREEN ACHIEVES ONE OF THE GREAT ENTERTAINMENTS
IN THE HISTORY OF MOTION PICTURES

MIRISCH PICTURES PRESENTS
"WEST SIDE STORY"
A ROBERT WISE PRODUCTION

STARRING NATALIE WOOD

RICHARD BEYMER RUSS TAMBLYN
RITA MORENO GEORGE CHAKIRIS
DIRECTED BY ROBERT WISE AND JEROME ROBBINS SCREENPLAY BY ERNEST LEHMAN
ASSOCIATE PRODUCER SAUL CHAPLIN CHOREOGRAPHY BY JEROME ROBBINS
MUSIC BY LEONARD BERNSTEIN LYRICS BY STEPHEN SONDHEIM
BASED UPON THE STAGE PLAY PRODUCED BY ROBERT E. GRIFFITH AND HAROLD S. PRINCE
BOOK BY ARTHUR LAURENTS
PLAY CONCEIVED, DIRECTED AND CHOREOGRAPHED BY JEROME ROBBINS
PRODUCTION DESIGNED BY BORIS LEVEN · FILMED IN PANAVISION® 70 · TECHNICOLOR®
PRESENTED BY MIRISCH PICTURES, INC. · IN ASSOCIATION WITH SEVEN ARTS PRODUCTIONS, INC.
RELEASED THRU UNITED ARTISTS

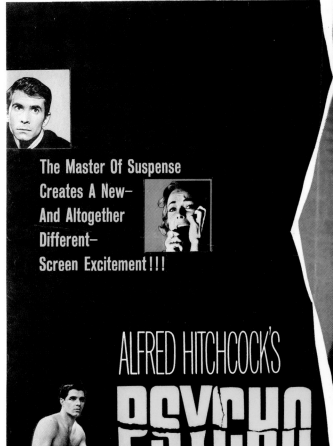

The Master Of Suspense
Creates A New—
And Altogether
Different—
Screen Excitement!!!

ALFRED HITCHCOCK'S
PSYCHO

Copyright ©1960 by Shamley Productions, Inc.   Country of Origin U.S.A.

STARRING ANTHONY
PERKINS
VERA
MILES
JOHN
GAVIN
CO-STARRING MARTIN
BALSAM
JOHN
McINTIRE
AND
JANET
LEIGH
AS
MARION
CRANE
DIRECTED BY
ALFRED
HITCHCOCK
SCREENPLAY BY
JOSEPH
STEFANO
A PARAMOUNT
Release

B

1970s

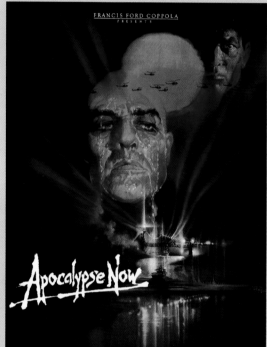

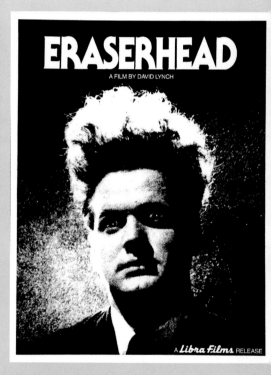

He was 25 years old • He combed his hair like James Dean •
He was very fastidious • People who littered bothered him •
She was 15 • She took music lessons and could twirl a
baton • She wasn't very popular at school • For awhile they
lived together in a tree house.

In 1959, she watched while he killed a lot of people.

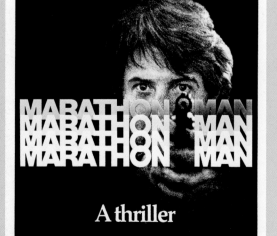

Darkness, grittiness, bleakness, and despair. Following the radiant designs that accompanied the majority of mainstream films around the world prior to the 1970s, a new aesthetic began to appear. A sense of threat had been present in low-budget films, or productions made outside the mainstream, for many years. But now even those in charge of the larger purses began to accept that sunlight and happiness weren't selling as well.

It was most noticeable in Hollywood. The rise of European art house cinema and its impact on a fresh generation of filmmakers resulted in the need to create a new image for a different kind of film, even among those most closely representing the establishment. In 1968, the poster for Don Siegel's *Madigan* featured Richard Widmark's cop facing off against an armed man. He looks dignified and calm. Just three years later, the poster for *Dirty Harry* (1971) depicted Clint Eastwood's character with a gun larger than his face, a bullet hole in glass, and no sign of provocation. In the same year, the poster for *The French Connection* (1971) showed Gene Hackman's wayward detective shooting an unarmed man in the back. These images seemed to represent a shift in how people—the audiences—perceived authority.

Klute (1971) and *The Parallax View* (1974) both hint at an unseen threat. While *All the President's Men* (1976), the third film in Alan J. Pakula's conspiracy trilogy, gives a documentary-style portrait of Dustin Hoffman and Robert Redford, the actors' expressions as they look off to something out of frame again prompt unease. Meanwhile, the popularity of Blaxploitation, Hong Kong martial arts films, and a more radical kind of horror signaled a dramatic shift in audience tastes.

The rise of European auteurs in the 1960s, such as Ingmar Bergman, Michelangelo Antonioni, and Luis Buñuel, whose darker themes were reflected in the way their films were promoted, not only had an impact on the way that films were being made around the world, but also on how they were sold to audiences. A character's actions no longer dominated a poster— their psychological state was also on show. Artists such as René Ferracci collaborated with filmmakers to produce imagery that provoked, and kicked against societal mores.

And yet, as the decade progressed, a new kind of mainstream cinema took hold. The blockbuster film had its roots in 1970s cinema, and its high concept approach to narrative and promotion would come to dominate subsequent decades.

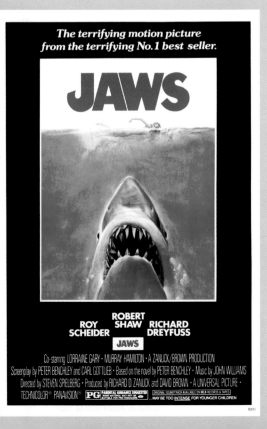

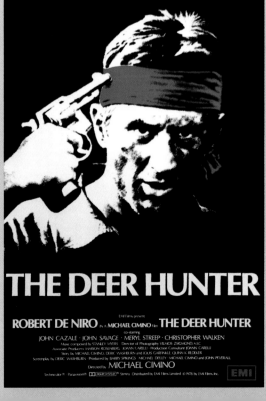

THE AGE OF ANXIETY

The 1970s witnessed a period of uncertainty in global politics. The decade was dominated by economic turmoil and civil strife. Regime change was in the air, as long-standing dictatorships ended and democratically elected governments were overthrown. Corruption was rife, and it was often accompanied by cover-ups and conspiracies. Political assassinations led to theories of a faceless corporate elite controlling the world. No wonder the cinema of the era evinced such a powerful mood of paranoia.

Although US cinema is most closely associated with the conspiracy films of the 1970s, countries farther afield, whose own political situations were unsteady, also saw instability reflected in their national cinema. Italian director Francesco Rosi made a name for himself with his portrait of Sicilian bandit *Salvatore Giuliano* (1962) and his study of corruption *Hands Over the City* (1963). A decade later, he produced two period films that also dealt with corruption, *The Mattei Affair* (1972) and *Lucky Luciano* (1973), before presenting a bleak portrait of political manipulation and murder with the complex procedural thriller *Illustrious Corpses* (1976). In this film, Lino Ventura plays an inspector investigating the murder of a district attorney, but as the film's poster suggests, no one is safe in this world.

Greek director Costa-Gavras followed up his Academy Award-winning *Z* (1969), which explores the events surrounding the assassination of Greek politician Grigoris Lambrakis in 1963, with *State of Siege* (1972), set in Uruguay. Loosely based on the activities of US police official and alleged torture expert Dan Mitrione, it looks at US involvement in Latin America and opened just prior to the overthrow of Chile's democratically elected President Salvador Allende.

The centerpiece of Hollywood's 1970s conspiracy thrillers is Alan J. Pakula's paranoia trilogy: *Klute* (1971, see page 166), *The Parallax View* (1974), and *All the President's Men* (1976). The first is a low-key, character-driven piece detailing the search for a missing man and his link to call girl Bree Daniels (played by Jane Fonda), whose own life may now be in danger. New York initially appears innocuous, but as the story progresses a sense of threat enters every corner of the city, including Bree's own apartment, where the constant ringing of her phone

Invasion of the Body Snatchers (1978)
The artwork recalls the use of color in the poster for Don Siegel's original version, but here the division between the colors is blurred. The double use of the same image reinforces the sense of danger.

"Illustrious CORPSES"

TECHNICOLOR®   United Artists

A
KNOCKOUT
OF A MOVIE
A superb and enthralling,
unforgettable film. — CBS-TV

STATE OF SIEGE

TOP

Illustrious Corpses (1976)
The main image and red
backdrop are clear in
their suggestion of the
film's bleak worldview.
The inset image (which
was also used alone as
the film's poster) hints at
the movie's conspiratorial
element, with Lino
Ventura's quizzical
expression appearing
below a figure forcibly
"vanished" from history.

BOTTOM

State of Siege (1972)
The use of monochrome
suggests a seriousness
that is heightened by the
film title's font and size,
which imply urgency. The
expressions of both men
reinforce the tone. Like
many stars of the era, Yves
Montand was pushing his
screen persona, and it is
not clear here what type
of role he is playing.

increases her paranoia. If that film plays up the threat of contemporary urban architecture as the representation of corporate power, the feeling is pushed further with *The Parallax View*. Warren Beatty stars as journalist Joseph Frady who, following the death of a friend, uncovers a series of assassination plots run by a mysterious organization. The poster for the film takes the form of a reflection in a building's window panes, hiding what goes on behind them. By contrast, *All the President's Men* is more sober—a detailed, stylishly unfussy account of the two journalists who brought the Watergate scandal to light. In the place of sensation is a more documentary-style image, reflecting the film's basis in actual events.

In addition, there were revisionist theories on a key moment of the 1960s. *Executive Action* (1973) suggests an alternative account of the assassination of President John F. Kennedy to the one that appeared in the Warren Commission report, whereas *Winter Kills* (1979), based on a satirical novel by Richard Condon, presents an even more bizarre scenario. In *Three Days of the Condor* (1975), Robert Redford plays a low-level CIA employee who is forced on the run after all his colleagues are assassinated and who uncovers a covert government-sponsored assassination program.

A government program gone awry is the subject of one of the decade's more outlandish conspiracy thrillers. *Capricorn One* (1977) makes the most of the theories that doubt the moon landings ever took place. When a mission to Mars goes wrong, three astronauts are pursued by the authorities before they can go public with the truth. Another science fiction thriller, Philip Kaufman's *Invasion of the Body Snatchers* (1978), offers a clever update on the classic 1950s version of the film and successfully taps into the mood of the time.

In the same year in which Dustin Hoffman made *All the President's Men*, he appeared in the taut New York-set thriller *Marathon Man* (1976). In this film, he plays the brother of a spy who becomes prey to Laurence Olivier's ageing Nazi. With its fine use of location, particularly New York's bustling street life and Central Park's reservoir, the film witnesses the transformation of Hoffman's solitary runner into a more ruthless character.

Between the first two *Godfather* films (1972 and 1974), Francis Ford Coppola directed the chamber piece *The Conversation* (1974). Gene Hackman's surveillance expert Harry Caul believes he may have overheard the discussion of a potential murder. His paranoia takes hold of him and gradually it tears his world apart. *The Conversation* is arguably the most compelling of all the conspiracy films of the era, suggesting the rot of corruption can come just as easily from within as it can from the outside world.

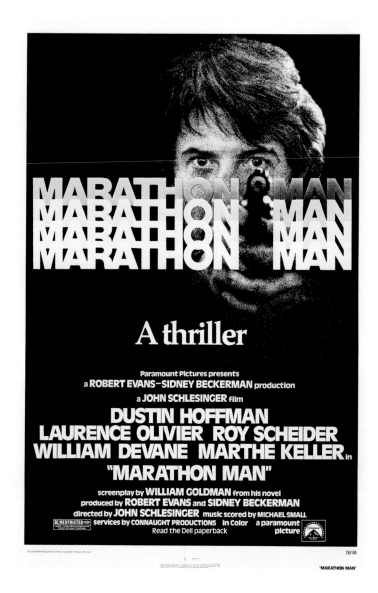

Marathon Man (1976)
The title design, which gives a sense of movement, and the simple caption suggest the kinetic trappings of the genre. The image of Hoffman and the gun adds urgency.

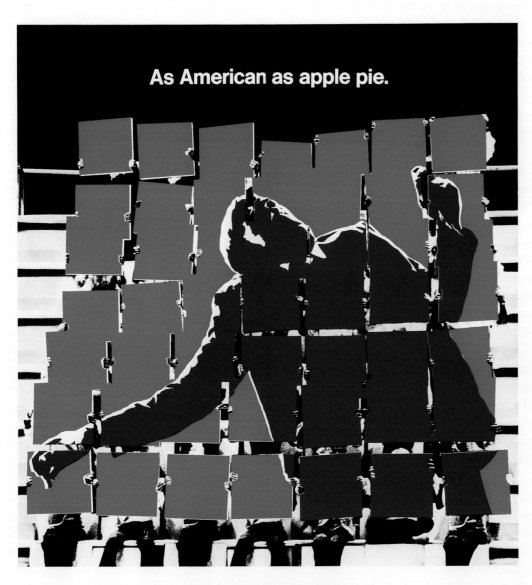

ABOVE

The Parallax View (1974)
What we see isn't always what is in front of us. That is the message behind this layering of imagery and the central conceit of Pakula's thriller.

TOP RIGHT

All the President's Men (1976)
The Watergate scandal was well known, so the poster only needs star wattage to sell the film version and a monochrome image to suggest journalistic integrity.

MIDDLE RIGHT

The Conversation (1974)
The black background underpins the covert nature of Harry Caul's profession, while his expression hints at the paranoia that permeates Coppola's film.

BOTTOM RIGHT

Capricorn One (1977)
The caption plays on conspiracy theories about the moon landings, and the star line-up links the film to the disaster film poster designs of the decade.

ERASERHEAD

A FILM BY DAVID LYNCH

A *Libra Films* RELEASE

MIDNIGHT MOVIES

OPPOSITE

Eraserhead (1977)
The harsh lighting, the ambiguous and vaguely threatening backdrop, Jack Nance's expression, and his wild hair were more than enough to sell David Lynch's genuinely strange journey into a dark dream of a film.

BELOW LEFT

El Topo (1970)
No single image could quite convey the strangeness of Alejandro Jodorowsky's surreal, south of the border Western. But an image of the main character and his son traveling across an otherworldly environment seems to suffice.

BELOW RIGHT

The Rocky Horror Picture Show (1975)
Released in the same year as Steven Spielberg's shark thriller, this film employs a caption that plays with that film's title. The simple design, featuring the lips of Playboy model Lorelei Shark, mirrors the film's opening credit sequence.

There is no specific genre and the film need not have achieved cult status, but there is definitely something about a midnight movie that makes it stand apart from any conventional film. It is the kind of film that plays well—best, perhaps—late at night and to an audience in the mood for something different.

The modern incarnation of the midnight movie is believed by some to have started at the Elgin Theater, in New York's Chelsea neighborhood. There are debates as to which film prompted it, but one of the most popular is *El Topo* (1970), Alejandro Jodorowsky's bizarre journey into the surreal. A Western of sorts, although set somewhere below the southern border of the United States, it features the director as a gunslinger who finds himself facing gunfighters who represent ideological or religious beliefs. It set the standard for an unconventional kind of film—one that was impossible to describe and tended to gain traction through word of mouth.

John Waters' *Pink Flamingos* (1972)—a film so outrageous and amateurish in production, it would never have had a life in mainstream cinema—followed suit. On the late night circuit, it thrived and made its director an icon of US popular culture. Likewise, *The Harder They Come* (1972) failed to ignite cinemas on its general release, but scored at late night screenings.

The Rocky Horror Picture Show (1975) seemed tailor-made for a midnight movie audience. Its blend of kitsch, camp, and knowing humor, with a dash of the surreal, guaranteed its success on limited release. More surprisingly, and thanks in no small part to a clever marketing campaign, the film became one of the year's sleeper hits.

The Warriors (1979) also proved popular with the midnight crowd, delivering a thrill ride in its portrayal of gang fights amid the detritus of a decrepit New York. But the one film whose sheer strangeness drew audiences was *Eraserhead* (1977), David Lynch's bizarre directorial debut. A tale of a young couple caring for an alien child, it defies description, but the film's poster is perhaps the most fitting representation of the midnight movie.

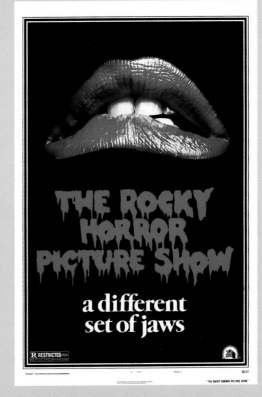

HORROR

George A. Romero's groundbreaking low-budget *Night of the Living Dead* (1968) once again transformed the horror genre, adding gore to the shocks that Alfred Hitchcock and Michael Powell introduced at the start of the 1960s. But his zombie classic only hinted at what lay around the corner in the 1970s.

Romero was one of the horror directors who dominated the decade. If his feature debut channeled the angst felt at the United States' involvement in Vietnam, its follow-up, *Dawn of the Dead* (1978), was a smart satire of the country's consumer culture, albeit with more than its fair share of flesh. In-between, he had a town lose its mind in *The Crazies* (1973) and redefined the vampire movie with *Martin* (1978). Each of these films is unique for its subversiveness, although their various artworks play more toward the staple elements of the genre.

Romero was the most prominent representative of the grittier 1970s horror film. Ranked alongside him was Wes Craven. His debut, like Romero's, deals with the fallout of Vietnam. But *Last House on the Left* (1972) eschews monsters or the undead in favor of a gang that enacts savage violence upon two girls and is then subject to brutal retribution. The film, which was banned or heavily censored in many countries, is notable for its stark realism, which is reflected in the artwork that promoted it. Similar controversy surrounded the release of *I Spit on Your Grave* (1978). Arguably the most famous film in the rape revenge sub-genre, it was shocking for its graphic scenes but was also defended for its feminist stance toward sexual violence.

David Cronenberg was another director who attracted acclaim and ire in equal measure. His early horror eschewed the genre's conventions, offering a more clinical approach to human depravity. Cronenberg's first two features, *Shivers* (1975) and *Rabid* (1977), were shocking for the way in which they employ a forensic examination of sexual activity, equating it with disease. *Rabid* in particular presents a disturbing account of a plague outbreak across one city, and the controversy surrounding the film was compounded by Cronenberg casting porn star Marilyn Chambers as the lead. Tobe Hooper's *The Texas Chainsaw Massacre* (1974) might have seemed more conventional, but it was still regarded as one of the best examples of independent

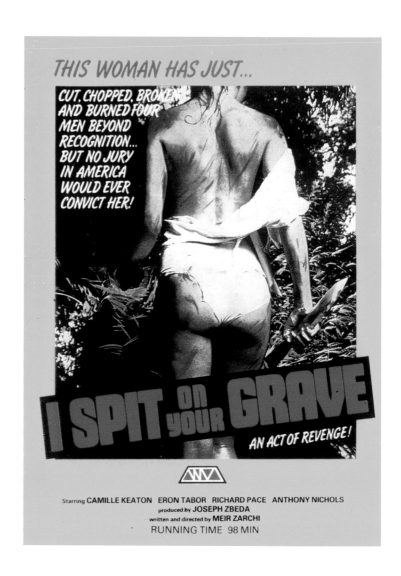

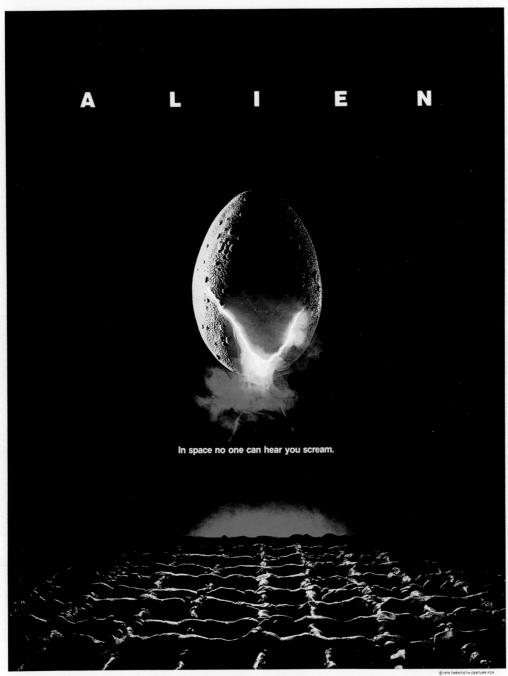

ABOVE

Alien (1979)
Stephen Frankfurt's design, along with
the inspired caption, steers clear of genre
conventions. Instead, it offers something
different, unidentifiable, which taps into
the film's blending of two popular genres.

TOP RIGHT

The Texas Chainsaw Massacre (1974)
This schlocky design hints at the film's
grindhouse tone, but in style it differs
from roughly hewn, low-budget horror.
The rudimentary design still gives enough
of an impression of what lies in store.

MIDDLE RIGHT

Last House on the Left (1972)
It may have been inspired by Ingmar
Bergman's The Virgin Spring (1960),
but the brilliance of this poster lies in
making the film look like it has been torn
from the headlines.

BOTTOM RIGHT

Dawn of the Dead (1978)
The selling point here is Romero's feature
debut breakout. This sequel might be
a smart satire, but its appeal lies in
audiences having the opportunity to
witness more zombies on the rampage.

horror filmmaking in the 1970s. It was made on a low budget and laced with humor in its representation of an "all-American" family, and its violence and Marilyn Burns' incessant screaming thrilled audiences.

Carrie (1976) and *Halloween* (1978) are very much the bridge between low-budget shockers and more mainstream horror. They are bloody, but the effects are less crude and the intention is to scare rather than outrage or provoke. *Carrie*'s director, Brian De Palma, belonged to the new wave of Hollywood filmmakers, and his adaptation of Stephen King's novel was his first major commercial success. Audiences were sold on the promise of a bloody prom night—a twisted take on a rite of passage event that most people experience. And the film's Grand Guignol climax delivered on the promise of its poster. *Halloween*, by contrast, was a low-budget breakthrough. It has no major stars and was directed by a filmmaker whose only previous commercial feature was a contemporary take on the Western *Rio Bravo* (1959). *Halloween* unfolds in suburbia and, after a thrilling prologue, takes its time to set its tone. But once the action begins and Jamie Lee Curtis finds herself running for her life, John Carpenter proves his mastery over sustained bouts of suspense. It is an expertly made slasher thriller whose unrelenting assailant has become an iconic figure in modern horror.

The slasher movie took another form, in a different genre, with Ridley Scott's *Alien* (1979). This film is a hybrid of two genres, moving between both as the story progresses, before its nerve-shredding climax aboard the *Nostromo* and Ripley's solo battle with the alien in a claustrophobic rescue craft. With its use of green, black, and burning yellow/white, the artwork hints at something terrible without identifying it.

The devil is the antagonist in two high-profile 1970s studio productions. In *The Omen* (1976), the Antichrist grows up as the son of a US ambassador and his wife. Anyone who suspects his identity is dispatched through a series of increasingly elaborate set pieces. The film's poster features stars Gregory Peck and Lee Remick, against a black background. Undoubtedly, there are scares, but it is the polar opposite to the intensity of William Friedkin's *The Exorcist* (1973). Indeed, if one film defined horror in the 1970s, it was this one. The story of an evil spirit that possesses a young girl, *The Exorcist* terrified audiences so much there were stories of people having to be hospitalized. Bill Gold's design for the poster employs the shot in the film when Max von Sydow's priest arrives to perform an exorcism. Its minimal palette sets the film's tone perfectly. It didn't so much sell a genre film as the idea that audiences were about to enter a world that would leave them changed in some way.

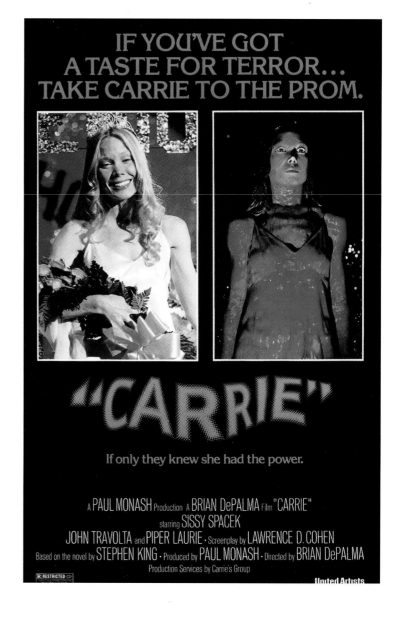

ABOVE

Carrie (1976)
The images say all you need to know about Brian De Palma's operatic bloodbath. It is ruthlessly simple. The homecoming queen becomes the avenging angel. Audiences just have to find out what happens in-between.

TOP LEFT

Rabid (1977)

The photograph of the rabid woman resembles a scientific experiment and taps into primal fears regarding the tenuousness of our existence.

TOP RIGHT

Halloween (1978)

The simplest way to promote a slasher film is to feature the movement of a blade. Bob Gleason's design also hints at what might be the killer's face in the blade's reflection.

ABOVE

The Exorcist (1973)

This simple treatment of a film shot uses yellow against a black backdrop to chilling effect. Whereas light offers relief in most horror films, here it appears foreboding.

NEW HOLLYWOOD

If the producer ruled classical Hollywood cinema, with the director frequently relegated to a lesser status, the disintegration of the studio system in the late 1960s saw a new breed of cine-literate filmmakers take control. Many cut their teeth on low-budget films before achieving mainstream commercial success. The 1970s was their decade: a once-in-a-lifetime opportunity to produce work that was uncompromising and groundbreaking, and that would go on to inspire subsequent generations.

The filmmakers were influenced as much by European cinema as by Hollywood movies. The techniques employed by the New Wave were incorporated into their work, breaking up the fluid style of conventional Hollywood narrative filmmaking. Resolution was less important than the attempt to be honest to character and motivation. And generally these films' outlooks were bleaker, more downbeat, sometimes despairing.

Bonnie and Clyde (1967), followed by Easy Rider (1969), led the way. The former was directed by Arthur Penn, who came from an older school of filmmaking but also embraced new ideas. Dennis Hopper went AWOL after Easy Rider, his era-defining road movie, only to return to direct The Last Movie (1971), a compelling piece of meta-cinema that cost a fortune to produce, was a commercial failure, and left many critics puzzled. During Hopper's absence, Head (1968) director Bob Rafelson made two intimate character-driven dramas starring Jack Nicholson: Five Easy Pieces (1970) and The King of Marvin Gardens (1972). Alongside Peter Bogdanovich's rural Texan coming-of-age tale The Last Picture Show (1971), these films were trailblazers for the new kind of cinema.

Hal Ashby may be less well-known as one of the New Hollywood filmmakers, but his work in the 1970s was a valuable, if mostly offbeat, addition to the decade. After his debut, The Landlord (1970), he directed the pitch-black comedy Harold and Maude (1971). Although the film was a commercial failure, its reputation has improved with time. The Last Detail (1973) gave Jack Nicholson one of his meatiest roles to date, but it was Shampoo (1975) and Coming Home (1978) that cemented Ashby's reputation. Both films contributed considerably to defining the spirit of the times.

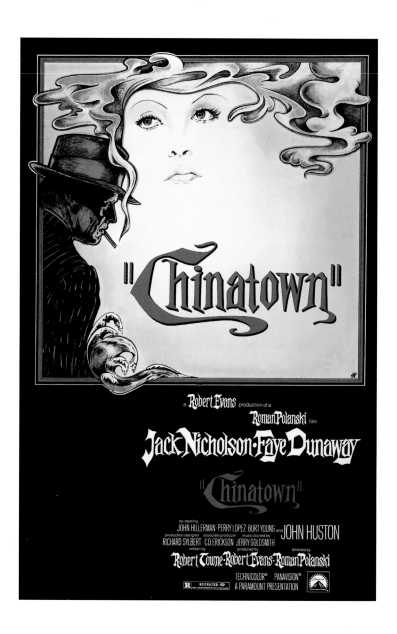

ABOVE

Chinatown (1974)
One of the most famous posters of 1970s US cinema, James Pearsall's design uses cigarette smoke to form Faye Dunaway's face, while also hinting at an earlier era of Hollywood.

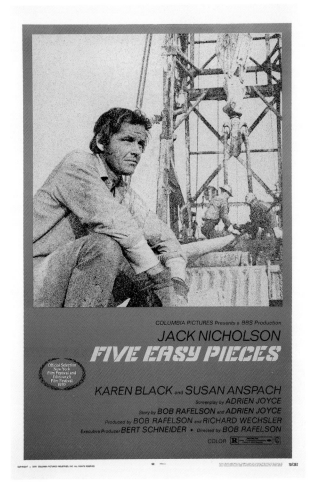

The Godfather (1972)
The novel was a runaway success, and the artwork for the film mirrors Neil Fujita's simple cover design for the book, underpinning the moral vacuity of Don Vito Corleone's world and his controlling influence.

The Godfather Part II (1974)
The return of Fujita's puppeteer design suggests the sequel is a continuation of the same story. But this time, power lies in the hands of Al Pacino's Michael Corleone, hence his presence in the artwork.

Five Easy Pieces (1970)
Jack Nicholson's expression, deep in thought, contrasts with the manual labor carried out in the background, and the coloring of the image adds ambiguity. The poster hints at the restlessness that permeates the lives of the characters who populate Rafelson's film.

The Last Picture Show (1971)
A small town and the group of teenagers who live there suggest the world in which Bogdanovich's film unfolds. The blank space in the poster reinforces the emptiness of the town and possibly the futures of the characters.

Monte Hellman and Terrence Malick were two of the outliers in the group. The latter's debut, *Badlands* (1973), is inspired by the true-life story of convicted killer Charles Starkweather. Malick's version creates a dream-like world, narrated by Sissy Spacek as an innocent teenage girl. Like his later *Days of Heaven* (1978), the film highlights the filmmaker's eye for rapturous beauty and was sold to audiences as much on the basis of its look as on its storytelling. Hellman's *Two-Lane Blacktop* (1971) follows *Easy Rider*'s route of a minimal dialogue, existentialist exploration of youthful rebellion, this time set along Route 66. It forms part of the countercultural road movie sub-genre that also includes *Electra Glide in Blue* (1973), but its principal selling point was the presence of popular singer-songwriter James Taylor.

Steven Spielberg and George Lucas were key members of the New Hollywood group. Spielberg got his first break in television, but came to notice with the knife-edge chase thriller *Duel* (1971) and the couple-on-the-run crime caper *The Sugarland Express* (1974). After directing the science fiction thriller *THX 1138* (1971), Lucas scored a huge commercial success with *American Graffiti* (1973, see page 199). However, the careers of both filmmakers altered dramatically with the commercial successes of *Jaws* (1975) and *Star Wars* (1977, for both see pages 216-217), which launched the modern blockbuster.

Francis Ford Coppola and William Friedkin were the first filmmakers of the new generation to win over mainstream audiences. After receiving an Academy Award for his screenplay for *Patton* (1970), Coppola wrote and directed the two *Godfather* films (1972 and 1974). They draw on classical Hollywood while offering a bleaker view of US society. Between them, the chamber thriller *The Conversation* (1974) explores paranoia, political assassinations, and institutional corruption. Coppola ended the decade with *Apocalypse Now* (1979), a war film as a surreal nightmare. Friedkin's *The French Connection* (1971) helped define New York in the 1970s, whereas *The Exorcist* (1973, see page 189) was one of cinema's most iconic horror films. All these films served to shape this new cinema.

Martin Scorsese is perhaps most closely associated with New Hollywood cinema. His third feature, *Mean Streets* (1973), was drawn from personal experiences growing up in New York and was his first collaboration with Robert De Niro, who had previously worked with another member of the group, Brian De Palma. Their collaboration on subsequent films throughout the decade, from *Taxi Driver* (1976, see page 217) and *New York, New York* (1977) to *Raging Bull* (1980), regarded by some as the last great film from this era, helped define this new age in US cinema.

TOP

Harold and Maude (1971)
The artwork attempts to convey the sweet-natured road movie aspect of the film alongside its pitch-black humor. The studio didn't know how to sell it, and this poster only goes so far in conveying the film's strangeness.

ABOVE

Shampoo (1975)
This minimalist design captures the movie's humor, as the film's title doubles up as the client's hair. If the caption hints at the tone of the movie, the poster design suggests that it is no conventional comedy.

He was 25 years old • He combed his hair like James Dean •
He was very fastidious • People who littered bothered him •
She was 15 • She took music lessons and could twirl a
baton • She wasn't very popular at school • For awhile they
lived together in a tree house.

In 1959, she watched while he killed a lot of people.

CLOCKWISE FROM TOP LEFT

Badlands (1973)
This beautiful shot takes
on a mythic resonance by
being silhouetted against a
setting sun, while the text
underpins the sense of
menace gleaned from the
characters' poses.

**Two-Lane
Blacktop (1971)**
The arrangement of
characters closely
resembles an album cover
of the era, reinforced by
the presence of James
Taylor. Like *Easy Rider* (see
page 176), the use of color
suggests a new kind of
road film.

**The French
Connection (1971)**
Like Friedkin's film, the
artwork here is direct and
uncompromising. Gene
Hackman's brooding cop,
pictured moodily in the
inset image, gives the
impression that he will
do anything to get his
job done.

Mean Streets (1973)
This is a triumph of
graphic design. The city
doesn't so much feature
violence as it is a part of
its very fabric. The gun
doubles up as another
structure on the skyline.
And the streetlight
resembles a gallows.

NEW HOLLYWOOD **193**

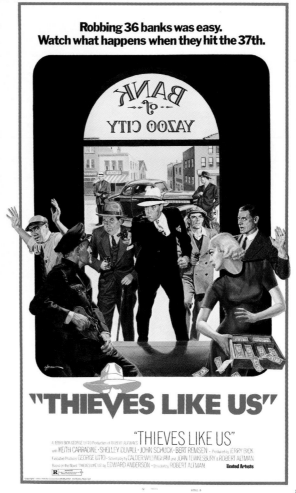

ROBERT ALTMAN

OPPOSITE
CLOCKWISE FROM TOP LEFT

The Long Goodbye (1973)
Jack Davis betrays his *MAD* magazine origins with this raucous cacophony of characters and captions, underpinning Altman's subversive take on a Philip Marlowe story.

McCabe and Mrs. Miller (1971)
Richard Amsel's design succeeds in being both old fashioned and contemporary, mixing classical Hollywood illustration with boldly colored type.

Thieves Like Us (1974)
George Gross' artwork taps into a nostalgic vein for this portrait of crime in 1930s America. Only the caption hints at the film's humor.

Nashville (1975)
Legendary design agency Diener-Hauser came up with the artwork for this country music epic. Rather than represent the vast canvas of characters and story lines, the poster instead finds one object to represent that world.

RIGHT

M*A*S*H (1970)
Anti-military and anti-authoritarian, Murray Duitz's design perfectly represents the anarchic nature of Altman's breakthrough film.

FAR RIGHT

Short Cuts (1993)
In contrast to *Nashville*, the artwork for Altman's 1993 ensemble drama underpins the fractured emotions of its large cast of characters.

Of all the directors to emerge from US cinema in the 1970s, no one was quite as anarchic, or as prolific, in their output as Robert Altman. He subverted almost every popular genre throughout the decade. And in the five years that began with his breakthrough war satire *M*A*S*H* (1970) and ended with *Nashville* (1975), an overview of the United States' country music scene, he achieved an unbroken run of creative brilliance. The only problem that his producers faced was how to sell these unique films to an audience.

During those five years, Altman directed eight films. Although the surreal comedy *Brewster McCloud* (1970), psychological drama *Images* (1972), and buddy gambling movie *California Split* (1974) are less known, they remain fascinating entries in Altman's 1970s filmography. And the remaining films from this period rank as some of the best US features of the decade.

The artwork for *M*A*S*H* is as iconic as the film itself. An anti-war comedy-drama set during the Korean conflict but clearly about Vietnam, it is raucous, disrespectful, and outrageous. In style, it captured the shifting tide of US cinema, particularly when compared with that year's other anti-war satire *Catch-22*. In the early 1970s, *McCabe and Mrs. Miller* (1971), *The Long Goodbye* (1973), and *Thieves Like Us* (1974) took three established genres—the Western, the detective, and the gangster film—mined them to their essence, then reconstructed them. As period films, *McCabe and Mrs. Miller* and *Thieves Like Us* retain more of their respective genres, and their promotional artwork suggests as much. But they are radical interpretations, particularly *McCabe and Mrs. Miller* with its experimentation with sound and dialogue. *The Long Goodbye* brings Philip Marlowe into the 1970s, and in the place of a whip-smart private dick, there is Elliott Gould's louche, cat-loving investigator. The various posters for the film, from Richard Amsel's quieter design to Murray Duitz's comic style, all identify Gould's shabby appearance as key to the film's offbeat charm.

Nashville, like Altman's later *Short Cuts* (1993), is a vast tableau of a film—a collection of tales whose narrative is more about a sense of place, or state of mind, than a linear story. Some artwork promoting the film places emphasis on the myriad of characters, but the most effective finds a common theme between them.

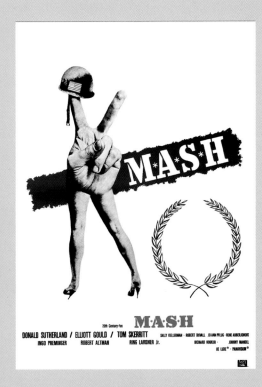

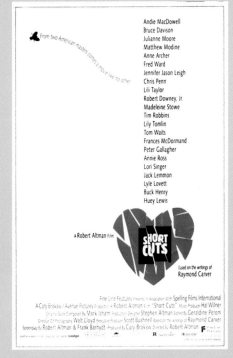

RICHARD AMSEL

Few artists working in film poster design have displayed such skill at evoking the past as Richard Amsel. His work taps into nostalgia, yet always draws on the present to avoid simply copying previous styles. Discussing his work, he once commented, "I'm interested in uncovering relationships between the past and the present, and in discovering how things have changed and grown. I don't see any point in copying the past, but I think the elements of the past can be taken to another realm."

Shortly after graduating from Philadelphia College of Art, he designed the artwork for *Hello, Dolly!* (1969). His image of Barbra Streisand and Walter Matthau subtly evokes the past, while the colors he employed boldly place them in the present. He subsequently designed the artwork for Bette Midler's debut album and was commissioned to design countless magazine covers, including a portrait of Lily Tomlin in 1977 for *Time* magazine, which now resides in the collection of the Smithsonian Institution, Washington, DC.

Amsel worked productively on film projects for fifteen years, before his untimely death at the age of thirty-seven, shortly after completing *Mad Max: Beyond Thunderdome* (1985). Much of his work in the 1970s skillfully drew on the past, whether it was to realize Robert Altman's vision of the West for *McCabe and Mrs. Miller* (1971, see previous page) or to create a more elegiac vision of that world for John Wayne's last feature, *The Shootist* (1976). Amsel balanced the gilded allure of Hollywood with the realities of life in Los Angeles during the 1920s and 1930s with his designs for *Chinatown* (1974) and *The Last Tycoon* (1976). By contrast, his celebrated artwork for *The Sting* (1973), set during the same period, evinces a more jocular tone as befits the story of two grifters (played by Paul Newman and Robert Redford) embarking on the con of their lives.

In 1981, Amsel was commissioned to create the artwork for Steven Spielberg's 1930s-era adventure series throwback *Raiders of the Lost Ark* (1981). Like his design for *McCabe and Mrs. Miller*, Amsel captured the milieu perfectly, but with the flaming title he gave the film a modern spin. It is the perfect illustration of his attention to time, place, character, and detail.

BELOW LEFT

The Shootist (1976)
As befits an elegy on the West and a tribute to the screen icon John Wayne, Amsel's artwork here is stately. He creates an image of a civilized world where the gun has no place, and so it exists outside of the tableau.

BELOW RIGHT

Raiders of the Lost Ark (1981)
Like the relics hunted by Indiana Jones, this image appears to have been etched into stone. The adventurer rises out of action scenes from the film but is not concerned by them. Instead, he looks to the future, holding the ultimate hero's pose. The image helped to establish Harrison Ford's star status.

OPPOSITE

The Sting (1973)
The presence of the cards and the drink denotes the characters' profession, and the clothes designate the era, but the emphasis of Amsel's design here is on the actors' faces. They are the stars of *Butch Cassidy and the Sundance Kid* (1969) once again getting into mischief.

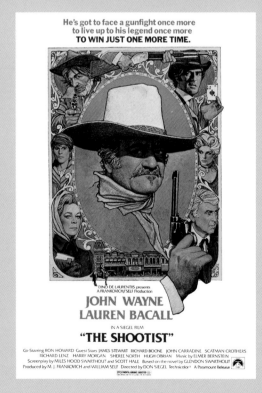

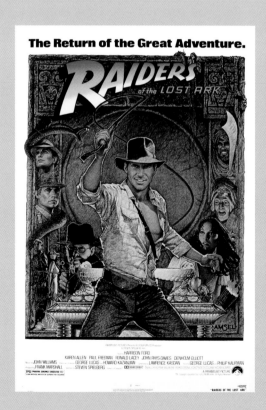

PAUL NEWMAN · ROBERT REDFORD ROBERT SHAW

IN A BILL/PHILLIPS PRODUCTION OF
A GEORGE ROY HILL FILM

THE STING

A RICHARD D. ZANUCK/DAVID BROWN PRESENTATION

…all it takes is a little Confidence.

Written by	Directed by	Produced by
DAVID S. WARD ·	GEORGE ROY HILL ·	TONY BILL, MICHAEL and JULIA PHILLIPS

Music Adapted by MARVIN HAMLISCH · A UNIVERSAL PICTURE · TECHNICOLOR®   ORIGINAL SOUNDTRACK AVAILABLE EXCLUSIVELY ON MCA RECORDS AND TAPES   **PG** PARENTAL GUIDANCE SUGGESTED SOME MATERIAL MAY NOT BE SUITABLE FOR PRE-TEENAGERS

NOSTALGIA SELLS

The new generation of filmmakers that dominated US cinema in the 1970s might have eschewed many of the conventions that defined classical Hollywood, but their work shows a noticeable engagement with the past. Nostalgia, in various forms, permeates many of the decade's key films.

Francis Ford Coppola's *The Godfather* (1972) is more brutal than the Warner Bros. gangster movies of the 1930s, but there is a clear romanticizing of the era in which the film is set. By contrast, *The Godfather: Part II* (1974) makes more of a break with the past, offering up a less glamorous representation of Michael Corleone's empire. In the same way, Roman Polanski's *Chinatown* (1974) and Martin Scorsese's *New York, New York* (1977) present rapturous evocations of earlier periods in the twentieth century. But their nostalgia was for the look of the worlds they presented. Life in them was morally bleak.

Other films were not so probing in their nostalgia. George Roy Hill's *The Sting* was one of the biggest hits of 1973, and its entire marketing campaign fetishized the world in which it is set. Written by and starring Sylvester Stallone, *Rocky* (1976), which went on to become the surprise winner of the Academy Award for Best Picture in 1977, may be set in a gritty present, but its comeback story of a boxer on the down-and-out who gets a shot at the world heavyweight title is the stuff of Hollywood at the peak of its golden age.

George Lucas' *Star Wars* (1977) might have been inspired by the films of Akira Kurosawa, but, like his later screenplay for *Raiders of the Lost Ark* (1981), it also draws on the old serials that used to play before the main feature during the 1930s. Steven Spielberg tried a similar approach, albeit less successfully, with his period comedy-action film *1941* (1979).

The best examples of US cinema's obsession with nostalgia in the 1970s were two films set in the 1960s. Lucas' semi-autobiographical *American Graffiti* (1973) and Randal Kleiser's musical hit *Grease* (1978) are both influential coming-of-age tales. Like the artwork that promoted these films, they offered contemporary moviegoers a vision of a world that was simpler, easier, and perhaps just a little more innocent. Even if, in truth, it wasn't.

ABOVE

Grease (1978)
Take a singer with a significant following and a newly minted star known for his incendiary screen presence, dress them so that their look isn't too old fashioned, and suggest that this is the only movie people should be seeing. The design for the *Grease* poster is simple but effective.

OPPOSITE

American Graffiti (1973)
With its busy style, the poster for Lucas' affectionate pastiche of baby boomers in the early 1960s is a forerunner of the artwork for *Star Wars* (see page 216). Everything that defines these characters' lives as being fun and adventurous appears in this cacophonous tapestry.

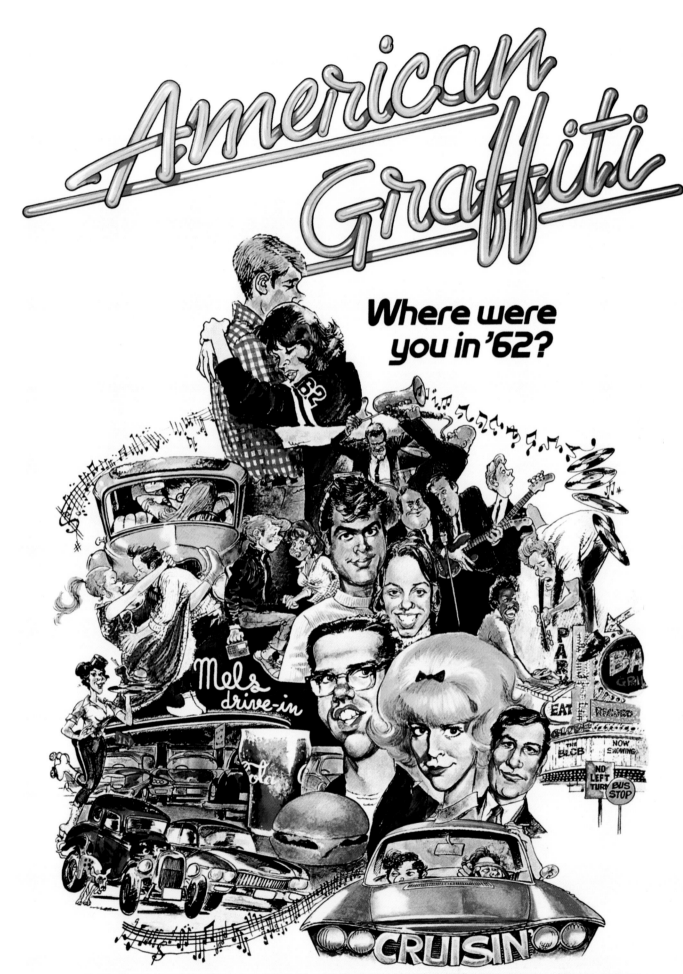

American Graffiti

Where were you in '62?

"AMERICAN GRAFFITI" • A LUCASFILM LTD./COPPOLA CO. Production • Starring RICHARD DREYFUSS • RONNY HOWARD
PAUL LE MAT • CHARLIE MARTIN SMITH • CANDY CLARK • MACKENZIE PHILLIPS • CINDY WILLIAMS • WOLFMAN JACK
Written by GEORGE LUCAS and GLORIA KATZ & WILLARD HUYCK • Directed by GEORGE LUCAS
Co-Produced by GARY KURTZ • Produced by FRANCIS FORD COPPOLA • A UNIVERSAL PICTURE • TECHNICOLOR®

STANLEY KUBRICK

From the early 1960s, Stanley Kubrick gained unprecedented control over his films, not only during production, but also in the way each release was promoted. From *Dr. Strangelove or: How I Learned to Stop Worrying and Love the Bomb* (1964) through to his final film *Eyes Wide Shut* (1999), Kubrick was involved in an intensive period of research and design to identify the key aspects of each film and how they could be presented to audiences. Nowhere is this more apparent than in the three films Kubrick shot during the 1970s: *A Clockwork Orange* (1971), *Barry Lyndon* (1975), and *The Shining* (1980). Each is wildly different in tone and style, and the various artworks reflect their uniqueness.

French designer Jouineau Bourduge's artwork for *Barry Lyndon* is deceptively simple. For Kubrick's adaptation of William Makepeace Thackeray's novel *The Luck of Barry Lyndon* (1844), Bourduge evokes a bygone era with elaborate typography. The image of a man's legs, boots, and hand holding a gun all appear in silhouette, like a cutout. The only color is the red of a single rose. With the man framed by a thick black border, the image is classical yet its roughness underpins the film's bleak tone.

   Philip Castle's airbrushed style made the poster for *A Clockwork Orange* one of the key images of 1970s cinema. (Castle would later work with Kubrick on the "Born to Kill" helmet design for 1987's *Full Metal Jacket*.) The artwork is intended to shock, from the blunt wording of the caption to the image of the delinquent protagonist Alex breaking out of the letter "A" of the film's title and the provocatively positioned mannequin beneath him. It exists outside any simple generic classification. And the white background suggests a world about to be torn apart by this young man.

   The history of Saul Bass' initial designs for *The Shining* is well documented. Kubrick, ever exacting in his desire to create the perfect encapsulation of the film's tone and themes, rejected a series of complex designs that play with the maze that appears in the film's climactic chase sequence between a psychotic Jack Torrance and his wife and child. Bass and Kubrick eventually settled on artwork that underpins the film's exploration of raw, primal fear.

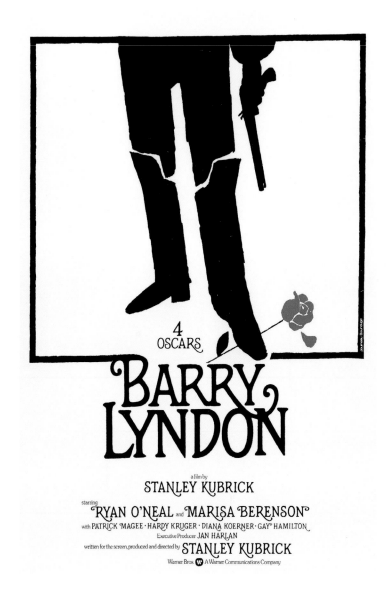

ABOVE

Barry Lyndon (1975)
There are hints of period drama, but it is a far cry from the opulent imagery normally associated with promoting this kind of cinema. Instead it is sparse, underpinning the film's glacial emotional tone.

A MASTERPIECE OF MODERN HORROR

A STANLEY KUBRICK FILM

STARRING
JACK NICHOLSON SHELLEY DUVALL "THE SHINING" WITH SCATMAN CROTHERS BASED ON THE NOVEL BY STEPHEN KING SCREENPLAY BY STANLEY KUBRICK & DIANE JOHNSON

PRODUCED AND DIRECTED BY
STANLEY KUBRICK EXECUTIVE PRODUCER JAN HARLAN PRODUCED IN ASSOCIATION WITH THE PRODUCER CIRCLE CO. **R** RESTRICTED · UNDER 17 REQUIRES ACCOMPANYING PARENT OR ADULT GUARDIAN From Warner Bros. ⓦ A Warner Communications Company ©Warner Bros.Inc.1980 All Rights Reserved.

Being the adventures of a young man whose principal interests are rape, ultra-violence and Beethoven.

'X'

A Stanley Kubrick Production "A CLOCKWORK ORANGE" Starring Malcolm McDowell,
Patrick Magee · Adrienne Corri and Miriam Karlin · Screenplay by Stanley Kubrick
Based on the novel by Anthony Burgess · Produced and Directed by Stanley Kubrick
Executive Producers Max L. Raab and S. Litvinoff · **From Warner Bros.** ⓦ A Warner Communications Company
Released by Columbia-Warner Distributors Ltd · Original Soundtrack recording on Warner Bros. K46127

TOP

The Shining (1980)
This artwork appeared in a number of versions, ranging from the yellow that appears in this example to red. The face looking out through the text appears to be an infant, whose expression conveys terror.

BOTTOM

A Clockwork Orange (1971)
The "A" of the title isn't immediately noticeable, as focus is directed toward the knife-wielding man emerging from it. The typography has a futuristic quality, but the film's title is almost comic-like.

"A COMIC MASTERPIECE
...FRIGHTENING, FUNNY,
PROFOUND, AND MYSTERIOUS"
JONATHAN ROSENBAUM

A SERGE SILBERMAN Production

A Film By LUIS BUÑUEL

15

40TH ANNIVERSARY REISSUE
BACK IN CINEMAS JUNE 29TH

The DISCREET CHARM
Of The BOURGEOISIE

SERGE SILBERMAN présente

LE FANTÔME
DE LA
LIBERTÉ

UN FILM DE LUIS BUNUEL

La plus *belle*
création de
CATHERINE
DENEUVE

Tristana

le film de LUIS BUÑUEL

BUÑUEL AND FERRACCI

The Discreet Charm of the Bourgeoisie (1972)
The first of Ferracci's cartoon designs for a Buñuel film bears a resemblance to Murray Duitz's design for *M*A*S*H* (1970; see page 195). However, the presence of the bowler hat denotes a comment on class, while the lips and legs hint at a common Buñuelian preoccupation: sex.

Tristana (1970)
The title design implies, from the personalized way the protagonist's name is written, that this is an intimate story. But the image isn't crisply clear, which suggests ambiguity. And Catherine Deneuve's expression, as she looks off to the side, hints at unease.

The Phantom of Liberty (1974)
Of the designs that Ferracci created for Buñuel's last three films, this is the most provocative. The Statue of Liberty is given a masculine makeover, with the torch of liberty now a flaccid object. It sums up the film's attack on Western mores and values.

That Obscure Object of Desire (1977)
Romantic and sexual desires are frustrated in Buñuel's final film. Fernando Rey is obsessed with a woman, played by two actors, but his advances remain unreciprocated. Ferracci's stitched lips hint at emasculation and emotional bondage.

One of the most prolific French film poster designers, René Ferracci studied under painter and engraver René Cottet. After completing his military service, Ferracci became head of advertising at MGM and then Cinédis. During the 1950s, he worked on film campaigns for directors such as Henri-Georges Clouzot, Jacques Becker, and Jean Renoir. However, it was after the emergence of the New Wave that Ferracci began to make a name for himself.

Remarkably prolific in the 1960s and 1970s, Ferracci produced artwork that is bold and provocative in the way that it eschews the design conventions of the time, favoring any approach that would best represent a given film. He championed a collage style, blending photography with offset printing, which can be seen in his designs for Jean-Luc Godard's *Made in U.S.A.* (1966) and *Two or Three Things I Know About Her …* (1967), and for Jacques Demy's *Les demoiselles de Rochefort* (1967).

In 1967, Ferracci embarked on his most ambitious collaboration, with Spanish filmmaker Luis Buñuel. Ferracci's designs for *Belle de jour* (1967, see page 164) might seem more conservative than some of his earlier work—an image of a bare-backed Catherine Deneuve with her head turned to face the audience—but their brilliance lies in the contrast between a classical painterly approach and the film's provocative subject matter. The designer would go on to work on four of the filmmaker's final five films, including *Tristana* (1970), which again stars Deneuve. Set in the late 1920s and early 1930s, Ferracci's poster evokes a distant age, again with the French actor dominating the design.

For Buñuel and Ferracci's remaining collaborations, each poster design employs an outrageous style that stands apart from the posters for any other films of that era. *The Discreet Charm of the Bourgeoisie* (1972), *The Phantom of Liberty* (1974), and *That Obscure Object of Desire* (1977) are all satires of social mores and bourgeois middle-class life. Instead of using stills, Ferracci created absurdist cartoon-like figures that capture each film's sense of anarchy. Like his iconic poster for Jean-Jacques Beineix's *Diva* (1981, see page 228), Ferracci's designs for these films are unique works of art.

BLAXPLOITATION

The Blaxploitation genre wasn't the first example of African American filmmaking. Earlier "race films" saw features and shorts made by and starring black filmmakers and actors. But the tumult of the 1960s, from the Civil Rights Movement to the widespread race riots across cities in the United States, provoked a new generation of filmmakers to respond. What resulted may initially have been sparked by a sense of revolution in the air, but the early success of Blaxploitation films saw the genre transform into a money-making machine. Its style, both on the screen and in the promotional posters, was seen by some as radical, but the place of the Blaxploitation genre in US film history is key, and its influence over a number of important contemporary filmmakers undeniable.

Melvin Van Peebles' first break came with his New Wave-inspired *The Story of a Three-Day Pass* (1968). After directing the studio-financed comedy *Watermelon Man* (1970), about a white bigot who wakes up one day to discover he is black, he went solo and self-financed *Sweet Sweetback's Baadasssss Song* (1971) when no one else would. He initially promoted the film through the release of its Earth, Wind, and Fire soundtrack, followed by a provocative advertising campaign. It was a significant success for an ultra-low budget film, and even became required viewing for Black Panther Party members.

Gordon Parks' *Shaft* (1971) became the archetype of the Blaxploitation genre. It features an iconic Isaac Hayes score and Richard Roundtree as the action lead, a role that would usually have been occupied by a white male star. Women entered into the act, too, with Pam Grier and Tamara Dobson leading the way. As the genre progressed, it blurred conventional boundaries, with drug dealers and mob bosses playing heroic roles and the (predominantly white) establishment portrayed as the villain. The response to the films was mixed, with some critics arguing that the way characters were "sold" to audiences perpetuated stereotypes of black people.

All manner of genres were absorbed into the films as the 1970s progressed, from horror and Westerns to knockabout comedy. In the 1990s, filmmakers and the hip-hop scene drew on the genre's iconography, and a series of film parodies exaggerated the way Blaxploitation represented the era in which it originated.

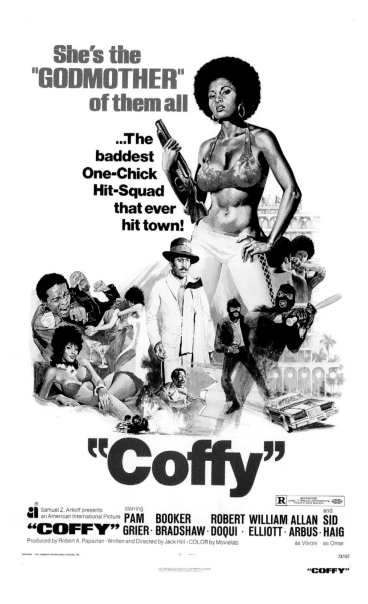

ABOVE

Coffy (1973)
Like the artwork for many Blaxploitation films, this poster features an amalgam of action scenes that bears comparison with the posters for the Bond films of the era. But here, the hero is female. Pam Grier followed this with *Foxy Brown* (1974), which made her a big star of the genre.

OPPOSITE

Shaft (1971)
The poster for Gordon Parks' film closely resembles a mainstream cinema release, but it would still have surprised audiences to see an African American portrayed as the heroic figure. This became the benchmark for subsequent crime or action films in the genre.

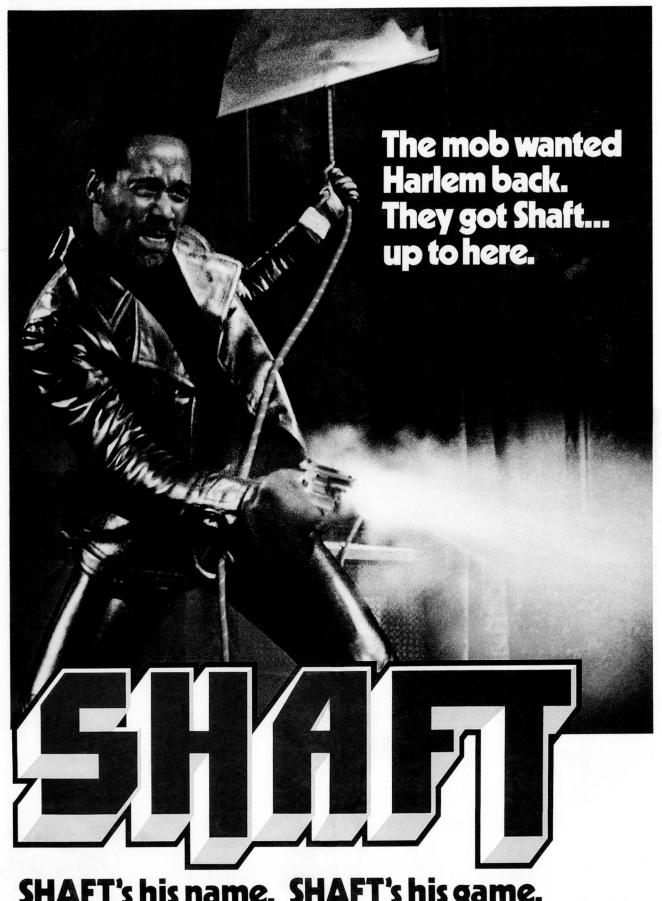

The mob wanted Harlem back. They got Shaft... up to here.

SHAFT

SHAFT's his name. SHAFT's his game.

METRO-GOLDWYN-MAYER Presents "SHAFT" Starring RICHARD ROUNDTREE · Co-Starring MOSES GUNN
Screenplay by ERNEST TIDYMAN and JOHN D. F. BLACK · Based upon the novel by ERNEST TIDYMAN
Music by ISAAC HAYES · Produced by JOEL FREEMAN · Directed by GORDON PARKS · METROCOLOR

R RESTRICTED
Under 17 Requires Accompanying
Parent or Adult Guardian

MGM

Their deadly mission: to crack the forbidden island of Han!

Enter The Dragon

The ultimate Martial Arts masterpiece! Lavishly filmed by Warner Bros. in Hong Kong and the China Sea!

BRUCE LEE · JOHN SAXON · AHNA CAPRI in "ENTER THE DRAGON" _{CO-STARRING} **BOB WALL · SHIH KIEN** and Introducing **JIM KELLY**

Music: Lalo Schifrin · Written by Michael Allin · Produced by Fred Weintraub and Paul Heller in association with Raymond Chow · Directed by Robert Clouse

R RESTRICTED Under 17 requires accompanying Parent or Adult Guardian · PANAVISION® · TECHNICOLOR® · Celebrating Warner Bros. 50th Anniversary · A Warner Communications Company

ORIGINAL SOUND TRACK ALBUM ON WARNER BROS. RECORDS

73/268

"ENTER THE DRAGON"

MARTIAL ARTS CINEMA

Martial arts films had been a staple of Asian cinema since the early years of narrative filmmaking, but their popularity around the world took off in the 1970s. The main production base was Hong Kong, which produced the genre's first global stars and with them a distinctive way of selling martial arts films that appealed to an international audience.

The Shaw Brothers, a major production company known by the late 1960s for producing opulent *wuxia* (period martial arts films) adventures, began the 1970s with the departure of two key executives to establish a new studio, Golden Harvest, which focused on more contemporary stories. The ace in this new studio's pack was the young, gifted martial artist Bruce Lee. After a minor stint in Hollywood, Lee had returned to Hong Kong and was cast in *The Big Boss* (1971). It was a massive hit in Asia and made him a star overnight.

The posters for *The Big Boss*, along with the subsequent *Fist of Fury* and *The Way of the Dragon* (both 1972), all saw Lee dominate the artwork with an action pose. Warner Bros. then approached Lee to star in *Enter the Dragon* (1973), the actor's last outing before his untimely death at the age of thirty-two, and this film was sold to audiences with Lee as part of an international cast. The huge success of *Enter the Dragon* guaranteed the proliferation of the martial arts genre and the distribution of films that would otherwise have been aimed solely at an Asian audience, such as *The 36th Chamber of Shaolin* (1978).

In both theme and content, *Enter the Dragon* bore similarities with Blaxploitation cinema, a link that was reinforced by the release of the Tamara Dobson vehicle *Cleopatra Jones and the Casino of Gold* (1975), the sequel to her character's eponymous action comedy debut of 1973. Martial arts films also drew on other genres, with varying degrees of success. They ranged from Western-style adventures to ludicrous attempts at horror.

By the late 1970s, Hong Kong cinema had found its new global star in Jackie Chan. *Snake in the Eagle's Shadow* (1978) was a significant success, and Chan became the perfect vehicle for martial arts films. His seamless blend of physical prowess and knockabout humor made the films an easy sell to most international markets and audiences.

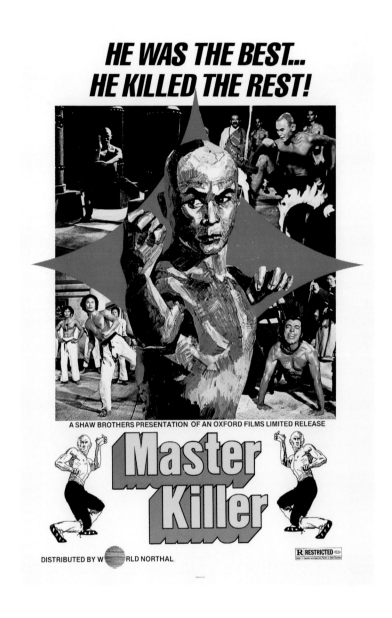

OPPOSITE

Enter the Dragon (1973)
Bruce Lee is very much the star of *Enter the Dragon*, his biggest budget and final film. However, Warner Bros. still hedged its bets with a Western audience by featuring an American supporting cast.

ABOVE

The 36th Chamber of Shaolin (1978, aka Master Killer)
One of the finest Hong Kong exports, the film delivers everything the poster promises. It remains a high point for Hong Kong martial arts cinema and the Shaw Brothers.

DISASTER FILMS

Films featuring disasters had been a staple of cinema since Italian director Giovanni Pastrone featured the eruption of Mount Etna and the destruction left in its wake in his silent movie *Cabiria* (1914). However, the 1970s witnessed the disaster movie emerge on an industrial scale, thanks in no small part to the promotional skills of producer Irwin Allen.

The film that set the template for the genre during the decade was *Airport* (1970). Adapted from Arthur Hailey's popular novel, it throws together a diverse group of individuals trapped on a plane whose mechanical problems threaten their lives. The humdrum narrative is bolstered by a stellar cast, who became the selling point of the film. Three sequels followed, with all but the final entry enjoying success at the box office.

Enter Irwin Allen. A successful television producer, he saw the potential in big-budget, concept-driven, all-star extravaganzas. He had already won an Academy Award with the marine documentary *The Sea Around Us* (1953) and had produced the adventure drama *Voyage to the Bottom of the Sea* (1961), so it was no surprise that his first disaster film would be ocean-bound. *The Poseidon Adventure* (1972) sees a tidal wave overturn a luxury liner, and a small group of passengers and crew make their way up to the underside of the ship in order to escape. In narrative terms, the film echoes the soapy travails of *Airport*, with each character experiencing their own personal crisis.

Allen followed the success of *Poseidon* with the even bigger *The Towering Inferno* (1974), which features another group of people trapped, but this time by a fire raging through a high-rise building. However, this film had to compete with Mark Robson's *Earthquake*, which came out in the same year and was also sold on the promise of state-of-the-art effects and a stellar cast being killed off one-by-one. These star actors featured heavily in both films' artwork, alongside a central concept that audiences could easily buy into.

By the late 1970s, the disaster at the center of each new film was reaching ridiculous levels of silliness, culminating in Allen's woeful *The Swarm* (1978), about African killer bees raging across the United States. Audiences stayed away, and the brief reign of the disaster film ended.

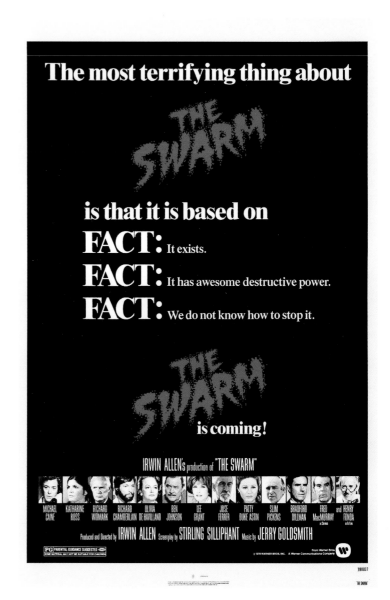

The Swarm (1978)
The story is apparently supported by science, but there is an air of desperation to this poster for one of the worst films of the 1970s. The cast is large, as evinced by the portraits at the bottom of the poster.

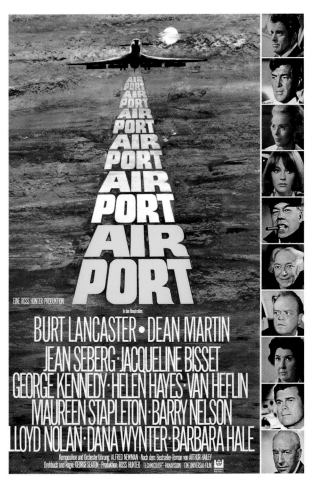

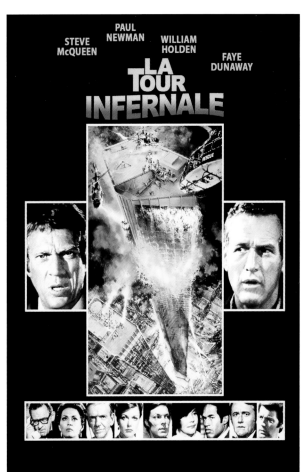

CLOCKWISE FROM TOP LEFT

Airport (1970)
The film that helped define the modern blockbuster disaster movie also set the template for the kind of design that would commonly be used. Most important is the emphasis on an all-star cast.

The Towering Inferno (1974)
Steve McQueen's name comes first, but Paul Newman's is higher up. The rest of the large, starry ensemble cast feature along the bottom of the poster. The central image promises spectacle on the grandest scale.

The Poseidon Adventure (1972)
This earlier entry in the genre remains one of the best and features the best caption. Once again, the design follows the template of cast member stills and an image of the disaster unfolding.

Earthquake (1974)
One of the more inventive posters for a big-budget disaster film has the title hint at the effects of an earthquake hitting central Los Angeles.

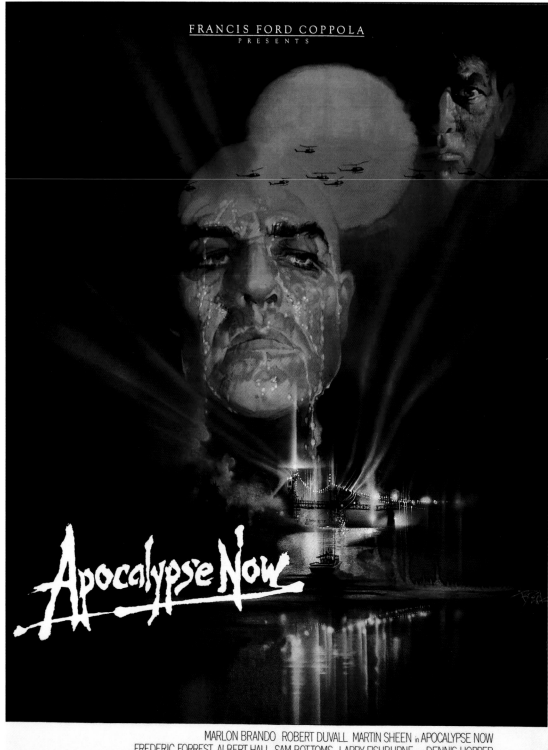

Apocalypse Now (1979)
Bob Peak's design is a fevered dream, no
less hallucinatory than the visions Martin
Sheen's character experiences at the start
of the film. It successfully conveys the
heart of darkness of Coppola's film.

Rolling Thunder (1977)
The artwork employs black and red to
stark effect, while both text and image are
repeated to suggest an unrelenting force.
The splayed hook as it impacts the title
also hints at the film's violence.

Coming Home (1978)
The image appears to suggest a tender
love story, but the addition of Bruce Dern
adds intrigue and threat. The anachronistic
look could be an attempt to distance the
film from a conventional war movie.

A VERY DIFFERENT WAR

Unlike the many propaganda films produced during World War II, only one Hollywood film was made about the Vietnam War while it still raged. *The Green Berets* (1968) was codirected by and starred John Wayne, and in its bravado and sentiment it was completely out of touch with the divisions that the war had created at home. It would be another decade before narrative cinema began to grapple with the complexity, guilt, and horror that resulted from the conflict.

The first two mainstream films to tackle the subject of the Vietnam War approached it from a domestic perspective. Following on from his searing screenplay for *Taxi Driver* (1976), whose references to the conflict were more oblique, Paul Schrader's story for *Rolling Thunder* (1977), like the one that features in the later *First Blood* (1982), links the bloody, vengeful actions of William Devane's Major Charles Rane directly to his wartime experiences. The film also touches on the veteran's inability to connect with any kind of intimacy, a theme that is explored in greater detail in *Coming Home* (1978). In contrast to the stark image for *Rolling Thunder*, Richard Amsel's design for the Jane Fonda and Jon Voight vehicle accentuates the tenderness derived from the main characters' adulterous relationship.

The 1970s ended with two films that defined the insanity of the conflict: *The Deer Hunter* (1978) and *Apocalypse Now* (1979). Robert De Niro headed the cast of *The Deer Hunter*, which is an account of three friends' experiences as prisoners of the Viet Cong. The war itself forms the center section of a triptych that ultimately highlights the veterans' inability to fit back into American society upon returning home. However, the defining image of the film comes from the Russian roulette game that the imprisoned soldiers are forced to play by their captors.

Bob Peak's celebrated poster for *Apocalypse Now* presents Francis Ford Coppola's vision of the conflict as some kind of nightmare. It features key moments from the film, but is dominated by Martin Sheen's protagonist and Marlon Brando's deranged colonel. Along with a blood-red sun, they float over the river upon which the film's action takes place, a journey that appears to lead into the jaws of hell.

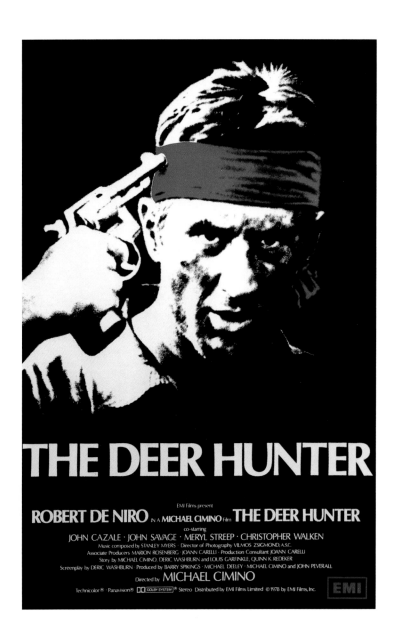

The Deer Hunter (1978)
Robert De Niro appears unsettled, all aggressive and confrontational. There is no color except for the blood-red bandana and no mention of Vietnam, but the nihilism of the image chimed with the times.

BOB PEAK

Bob Peak had been in the advertising world for a decade when he was hired by United Artists in 1961. His work on the campaign for *West Side Story* (1961) led to his collaborating with legendary designer Bill Gold on the big-budget musicals *My Fair Lady* (1964) and *Camelot* (1967). However, it was in the 1970s that his reputation grew, and his unique style saw him labeled "The Father of Modern Movie Posters."

Peak's skill lay in his innate abilities as a draftsman —his subtle command of portraiture and a striking compositional sense—and also in his thorough grounding in art history and techniques. He incorporated the influence of art movements, from cubism and fauvism to futurism, impressionism, and art nouveau, into his poster designs. There was elegance in his work, even when he was depicting chaos. His poster for *Apocalypse Now* (1979, see page 210) is one of the best examples of his style. The heads of the main protagonists loom over a world at war, but the effect is more hallucinatory than horrific.

A more rigid style can be seen in Peak's design for Sydney Pollack's *The Yakuza* (1974), while his work on *The Spy Who Loved Me* (1977) was a marked shift away from the more comic book approach that Robert E. McGinnis used in his Bond posters of the 1960s and early 1970s.

Peak's design for *Rollerball* (1975) is another high point of his career. Norman Jewison's dystopian science fiction film depicts a world run by corporations that use a violent, gladiatorial sport as a way of channeling the populace's lust for violence. The poster is confrontational and threatening, but also dream-like, as if this world is a nightmare of what could be. Peak's work on *Excalibur* (1981) also evinces a dreamy texture.

In 1978, Peak designed artwork for *Superman* (1978). The following year, he was commissioned to design the poster for *Star Trek: The Motion Picture* (1979), and went on to design the posters for four sequels. They are notable for the way in which Peak utilizes lines of light and color, and the artwork set the standard for how big-budget movies were sold to audiences.

BELOW LEFT

Rollerball (1975)
James Caan's sports star may be confused by the world he resides in when he is not at work, but on the track he is a primal beast. His aggression is channeled into this image: his spiked glove raised in provocation, the bacchanalian festivities beneath almost crushed by it.

BELOW RIGHT

Superman (1978)
This is another example of Peak using lines of color to divide an image. Here, the shift from blue, through yellow, to red denotes speed. The icon takes the place of a title. It is simple but ruthlessly effective in selling its concept.

OPPOSITE

Star Trek: The Motion Picture (1979)

Peak makes clever use of the USS *Enterprise*'s teleport machine as the central concept in his artwork. But rather than a single block of light, he creates a vertical spectrum of color, from which Kirk and Spock appear.

The
Human
Adventure
Is Just
Beginning.

STAR TREK
THE MOTION PICTURE ™

THE BOLLYWOOD ACTION HERO

The term Bollywood was coined in the early 1970s. To international audiences, it represents an explosion of color, with action, music, and dance. To a local Indian audience, it is best represented by the masala film, which takes its name from the spices of Indian cuisine. Not so much a genre in itself, a masala film is a melding of genre conventions. The action film merges with comedy, melodrama, romance, and musical to produce a hybrid movie with universal appeal.

Two notable examples are Nasir Hussain's *Procession of Memories* (1973) and Manmohan Desai's *Amar Akbar Anthony* (1977). The poster promoting the former features a couple dancing and kissing, as well as a villain—dressed in black—wielding a knife, while the latter showcases its stars and hints at the various genre styles incorporated into its narrative. Desai's film was so popular it was remade into three different versions for Tamil (*Shankar Salim Simon*, 1978), Telugu (*Ram Robert Rahim*, 1980), and Malayalam (*John Jaffer Janardhanan*, 1982) audiences.

One of the subgenres to emerge out of masala film was the Curry Western. A none-too-subtle appropriation of the Spaghetti Western, the first entry was *Khote Sikkay* (1974), which tells the story of a group hired by a defenseless village to protect it from marauding bandits. The poster for the film features action and romance and is richly colorful, even by the standards of the average Bollywood film. The following year, director Ramesh Sippy teamed up with Amitabh Bachchan, the newly minted star of *Deewaar* (1975), for the epic *Sholay* (1975). It is often cited as one of the greatest Indian films, and its scale—particularly its 70mm format—was a major selling point. One promotional poster featured the all-star cast in similar fashion to the US disaster movies of the time—with head shots lining the top of the poster—but here they are against a background of flames. In another, Bachchan features in an expressively heroic posture next to costar Jaya Bhaduri.

Over the next decade, the Bollywood action movie expanded its range, encompassing an increasing number of genres and periods. Bachchan continued to star in action films, such as *Ram Balram* (1980), which attracted huge audiences. And the inclusion of musical numbers, no matter how dark the narrative, remained a fixture.

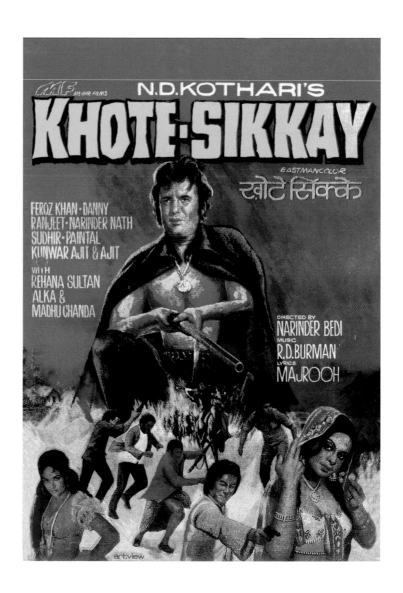

ABOVE

Khote Sikkay (1974)
The contrasting figures, from the hero rising above the action to the woman in the right corner and the gun-wielding man, hint at the melding of genre elements in this early example of a masala film.

OPPOSITE

Sholay (1975)
Everything about this poster, from the stars appearing to rise out of flames to the design of the film's title, hints at the epic. Like the artwork for the Hollywood epics of the 1950s, this poster is selling scale.

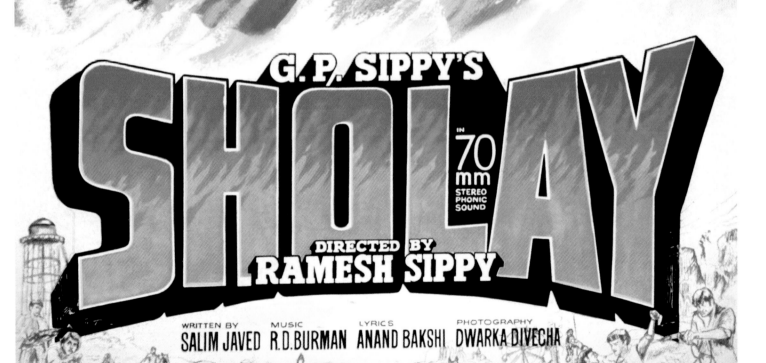

A long time ago in a galaxy far, far away...

©1977 Twentieth Century-Fox

STAR WARS

TWENTIETH CENTURY-FOX Presents
A LUCASFILM LTD. PRODUCTION
STAR WARS
Starring MARK HAMILL HARRISON FORD CARRIE FISHER
PETER CUSHING
and
ALEC GUINNESS
Written and Directed by GEORGE LUCAS Produced by GARY KURTZ Music by JOHN WILLIAMS
PANAVISION® PRINTS BY DE LUXE® TECHNICOLOR®
Original Motion Picture Soundtrack on 20th Century Records and Tapes

Making Films Sound Better
DOLBY SYSTEM
Noise Reduction · High Fidelity

POSTERS OF THE DECADE

By the end of the 1970s, Hollywood had identified a style of cinema that would allow it to gain dominance at the global box office. It was a world away from the kind of US cinema that was being produced at the beginning of the decade. Steven Spielberg and George Lucas led the way, forging the path for the modern blockbuster—albeit imbued with more grittiness than this kind of film would display in subsequent decades. The posters that accompanied these movies would help define American cinema of this era, but this kind of film was not alone in creating iconic imagery.

There are few better examples of the searing intensity of deeply personal, cathartic cinema than *Taxi Driver* (1976). Written by Paul Schrader during a particularly dark night of the soul and directed by Martin Scorsese with a verve that saw him win the Palme d'Or at the Cannes Film Festival (the film lost out to *Rocky* in the Best Picture category at the Academy Awards), it presents a bleak portrait of life on the streets of New York. Robert De Niro is incendiary in the lead role, and his presence, with the city in the background, was all that was needed to sell the film. Like the bold monochrome poster for *Scarface* (1983), the photograph of Travis Bickle walking along a New York street would soon represent an image

of rebellion and a become regular sight on the walls of student dorms.

Jaws (1975) marked a turning point in US film and cemented Steven Spielberg's position as US cinema's preeminent entertainer. It set the parameters for the blockbuster film, both in terms of marketing and merchandising. Furthermore, it lay the groundwork for the kind of high-concept film that dominated cinema throughout the 1980s. That concept was memorably encapsulated in the film's poster, which was lifted directly from Roger Kastel's cover design for Peter Benchley's book. It told audiences everything they needed to know about the film.

There is a story about a screening of a rough cut of George Lucas' space opera. Present were many of Lucas' peers. He had yet to create the battle scenes in space so footage of aerial dogfights from earlier war movies was intercut with the action. After the screening, the response was mostly mute. Spielberg was the exception, noting that *Star Wars* (1977) was going to be a huge success. However, he might not have foreseen the existence of a forty-year (and counting) legacy that has resulted in one of the most successful franchises in cinema history.

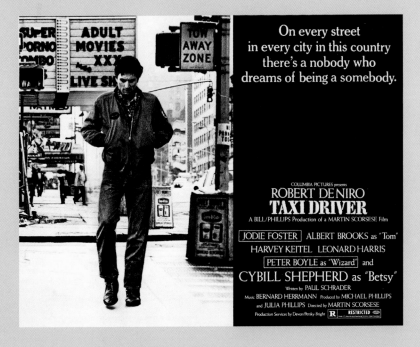

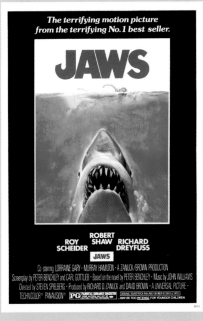

1980s

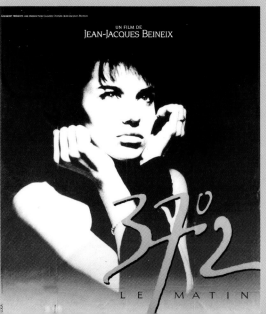

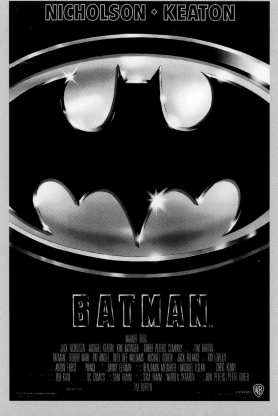

The 1980s may have witnessed stagnation in mainstream cinema, but it also saw the appearance of movements that reveled in visual style and the gradual return of a rejuvenated genre. High concept blockbusters dominated, Steven Spielberg became Hollywood's supreme entertainer, and action heroes run the gamut from beefcake to blue-collar cop.

The 1980s has widely been regarded as the nadir for mainstream Hollywood cinema. Like television three decades earlier, the rise in popularity of video saw ticket sales at the box office plummet. At the same time, producers who were interested in earning quick money realized that straight-to-video movies could reap greater rewards. The prevailing opinion seemed to be, if it is not working, dumb it down.

The notion of high concept movies was to take a simple idea, one that could be summed up in a caption or sentence, and transform it into a crowd-pleasing spectacle. Better still—build a franchise from it. The artwork around these films generally focused on the star and the motif or theme that drove the narrative. So, a disheveled Eddie Murphy against the plush environs of

Beverly Hills, or Tom Cruise on a bike with fighter planes in the background, was all an audience needed to know.

There were more interesting concepts in 1980s US cinema, though, such as David Lynch's visions of suburbia in his neo-noir thriller *Blue Velvet* (1986) and Jim Jarmusch's adventures in low-budget, off-beat comedy, such as *Stranger Than Paradise* (1984), which presaged indie cinema in the 1990s. Crime films also made a welcome return. Michael Mann and Brian De Palma brought out the big guns with their spectacular, operatic set pieces, Joel and Ethan Coen made their directorial debut with the smart *Blood Simple* (1984), and John Cassavetes transformed Gena Rowlands into a gun-toting con in *Gloria* (1980).

China's Fifth Generation of filmmakers provided some of the most delicate images of any film across the decade as they examined their country's recent past. The promotional artwork for the films was initially understated. However, when acclaimed cinematographer Zhang Yimou turned to directing, the posters for his films were awash with color. Similarly, the short-lived Cinéma du look was all about style and what it said about contemporary life.

HIGH CONCEPT HOLLYWOOD

If certain US films—narratively open-ended, with complex characterization, tonally dark—evaded easy description in the 1970s, others laid the groundwork for what became known as high concept filmmaking. The idea behind these films was simple: a narrative that could be encapsulated in one or two sentences. *Alien* (1979), for example, was described as "*Jaws* in space." Steven Spielberg's 1975 shark thriller, promoted by a poster that tells audiences everything they need to know about the film (see page 217), was an early example of this type of film. But high concept filmmaking was to become ruthlessly effective in the hands of two producers who emerged in the 1980s.

Jerry Bruckheimer had been producing films since the mid 1970s, including *Farewell, My Lovely* (1975), *American Gigolo* (1980), and *Thief* (1981), but it was when he teamed up with Paramount's former head of production, Don Simpson, that he scored his first big hit: *Flashdance* (1983). Together, they created a cinema that eschewed depth in favor of quick thrills and pulse-racing action. The success of the story of a woman who is a welder by day, and a stripper who dreams of a career in dance by night, proved that the producers were on to a good thing. Although *Flashdance* was a contrast to the male-driven action films that dominated their collaboration (the Michelle Pfeiffer vehicle *Dangerous Minds*, 1995, is the sole exception), the way in which Bruckheimer and Simpson films were sold to audiences was no less brash.

Like *Flashdance*, *Beverly Hills Cop* (1984) features a duck-out-of-water narrative—its premise little more than the juxtaposition of a smart-talking, streetwise black cop from Detroit running wild in the exclusive West Coast city. That film's runaway success saw the rebel-versus-the-system plot played out in various scenarios, from Tom Cruise's loner fighting to be the best in *Top Gun* (1986) and *Days of Thunder* (1990), to Will Smith and Martin Lawrence fighting everyone in *Bad Boys* (1995).

Action cinema—from buddy movies *48 Hrs.* (1982) and *Lethal Weapon* (1987), to science fiction extravaganzas *The Terminator* (1984) and *Predator* (1987), and the ultimate action thriller *Die Hard* (1988)—profited from the easy sell of being able to condense a film's plot into a simple brief pitch, illustrated by an equally forthright marketing campaign.

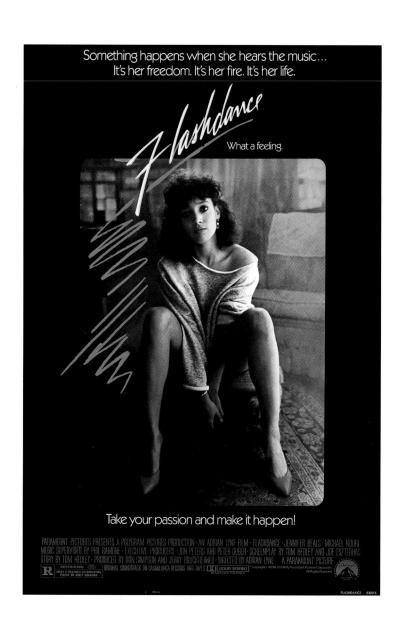

ABOVE

Flashdance (1983)
The success of this simple design lies in the caption "What a feeling." It is the title of Irene Cara's euphoric song, which was released to coincide with the film's opening and represents the hopes and dreams of Jennifer Beals' dancer.

OPPOSITE

Top Gun (1986)
The image of Tom Cruise and Kelly McGillis was used in various versions of artwork for Tony Scott's gung-ho action drama. Cruise is all attitude, and the airplanes in this image suggest, with no hint of subtlety, male virility.

UP THERE WITH THE BEST OF THE BEST.

A DON SIMPSON/JERRY BRUCKHEIMER PRODUCTION

TOM CRUISE · KELLY McGILLIS

TOP GUN

PARAMOUNT PICTURES PRESENTS · A DON SIMPSON/JERRY BRUCKHEIMER PRODUCTION · A TONY SCOTT FILM · TOM CRUISE · TOP GUN · KELLY McGILLIS · VAL KILMER · ANTHONY EDWARDS
TOM SKERRITT · MUSIC SCORE BY HAROLD FALTERMEYER · WRITTEN BY JIM CASH & JACK EPPS, JR. · PRODUCED BY DON SIMPSON AND JERRY BRUCKHEIMER · A PARAMOUNT PICTURE
PG PARENTAL GUIDANCE SUGGESTED ⊲▷ · DOLBY STEREO · DIRECTED BY TONY SCOTT · ORIGINAL MOTION PICTURE SOUNDTRACK ALBUM AVAILABLE ON COLUMBIA RECORDS CASSETTES AND COMPACT DISCS
SOME MATERIAL MAY NOT BE SUITABLE FOR CHILDREN · IN SELECTED THEATRES · READ THE PAPERBACK FROM POCKET BOOKS · COPYRIGHT 1986 BY PARAMOUNT PICTURES CORPORATION. ALL RIGHTS RESERVED

JOHN ALVIN

Shortly after graduating from the Art Center College of Design in Los Angeles, John Alvin established his reputation in Hollywood with his design for Mel Brooks' Western parody *Blazing Saddles* (1974). Over the course of the next three decades, Alvin helped forge the look of big-budget Hollywood films.

Although not averse to the use of more conventional photography—he selected the stills for the artwork for *The Mosquito Coast* (1986) and *Rain Man* (1988)—in some of his most notable work, Alvin employed a single painted image or layers of imagery to represent a film. He created the artwork for *Blade Runner* (1982), with Harrison Ford and Sean Young atop a futuristic Los Angeles, and obscured Meryl Streep and Jack Nicholson's faces for the Depression-era drama *Ironweed* (1987). Alvin worked on a variety of films in the 1980s, from action vehicles for Arnold Schwarzenegger and Eddie Murphy to the science fiction and fantasy worlds of *Cocoon*, *Legend* (both 1985), and *Short Circuit* (1986).

In the 1990s, he was responsible for relaunching a reinvigorated Disney, first with *Beauty and the Beast* (1991), followed by *Aladdin* (1992) and *The Lion King* (1994). His images employed a "heavy light" source, and from the silhouette formed in front of it he would build up character detail. (In the case of *Beauty and the Beast*, this was a practical process as the poster concept was completed before the character details were finalized.) This approach was a world away from Disney's older animated classics and hinted at the level of sophistication that was available at the time through the use of computerized techniques. But like all of Alvin's work, these images emphasize the power of storytelling. Nowhere is this more apparent than in his collaboration with Steven Spielberg.

Alvin oversaw the artwork design of five Spielberg films, along with many other projects the filmmaker produced. Of these, *E.T. the Extra-Terrestrial* (1982) remains the most iconic, and also Alvin's favorite of all his film work. A series of images was created for the film, which would work together as an overarching concept. Like so many of Alvin's designs, they evince a sense of wonder at the world created in the film.

BELOW LEFT

Blade Runner (1982)
Alvin draws on film noir iconography to portray a future Los Angeles, replete with an anti-hero and a femme fatale.

BELOW RIGHT

Ironweed (1987)
Alvin employs the star wattage of Meryl Streep and Jack Nicholson to sell this Depression-era film. Its minimal design hints at the period in which the film is set and its seriousness.

OPPOSITE
CLOCKWISE FROM TOP LEFT
E.T. the
Extra-Terrestrial (1982)
Michelangelo's *Creation of Adam*, which appears on the ceiling of the Vatican's Sistine Chapel, inspired this image of first contact with an alien life form.

This lesser-known version replaces the image of the child and alien's hands with a constellation-like outline. Once again, the first contact produces the brightest light.

For the twentieth anniversary re-release, Alvin worked the two key images of the original campaign into one. There is more detail, such as E.T.'s fingers poking out of the bike's basket.

This image recreates arguably the most magical moment in Spielberg's film and the first real bonding between E.T. and Elliott. Here, the oversized moon becomes a thing of magic and wonder.

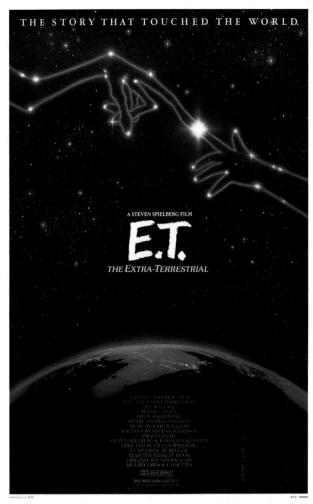

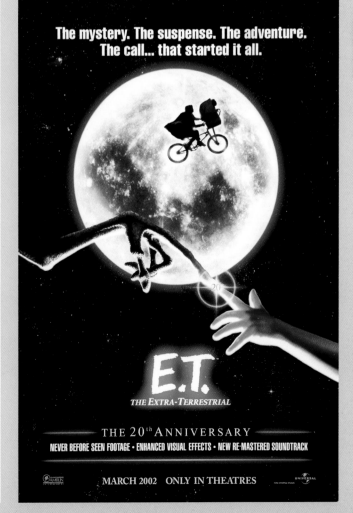

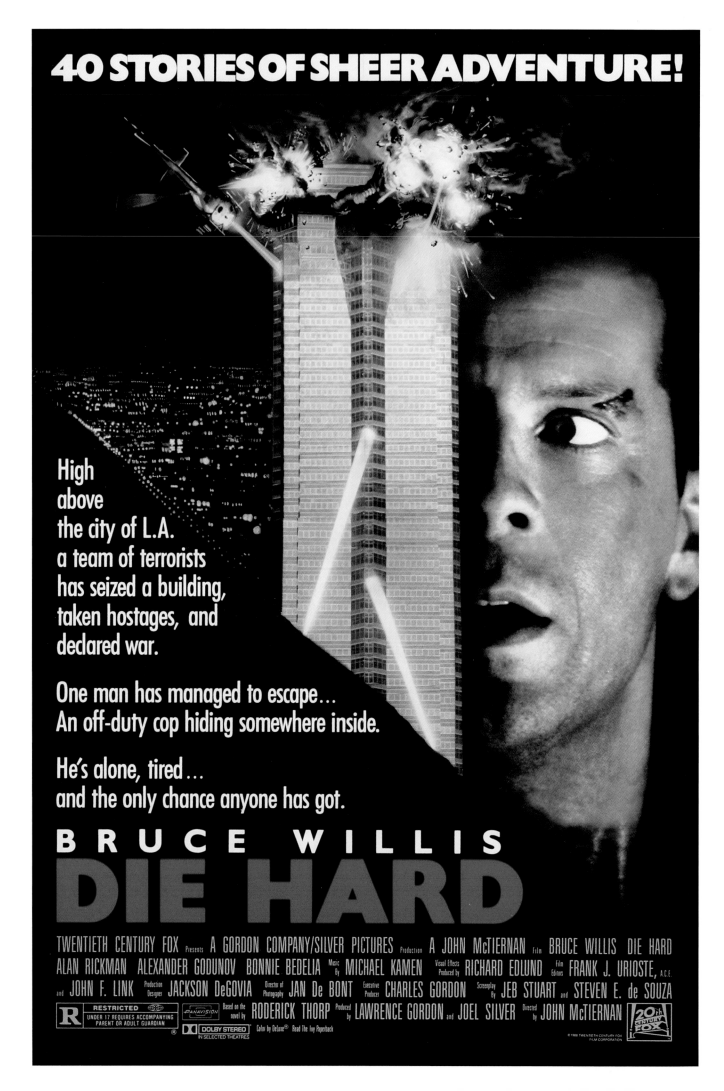

THE ACTION HERO

The action movie ran the gamut, from big-budget vehicle to low-rent fare. In the 1980s, there was an incredible demand for all manner of genre films, fueled by the arrival of home video players. There was an upsurge in the production of low-budget horror films, and the action movie soon followed suit. At the same time, a number of action stars dominated mainstream cinema. If the decade began with bulked-up, muscle-bound icons, it ended with the rise of the everyman action star.

At the low end of the spectrum, the popularity of martial arts films and gritty action thrillers in the 1970s formed the bedrock of companies such as Canon, who profited from the familiarity of stars Charles Bronson and Chuck Norris. Bronson's popularity in *Death Wish* (1974) resulted in four sequels and other similarly themed action dramas, while Chuck Norris became the all-American go-to guy for hand-to-hand combat. By the end of the 1980s, he had been replaced by Jean-Claude Van Damme. The promotional material for all these action films placed their heroes front and center, more often than not armed or ready to fight.

Sylvester Stallone and Arnold Schwarzenegger dominated action cinema in the early 1980s. Outside of their *Rocky*, *Rambo*, and *Terminator* franchises, their action films were larger in scale and bigger in budget than their straight-to-video counterparts. Moreover, the way in which they were sold was almost interchangeable. John Alvin's artwork for Stallone's *Cobra* and Schwarzenegger's *Raw Deal* (both 1986) is one such example. Audience tastes changed toward the end of the decade, and both these stars' action personas became more integrated within a film's concept or narrative.

Lethal Weapon (1987) and *Die Hard* (1988) did much to develop the genre. The action star was no longer all brawn, but an ordinary guy in extraordinary circumstances. Mel Gibson, Danny Glover, and Bruce Willis were still primarily sold as men of action, but there was less emphasis on their physical strength.

Recent years have seen the old-school action movie return, in the form of the ever-expanding *Expendables* franchise (2010–). Almost every star from the past forty years of US action cinema has played a role, and the posters promoting them appear almost nostalgic.

OPPOSITE

Die Hard (1988)
Bruce Willis turned a New York cop into an everyman hero with his portrayal of John McClane. In this poster, his gun represents the tower in which he fights a group of criminals, using the building as a weapon.

ABOVE

Commando (1985)
Arnie's one-liners were an integral part of his act by the time this film was released, as were his muscles and weapons. This look was parodied by Ben Stiller for the poster of *Tropic Thunder* (2008).

CRIME FILMS

Perhaps not since Warner Bros.' dominance of the gangster movie genre in the 1930s had the US crime film enjoyed such a killing at the box office as it did in the 1980s. Unlike that earlier period, which focused on the war between gangsters and law enforcement officers during the Prohibition era, the new batch of crime thrillers varied in style and look.

There are echoes of Warner's classic gangster films in Sergio Leone's epic *Once Upon a Time in America* (1984). Its poster features a sepia-tinted image of a memorable early scene in the film, which takes place in the shadow of the Manhattan Bridge. And Al Capone's Chicago resurfaces in Brian De Palma's *The Untouchables* (1987), with Robert De Niro's mobster looming large over the city and Eliot Ness' small gang of law enforcers.

The mob are connected peripherally to the protagonists of John Cassavetes' *Gloria* (1980) and Michael Mann's *Thief* (1981). Gena Rowlands appears as the eponymous action figure in the poster for *Gloria*, tough and solitary but ready to fight. By contrast, James Caan, the anti-hero of Mann's heist movie, is little more than an outline lit up by the flare of the tools he uses to break into safes. Both designs contrast starkly with the poster for William Friedkin's *To Live and Die in L.A.* (1985), one of the key West Coast crime films of the decade. Like the film, the artwork blurs the identity of cop and criminal, with the "L.A." of the title daubed in a blood-red scrawl across a cityscape at sunset.

The serial killer genre gained momentum toward the end of the decade. Mann returned with *Manhunter* (1986), his adaptation of Thomas Harris' first Hannibal Lecter novel, *Red Dragon* (1981). But arguably the most disturbing film of the period was *Henry: Portrait of a Serial Killer* (1986). As John McNaughton's thriller eschews Hollywood conventions, employing a documentary-like aesthetic in its portrayal of a sociopath, so its artwork presents an unvarnished image of the killer played by Michael Rooker.

Of all the 1980s US crime films, Brian De Palma's *Scarface* (1983) dominated the decade. The haunted image of Al Pacino's immigrant-turned-crime boss has become one of the most popular movie posters of the past three decades, and its simple monochrome design underpins Tony Montana's ruthless ambition.

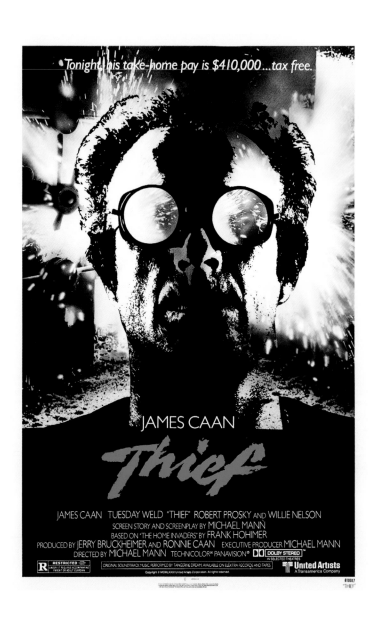

ABOVE

Thief (1981)
James Caan's face appears like a mask in this design. It is an accurate portrait of a man who barely expresses emotion and whose thought process is kept from view. But the image suggests an inner rage that edges toward the incandescent.

OPPOSITE

Scarface (1983)
The film's title and credits appear boldly in upper case. They accentuate the scale of De Palma's bloody thriller. The use of monochrome hints at a journey between two worlds: the one Tony Montana comes from and the darker one he enters into.

AL PACINO SCARFACE

In the spring of 1980, the port at Mariel Harbor was opened, and thousands set sail for the United States. They came in search of the American Dream.

One of them found it on the sun-washed avenues of Miami…wealth, power and passion beyond his wildest dreams.

He was Tony Montana. The world will remember him by another name …SCARFACE.

He loved the American Dream. With a vengeance.

A MARTIN BREGMAN PRODUCTION

A BRIAN De PALMA FILM

AL PACINO "SCARFACE"

SCREENPLAY BY OLIVER STONE

MUSIC BY GIORGIO MORODER

DIRECTOR OF PHOTOGRAPHY JOHN A. ALONZO A.S.C.

EXECUTIVE PRODUCER LOUIS A. STROLLER

PRODUCED BY MARTIN BREGMAN

DIRECTED BY BRIAN De PALMA

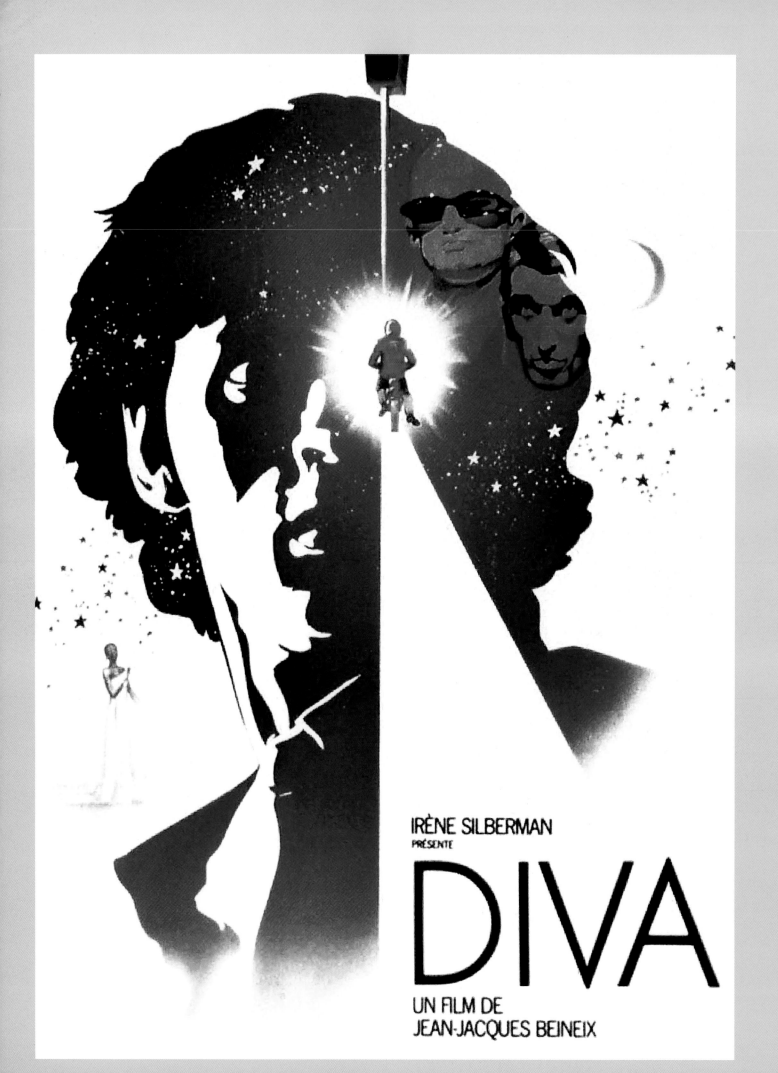

IRÈNE SILBERMAN
PRÉSENTE

DIVA

UN FILM DE
JEAN-JACQUES BEINEIX

CINÉMA DU LOOK

OPPOSITE

Diva (1981)
This is one of the key artworks of the 1980s French film wave. The narrative elements of the film are all present, but there is a hint that many of them may be taking place inside the head of the protagonist. It is fantastical and imbued with threat.

BELOW LEFT

Subway (1985)
Luc Besson's defining film of this movement is arguably the most chic, employing the Paris Metro and subterranean world to moody effect, as Christopher Lambert and Isabelle Adjani play out their dangerous romance.

BELOW RIGHT

Mauvais Sang (1986)
The poster for Leos Carax's feature is all longing looks and drama. A man running with abandon is watched by a woman—his lover, perhaps. There is an air of danger—possibly something forbidden—in their connection.

This short-lived movement in French filmmaking, which made an important contribution to 1980s cinema, was defined by its visual style. The films are all about "surface," a commentary on the state of the country at the time according to Raphaël Bassan, the critic who coined the term Cinéma du look. The disaffected youth were fed up with politics, and the general direction of French society, and more interested in easy thrills. These films represent that desire. Everything was about the look.

The movement began with Jean-Jacques Beineix's *Diva* (1981), which plays with multiple genres while never truly aligning itself to any of them. The artwork is similarly schizophrenic. In one poster, there is a silhouette of a man's head, mostly blue against a white background, with images of two villains superimposed. The other poster is more abstract and features two identical images of a mannequin wearing a helmet, with the second image torn to reveal the skinhead psycho cop from the film.

Leos Carax's *Boy Meets Girl* (1984) and *Mauvais Sang* (1986) are deeply romantic. The films' artwork emphasizes the tragic nature of love affairs—their fleeting moments of passion and the despair that awaits. If Carax was the poster boy for the Cinéma du look movement, the artwork that accompanied his films embellished that status. The director's romanticism grew as his work progressed, culminating in the operatic *The Lovers on the Bridge* (1991).

Like Beineix's *Diva*, Luc Besson's entry into the movement blends hopeless romanticism with a punk aesthetic. *Subway* (1985), the director's second film after the post-apocalyptic *The Last Battle* (1983), defines the movement in no uncertain terms, traveling into Paris' subterranean Metro system for the most part, and thus reinforcing just how "underground" the film is. It redefined the notion of cool.

The poster presents a combination of grunge and chic, perfectly reflecting the aesthetic championed by this band of rebellious filmmakers. Besson's later *Nikita* (1990) employs a similar visual aesthetic, fetishizing through neon-soaked images his tough addict-turned-assassin. But by that time, the only aspect of Cinéma du look that remained was the visual style.

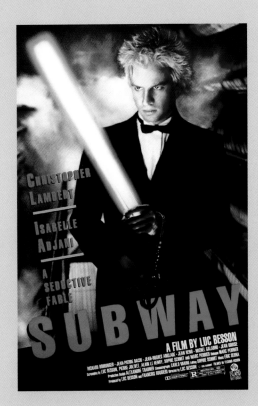

CHINA'S FIFTH GENERATION

Trained at Beijing's legendary Film Academy, China's Fifth Generation of filmmakers were the first to emerge from the Cultural Revolution. The directors who made up the core of the group—Zhang Yimou, Tian Zhuangzhuang, Chen Kaige, and Zhang Junzhao— all graduated from the class of 1982. The first films appeared soon after and announced a break with the social realist tradition of the previous generation. Chen Kaige's *Yellow Earth* (1984) and Zhang Junzhao's *One and Eight* (1983) are both set in the near past and feature a stark beauty and minimal dialogue. They announced a paradigm shift away from propagandist themes toward a more humanist narrative cinema.

Thematically, the Fifth Generation films differ greatly, although most of the early films are located in rural landscapes, allowing the filmmakers complete control over their environments. Tian Zhuangzhuang's *On the Hunting Ground* (1985) and *The Horse Thief* (1986) evince a documentary style that contrasts with Chen's work. Many of these films played at international festivals, but it was with Zhang Yimou's debut as a director that international audiences took notice.

  Zhang was the cinematographer on *Yellow Earth* and *One and Eight* and displayed extraordinary skill in his juxtaposition of colors against natural backdrops. His debut, *Red Sorghum* (1987), went further, particularly in its use of red. Rather than play up to this, the international artwork for the film was modulated to accentuate the film's artfulness. The reeds that play a central role in the film appear like Chinese characters, while the faint image of a character appears in the celestial object floating above. A similar approach was employed for the design of Zhang's third feature, *Ju Dou* (1990). But by the time of his celebrated *Raise the Red Lantern* (1991), audiences were aware of the visual style and the artwork reflected the richness of the film's palette.

  Chen's *Farewell My Concubine* (1993) is one of the Fifth Generation films that charts the impact of various radical movements on Chinese life and culture in the mid twentieth century. With its focus on members of the Peking Opera's company, the sumptuous artwork for the film plays with the idea of identity. The film won the Palme d'Or at the Cannes Film Festival and remains the quintessential example of Fifth Generation cinema.

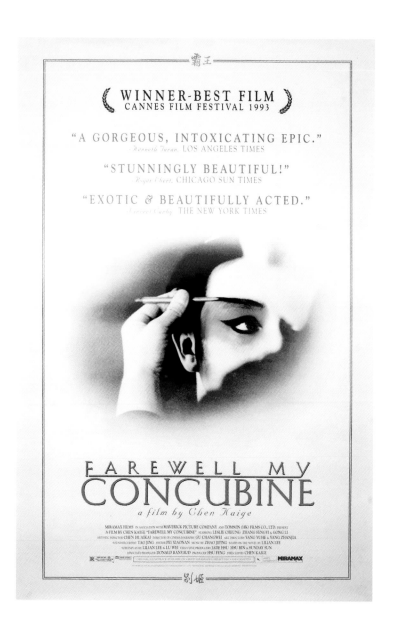

ABOVE

Farewell My Concubine (1993)
The central image appears so fragile it is already dissolving at its edges. It is a beautifully illustrated metaphor for loss of identity in the strict conformist regime presented in Chen's film.

OPPOSITE

Red Sorghum (1987)
The film's title hints at the colors the film exudes, while the simple silhouetted imagery is captivating—particularly the roughly drawn reeds that break up the center of the poster.

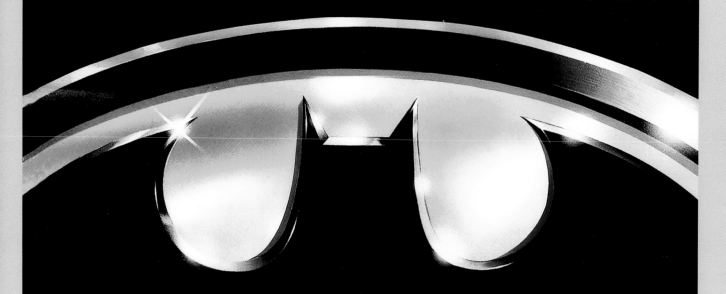

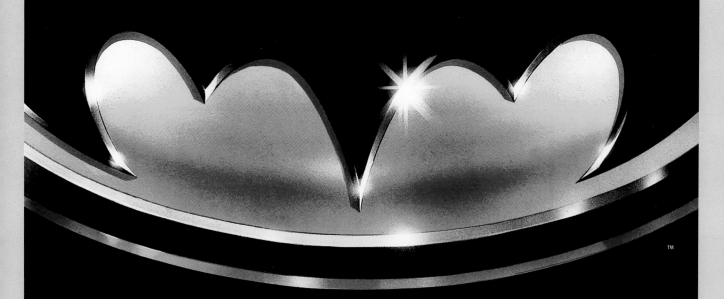

NICHOLSON · KEATON

BATMAN

WARNER BROS.

JACK NICHOLSON MICHAEL KEATON KIM BASINGER GUBER-PETERS COMPANY TIM BURTON

"BATMAN" ROBERT WUHL PAT HINGLE BILLY DEE WILLIAMS MICHAEL GOUGH JACK PALANCE RAY LOVEJOY

ANTON FURST PRINCE DANNY ELFMAN BENJAMIN MELNIKER MICHAEL USLAN CHRIS KENNY

BOB KANE DC COMICS SAM HAMM SAM HAMM WARREN SKAAREN JON PETERS PETER GUBER

TIM BURTON

PG-13 PARENTS STRONGLY CAUTIONED DOLBY STEREO WARNER BROS.

POSTERS OF THE DECADE

OPPOSITE

Batman (1989)
Anton Furst, the film's
production designer, came
up with the revitalized
Bat logo. He made it gold
and black—instead of the
traditional yellow—which
added class and shifted
the image away from
any notion of kitsch. Jack
Nicholson was a bigger
star than Michael Keaton
so his name came first.

BELOW LEFT

Betty Blue (1986)
The film's French title (the
normal temperature of a
pregnant woman in the
morning) is emblazoned
across an image of the
film's star, Béatrice Dalle,
and a house in the middle
of nowhere as the morning
sun rises. Her expression
is troubled and it sets the
tone of the film.

BELOW RIGHT

Blue Velvet (1986)
A couple are entwined,
but the image is not one
of affection. There is a
palpable sense of desire
in the still used for this
artwork, but there is also
threat. Isabella Rossellini's
character appears to be
the victim. The pair are
adrift—not at sea, but
upon the folds of rich
velvet that surround them.
We are being told that this
is a strange world.

Of the best film poster artwork created throughout the 1980s, a few examples transcended their original remit—of selling a film to a large audience—to become culturally significant artifacts. They represent rebellion, escapism, desire, and the dream of an alternate world.

There was a time when superhero movies made only occasional appearances on cinema screens. All that changed when Marvel and DC transformed into studio behemoths. *Superman* (1978) set the template for the tentpole blockbuster release, but it was Tim Burton's *Batman* (1989) that truly brought the comic book hero into the modern age. A world away from the kitsch 1966 movie spin-off of the popular television series, Burton created a world that was dark, menacing, and mordantly funny. The director had made only two features previously, the offbeat *Pee-wee's Big Adventure* (1985) and the bizarre *Beetlejuice* (1988), but both had been successes. However, fans of the comic book were worried about Burton's credentials and Michael Keaton's casting as the Dark Knight. Rather than offer up images of the film to attract audiences, the producers decided on a revised version of the Batman logo. It appeared months before the film's release and worked its way into the cultural psyche.

David Lynch was also regarded with suspicion prior to the release of *Blue Velvet* (1986). *Eraserhead* (1977) had marked him out as a cult director and *The Elephant Man* (1980) was an offbeat triumph. The latter tells the story of John Merrick, a disfigured man who with the help of a doctor finds some happiness. Lynch was offered *Star Wars: Return of the Jedi* (1983), but instead embarked on an ambitious adaptation of Frank Herbert's *Dune* (1984). It was a creative and commercial disaster and proved that the director was better suited to pursuing his own path, which is what he did with his deconstruction of small-town America. The poster for *Blue Velvet* hints at illicit desires, framed against a lush blue background.

In France, the films that fell into the critic-created category Cinéma du look attracted admiration and ire in equal measure. They were either films that spoke to the younger generation about the malaise in contemporary French life or solipsistic dramas that privileged style over substance. Jean-Jacques Beineix followed his era-defining *Diva* (1981) and atmospheric *The Moon in the Gutter* (1983) with the romantic drama *Betty Blue* (1986). It made a star of Béatrice Dalle, and Christian Blondel's evocative artwork adorned the bedroom walls of love-struck students around the world.

1990s

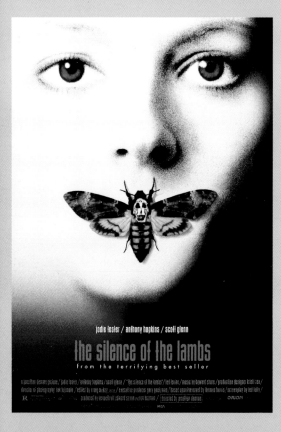

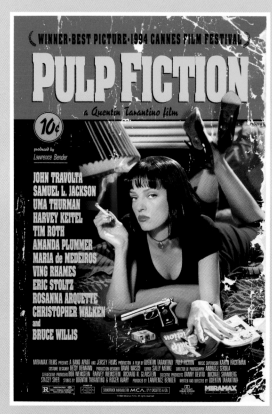

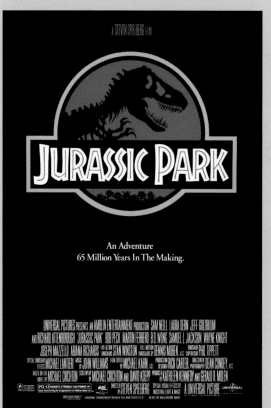

The 1990s saw a resurgence in the number of cinemagoers around the world. US cinema seemed more fractured than ever and was all the better for it, whereas Asian horror became the byword for fear. The noir thriller arrived with an added twist, and it appeared that audiences could not get enough of the end of the world, if the number of disaster and alien invasion blockbusters was anything to go by.

The independent film movement that had gradually been growing in the United States during the 1980s exploded onto the scene at the end of the decade. And with the arrival of American indie films came poster designs that attempted to separate these movies from mainstream Hollywood fare. At the same time, African American cinema increased its presence, led by the success of and controversy around Spike Lee's films. Furthermore, although new queer cinema started the decade on the fringes of US cinema, by the end of the 1990s it witnessed mainstream success.

The indie film found its champion in Quentin Tarantino, a filmmaker immersed in popular culture. The designs for his films possess a retro feel that makes them familiar yet offers something new. The motley bunch of criminals in *Reservoir Dogs* (1992) could have come from a hardboiled crime film of old, yet still feel contemporary, while the book cover look of the poster for *Pulp Fiction* (1994) promises nostalgia with a modern twist. These works heralded a resurgence in noir-tinged films, which had already made the odd appearance in the 1980s with the likes of *Blood Simple* (1984). They range from period noirs through to rural thrillers, but all have one eye on the morally ambivalent films of the classic noir period in the 1940s and 1950s. This was often reflected in the way the films were promoted. Both *L.A. Confidential* (1997) and *Devil in a Blue Dress* (1995) play with the recognizable tropes of that era, although Carl Franklin's Denzel Washington vehicle engages with race in a way that would never have been approached by any major studio during the period in which the film is set.

There is the occasional noir element in Pedro Almodóvar's unique body of work. Few filmmakers provided such a rich vein of inspiration for poster designers around the world, but Almodóvar's fruitful collaboration with artist Juan Gatti resulted in posters that rank among the best of the decade.

THE AMERICAN INDIE

The American indie scene was less a homogenous group and more a collection of distinctive voices helping to shape the landscape of contemporary US cinema. Its roots can be found in the spirit of John Cassavetes, whose directorial debut *Shadows* (1959) might not have been the first independent production but became the film to which subsequent generations aspired. In fact, indie cinema was more disparate than the group of filmmakers who comprised New Hollywood in the 1970s—both groups were linked by the desire to break free from mainstream conventions—which is evinced in the way indie films were promoted.

The breadth of indie cinema can be seen in the breakthrough films of three key directors who emerged as this landscape was in its nascence. Jim Jarmusch was an early example. His sophomore film *Stranger Than Paradise* (1984) pretty much defined the look of the archetypal indie movie. Three characters appear in a monochrome image (the film was shot in black and white) against a white background. The type is unfussy, while the caption—"A new American film"—seems more significant in hindsight. *Stranger Than Paradise* was only a minor commercial success, but Jarmusch's use of long takes within a freewheeling narrative and smart, humor-tinged dialogue set the template for the films that followed.

Steven Soderbergh's *Sex, Lies and Videotape* (1989) was a breakthrough film. It won the top prize at the Cannes Film Festival and went on to lead the way for a new generation of filmmakers. It was followed, two years later, by Richard Linklater's *Slacker* (1991). Like *Stranger Than Paradise*, both these films are performance-based and dialogue-heavy. Yet all three are tonally, thematically, and visually distinct from one another. In terms of the way the films were sold, *Sex, Lies and Videotape* was arguably more conventional, with Laura San Giacomo sitting on the edge of a bed, looking directly at the audience. Yet the "i" of "Videotape" is inverted and the hyphen linking "Sex" and "Lies" hints at something unconventional. By contrast, the poster for *Slacker* could have been designed to promote a drug-addled road movie. Instead, it hints at the strangeness that can be found in everyday life. A portrait of Austin, Texas, it evokes Arthur Schnitzler's play

ABOVE

Sex, Lies and Videotape (1989)
The blue backdrop, contrasting with Laura San Giacomo's Cynthia, suggests a false reality. It hints at the layers of deception that mask the real feelings of the four protagonists in Steven Soderbergh's debut.

OPPOSITE

Slacker (1991)
The design could be for an offbeat stoner comedy. Instead it highlights the invention of Richard Linklater's breakthrough feature, whose narrative structure suggests everyday life is often stranger than we think.

SLACKER

Written, Produced and Directed by RICHARD LINKLATER
Cameraman LEE DANIEL Production Manager, Casting ANNE WALKER-McBAY Dolly Grip, Assistant Camera CLARK WALKER Sound DENISE MONTGOMERY
Editor SCOTT RHODES Script Supervisor MEG BRENNAN A Detour Filmproduction Cast A LOT OF PEOPLE

An ORION CLASSICS Release

© 1991 Orion Pictures Corp.

La Ronde (1897) in the way that it features a series of one-off encounters between people.

The increasing importance of the Sundance Film Festival—the decade's key platform for promoting US independent features—and the rise of independent production companies such as Miramax saw the indie scene expand significantly in the early 1990s. And in Quentin Tarantino, it found its most outspoken representative. A cinephile who had gorged himself on movies while growing up and working in a video store, Tarantino consumed books on cinema and was an avid fan of crime fiction. His debut film, *Reservoir Dogs* (1992), divided opinion because of its extreme violence, but there is no denying the force of the film. Its artwork draws on the credit sequence, underpinning its inherent "coolness" and featuring a gang of criminals dressed in black suits about to carry out a bank job. (In the film, Chris Penn's Nice Guy Eddie character is actually wearing a garish tracksuit, but here he is dressed the same as his colleagues.) Robert Rodriguez's *El Mariachi* (1992) hints at a different kind of violent world to that portrayed in *Reservoir Dogs*, illustrated by a lone gunman with a guitar case walking in the middle of a desolate highway.

Tarantino's ear for whip-smart dialogue that mines popular culture references and movie lore is also a notable feature of Kevin Smith's *Clerks* (1994), an ultra-low-budget black-and-white comedy, set in a convenience store. This film's amateurish poster, featuring a slightly distorted portrait of the cast, block titles, and the caption "Just because they serve you doesn't mean they like you," perfectly encapsulates the film's tone.

At the Sundance Film Festival in 1992, Alexandre Rockwell won the top prize with the comedy drama *In the Soup* (1992), whose monochrome imagery harks back to Jarmusch and Cassavetes. In the same year, Allison Anders offered a different variation of the archetypal indie movie with the thoughtful, low-key *Gas, Food Lodging* (1992). An intimate female-driven drama, its warm tones are reflected in the film's poster. A more complex image, again flooded with golden hues, promoted Anders' drama about an aspiring female singer-songwriter, *Grace of My Heart* (1996).

The extreme edges of American indie cinema were defined by Larry Clark's controversial *Kids* (1995), which focuses on underage sex among a group of New York City teenagers, along with *Kids*' screenwriter Harmony Korine's directorial debut, *Gummo* (1997), and Darren Aronofsky's *Pi* (1998). These last two films are virtually unclassifiable, as proven by their oblique posters, and pushed at the envelope of what came to be recognized as indie cinema.

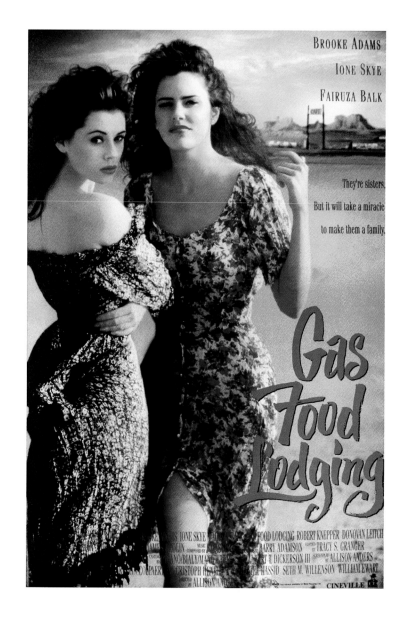

ABOVE

Gas, Food Lodging (1992)
An archetypal image for the American indie character drama, its warm tones suggest a slow-burn, low-key narrative, which is exactly what this intelligent and heartfelt study of an all-female family is.

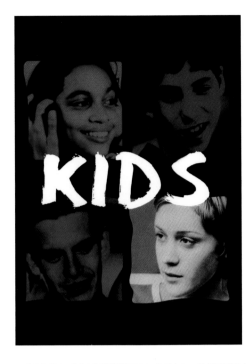

TOP LEFT

Kids (1995)
The coloring hints at different personalities, and the way the title is superimposed emphasizes their age. Little else prepares audiences for how provocative the film is.

TOP MIDDLE

Stranger Than Paradise (1984)
The poster for this deadpan road movie exudes an air of melancholy that suffuses the dialogue between the three main characters. It defined the filmmaker's style.

TOP RIGHT

Gummo (1997)
The out of focus image perfectly underpins the strangeness of Harmony Korine's debut: an unsettling, but ultimately affecting portrait of America's underbelly.

ABOVE

Reservoir Dogs (1992)
The cast of Tarantino's heist-gone-wrong thriller might resemble a motley crew of individuals but the splash of red hints at the bloodshed to come.

ABOVE

Boyz n the Hood (1991)
The blue backdrop to this image hints at the danger ever present on the streets of South Central, as does the blood-red title. The presence of N.W.A. member Ice Cube gives the film factual credence.

TOP RIGHT

New Jack City (1991)
Wesley Snipes looms large, announcing a new godfather of movie criminality. Rapper-turned-actor Ice-T's posture is in stark contrast to those of Mario Van Peebles and Judd Nelson's cops.

MIDDLE RIGHT

Set It Off (1996)
F. Gary Gray challenges the perception of what female-led African American cinema should be with this heist-thriller. The selling point was the cast who dominate the film's artwork.

BOTTOM RIGHT

Above the Rim (1994)
The poster details the conflict at the heart of the film—between sporting ambition that offers opportunity and the streets that threaten to thwart it. The presence of Tupac Shakur adds an edge.

AFRICAN AMERICAN CINEMA

In the early 1990s, US cinema seemed to finally acknowledge that the United States was a diverse place with many communities underrepresented on the screen. Popular culture began to see a shift in the representation of African Americans. In film, following the example of Spike Lee (see overleaf), black filmmakers and subjects appeared to be on the increase. It didn't last, but at the time, as one *New York Times* journalist put it, "Black film properties may be to the 90s what the carphone was to the 80s; every studio executive has to have one."

Early in the decade, the key voices belonged to John Singleton and Julie Dash. *Boyz n the Hood* (1991) and *Daughters of the Dust* (1991) each broke down barriers. Singleton was the first African American to be nominated for a Best Director Academy Award for his account of the lives of three young black men living in Los Angeles, and Dash was the first African American woman to have a film theatrically released in the United States. Her story of three generations of Gullah women living off the South Carolina–Georgia coastline remains a key feminist work, and its promotion highlighted the film's predominantly female cast. Dash continued to focus on female African American-related topics, and other films followed suit, such as Singleton's *Poetic Justice* (1993), which stars Janet Jackson (who dominates the posters for the film) and F. Gary Gray's thriller *Set It Off* (1996), in which a group of women carry out a bank robbery.

The *Boyz n the Hood* poster features its three lead actors against a blue-tinted image of their home, underpinning the sense of danger on Los Angeles' streets for young black men. *New Jack City* (1991) was more incendiary in its worldview. Echoing the posters of the Blaxploitation era, the artwork for Mario Van Peebles' film takes a more sensationalist approach. In its wake, other films presented bleak portraits of contemporary African American life, from *South Central* and *Juice* (both 1992) to *Menace II Society* (1993) and *Fresh* (1994). They were a stark contrast to the lighter films, such as the *House Party* series (1990–1993) and the hugely popular *Friday* (1995). But what underpinned them all, as evinced in their posters, was a keen eye for up-to-the-minute fashion and a street-smart attitude that was no less forthright than the accompanying soundtracks.

Friday (1995)
Ice Cube's autobiographical tale finds the rapper-turned-actor performing in a lighter register. This is evinced by the poster design, in which the use of bold primary colors mirrors the style of the time.

SPIKE LEE

Of the wave of African American filmmakers who emerged in the late 1980s and early 1990s, none was more prominent than Spike Lee. His confrontational approach to race, history, and politics chimed perfectly with the times, and his best work continues to resonate.

Lee's position as a provocative filmmaker was fully realized with his third feature, *Do the Right Thing* (1989). It unfolds over the course of one baking hot summer's day in Brooklyn, eventually erupting with violence following the death of a young black man at the hands of the police. The poster for the film features an overhead shot of Lee's Mookie and Danny Aiello's Sal, standing on a blue pavement, with near blank expressions. Rather than reveal what takes place, it hints instead at the film's texture.

The use of color and mood dominates Lee's subsequent *Mo' Better Blues* (1990), a portrait of a jazz musician played by Denzel Washington. In the film's artwork, he appears with the two women in his life on a poster that has been pasted on a wall, over the poster for *Do the Right Thing*. Like Lee's subsequent *Crooklyn* (1994), *Girl 6* (1996), and *She Hate Me* (2004),

the image is saturated with color, once again reflecting the filmmaker's signature style, which combines a contrasting palette—both in costume and production style—with heightened emotions.

Jungle Fever's (1991) focus on a mixed race relationship, between Wesley Snipes' married architect and Annabella Sciorra's temp, was a marked change in tone for Lee. It also signaled a shift in how his films were promoted. The poster features only the intertwined fingers of a black man and white woman's hands, leaving the interpretation of the image to the audience.

The posters for three of Lee's other key films of the 1990s also differ in style. *Malcolm X* (1992) provocatively features an "X" filled with an image of Denzel Washington as the outspoken 1960s icon set against the American flag. The crime film *Clockers* (1995), like Lee's later *25th Hour* (2002), is a minimal three-tone design, in which Art Sims' silhouette of a disembodied corpse recalls the work of Saul Bass. And although *Summer of Sam* (1999) returns to the fire and fury of *Do the Right Thing*, its contrasting artwork informs audiences that this is a very different kind of New York.

BELOW LEFT

Malcolm X (1992)
Like the film's opening sequence, which shows an American flag burning into the shape of an "X," intercut with footage of the Rodney King beating, this image was created to be provocative.

BELOW RIGHT

Summer of Sam (1999)
In contrast to most of the posters that promote Lee's films, the only bold color here is the red of the title, underpinning the drama's violence. The newspaper backdrop places the film within its historical context.

OPPOSITE

Do the Right Thing (1989)
Echoing the use of color in Lee's film, everything is heightened in this image, from the blue of the pavement and the red of the car to the clothing. There is an element of volatility in this combination.

It's the hottest day of the summer.
You can do nothing,
you can do something,
or you can...

Do The Right Thing

Bed-Stuy

A SPIKE LEE JOINT

A 40 ACRES AND A MULE FILMWORKS PRODUCTION
A SPIKE LEE JOINT "DO THE RIGHT THING" DANNY AIELLO
OSSIE DAVIS · RUBY DEE · RICHARD EDSON · GIANCARLO ESPOSITO
SPIKE LEE · BILL NUNN · JOHN TURTURRO and JOHN SAVAGE as Clifton   Casting ROBI REED
Production Design WYNN THOMAS   Original Music Score BILL LEE   Editor BARRY ALEXANDER BROWN   Photographed by ERNEST DICKERSON

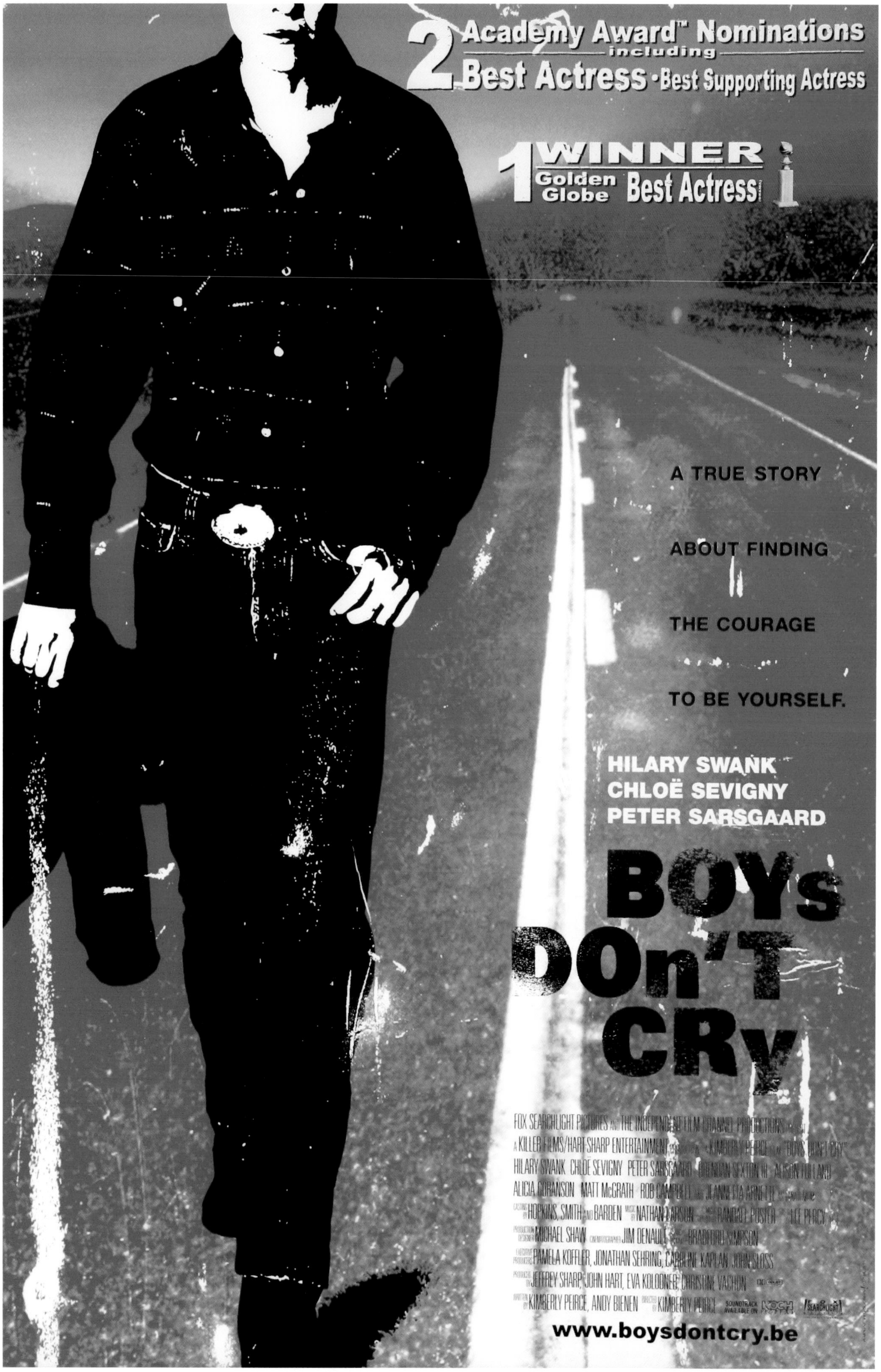
2 Academy Award™ Nominations
including
Best Actress • Best Supporting Actress
1 WINNER
Golden Globe Best Actress
A TRUE STORY
ABOUT FINDING
THE COURAGE
TO BE YOURSELF.
HILARY SWANK
CHLOË SEVIGNY
PETER SARSGAARD
BOYs DOn'T CRy
FOX SEARCHLIGHT PICTURES AND THE INDEPENDENT FILM CHANNEL PRODUCTIONS
A KILLER FILMS/HART-SHARP ENTERTAINMENT KIMBERLY PEIRCE "BOYS DON'T CRY"
HILARY SWANK CHLOË SEVIGNY PETER SARSGAARD BRENDAN SEXTON III ALISON FOLLAND
ALICIA GORANSON MATT McGRATH ROB CAMPBELL JEANNETTA ARNETTE
CASTING BY HOPKINS, SMITH AND BARDEN MUSIC BY NATHAN LARSON RANDALL POSTER LEE PERCY
PRODUCTION DESIGNER MICHAEL SHAW CINEMATOGRAPHER JIM DENAULT BRADFORD SIMPSON
EXECUTIVE PRODUCERS PAMELA KOFFLER, JONATHAN SEHRING, CAROLINE KAPLAN, JOHN SLOSS
PRODUCED BY JEFFREY SHARP, JOHN HART, EVA KOLODNER, CHRISTINE VACHON
WRITTEN BY KIMBERLY PEIRCE, ANDY BIENEN DIRECTED BY KIMBERLY PEIRCE
SOUNDTRACK AVAILABLE ON KOCH
SEARCHLIGHT
www.boysdontcry.be

NEW QUEER CINEMA

New queer cinema grew out of the American indie scene, but soon became a distinct, if diverse, movement in itself. The popularity of the films helped raise awareness of issues regarding gender and sexuality, which often counter mainstream representations of LGBTQ life and culture. New queer cinema also explored a world still living in the shadow of the AIDS crisis.

The critic B. Ruby Rich first coined the term "new queer cinema" in 1992 in an article for the film journal *Sight & Sound*. By that time, a number of key films had already been released. For example, Todd Haynes, who would come to be seen as a leading figure, had already made the cine-literate *Poison* (1991). The film's triple-narrative exploration of identity and sexuality is reflected in its artful, ambiguous poster. Fractured identities, played out by Keanu Reeves and River Phoenix, were also key to the appeal of Gus Van Sant's critically acclaimed *My Own Private Idaho* (1991). Next, Van Sant made *Even Cowgirls Get the Blues* (1993) and then returned to queer cinema in 2008 with the Academy Award-winning *Milk*.

Alongside Haynes, Tom Kalin directed a queer take on the Leopold and Loeb story titled *Swoon* (1992), whose poster image recalls German expressionism. In addition, Gregg Araki made *The Living End* (1992), *Totally F***ed Up* (1993), and *The Doom Generation* (1995), which were promoted for their visceral qualities and nihilistic edge.

Rose Troche's *Go Fish* (1994) was one of the key lesbian-themed features of the decade. It sensitively charts the burgeoning relationship between two women. Likewise, Lisa Cholodenko's later *High Art* (1998) offers an intelligent account of a woman's increasing attraction to her neighbor. The posters for both films accentuate the intimacy of their characters' relationships.

As transgender issues became more prominent in our culture, cinema followed suit. Kimberly Peirce's *Boys Don't Cry* (1999) is based on the true story of Brandon Teena, a US trans man who was brutally murdered. Hilary Swank won an Academy Award for her performance, but the film's artwork smartly avoids simple genre classification. The success of that film also preempted a shift in queer cinema in the 2000s, which saw mainstream productions such as *Brokeback Mountain* (2005), *Milk*, and *The Kids Are All Right* (2010) play to large audiences.

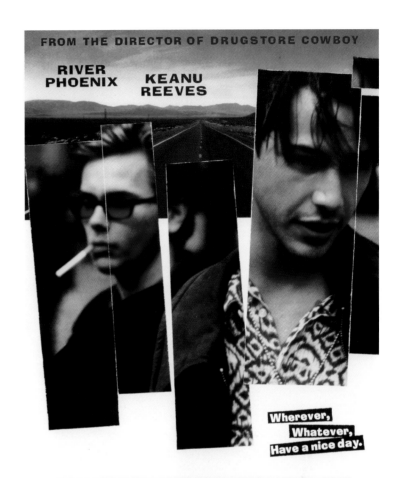

OPPOSITE

Boys Don't Cry (1999)
Like the accompanying poster, which only reveals the lower half of Hilary Swank's face and body, this image blurs gender classification. Instead, we are invited to look at the person and not judge by conventions.

ABOVE

My Own Private Idaho (1991)
The fractured images of Keanu Reeves and River Phoenix's characters accurately represent their psychological state, while the open road either hints at a destination yet reached or the possibility of escape.

NEO-NOIR

No less dark or labyrinthine in exploring moral conundrums than the film noir thrillers that preceded it, the neo-noir genre has been a presence in cinema since the 1960s. Key examples include *The Long Goodbye* (1973), *Chinatown* (1974), *The Postman Always Rings Twice* (1981), and *Blood Simple* (1984). By the 1990s, neo-noir had diversified into different avenues.

John Dahl's *Red Rock West* (1993) is an archetypal neo-noir and offers up a perfect slice of Texarkana, with Nicolas Cage's huckster caught between a double-dealing couple and a ruthless assassin. It is a perfectly executed thriller, whose poster hints at its violence. Dahl went further in exploring the lives of remorseless characters with *The Last Seduction* (1994), in which Linda Fiorentino plays one of the finest femme fatales in contemporary cinema. She was the film's selling point and presented as a modern variation of Veronica Lake.

Two women hold all the cards in *Bound* (1996), which offers audiences a queer take on the genre. Visually stylish and cleverly plotted, the film successfully balances its crime story with the tale of two women falling in love, although never fully enough to trust one another. Like Fiorentino in *The Last Seduction*, Jennifer Tilly and Gina Gershon were *Bound*'s selling point.

Two different visions of Los Angeles appear in *Devil in a Blue Dress* (1995) and *L.A. Confidential* (1997). Both unfold in the immediate aftermath of World War II—as evinced by the characters' costumes in the promotional artwork—and play to audiences' knowledge of the films from this period. However, *Devil in a Blue Dress* is a portrait of life for black people during this era, whereas *L.A. Confidential* explores the corruption endemic in the upper echelons of the city's white society.

The poster for *The Usual Suspects* (1995) could be from any era, with its protagonists standing in a police lineup, and it is this familiarity with the tropes of the noir genre that allows director Bryan Singer to play with audience expectations. David Lynch employed a similar tactic with *Lost Highway* (1997), featuring a guy driving late at night on an open road and an archetypal femme fatale in the form of Patricia Arquette's platinum blond. Although most filmmakers were content to stay within the criminal fraternity, Lynch takes his audience into a surreal, nightmarish world that touches on horror.

L.A. Confidential (1997)
The title design harks back to classical Hollywood, but the cast list is more contemporary. The overall look plays with nostalgia for Tinseltown's past while imbuing it with a modern spin.

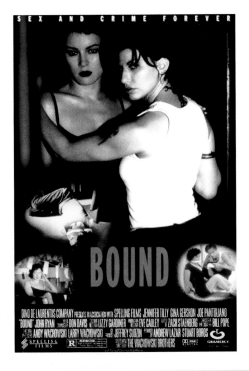

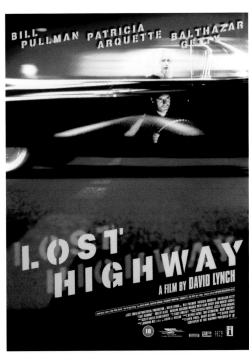

TOP LEFT

Bound (1996)

The tinted main image implies something illicit, reinforced by the characters' expressions, while the inserts suggest one interpretation of the film's title.

TOP MIDDLE

Lost Highway (1997)

Patricia Arquette appears like a dream over Bill Pullman's late night driver. But his car transforms into a highway. Together, they present the road movie as a nightmare.

TOP RIGHT

Devil in a Blue Dress (1995)

The shadows, Denzel Washington's hat, and the femme fatale figure all point to Carl Franklin's film being an African American take on the classic film noir.

ABOVE

Red Rock West (1993)

In this simple design for a slice of Texas noir, the film's title fractures the characters' features, thereby emphasizing the flawed personality of each one.

There are some places in the universe
you don't go alone.

ALIENS
The New Movie

TWENTIETH CENTURY FOX Presents A BRANDYWINE Production A JAMES CAMERON Film ALIENS SIGOURNEY WEAVER Music by JAMES HORNER
Executive Producers GORDON CARROLL, DAVID GILER and WALTER HILL Based on Characters Created by DAN O'BANNON and RONALD SHUSETT Story by JAMES CAMERON
and DAVID GILER & WALTER HILL Screenplay by JAMES CAMERON Produced by GALE ANNE HURD Directed by JAMES CAMERON Prints by DeLuxe 20th CENTURY FOX ™

 DOLBY STEREO ®
IN SELECTED THEATRES   READ THE WARNER BOOK   Original Soundtrack Available On
Varese Sarabande Records And Cassettes   © 1986 TWENTIETH CENTURY FOX

THE FEMALE ACTION HERO

The action movie has never been solely the domain of men, but the way in which action films are sold to audiences has seen them skew more toward male characters. Only in rare exceptions, outside of specific genres, has a women been seen as the action lead in mainstream cinema. However, times have changed, and since the 1990s there has been a shift in the way female-led action movies are promoted.

Joan Crawford in *Johnny Guitar* (1954) is a rare example in classical Hollywood of an A-list female star dominating the poster for a Western, wearing a holster and looking as though she is about to draw. Elsewhere, even if a female character was tough, she may not have been portrayed as such in a film's artwork. Furthermore, some of the key female action characters from recent years never appeared on their film's posters. Ellen Ripley and Sarah Connor were leading female action characters of the 1980s and 1990s, but neither of them was featured in the artwork for the *Alien* and *Terminator* series. Compare that to the Blaxploitation films of the 1970s, with Pam Grier and Tamara Dobson (see page 204), or the many Hong Kong martial arts films of the 1960s and 1970s that regularly featured female fighters.

In 1990, Anne Parillaud played an ex-drug addict-turned-assassin in Luc Besson's *La Femme Nikita*. It began a wave of films that not only starred women in action roles, but also placed them front and center on the posters. *Thelma & Louise* (1991, see page 261) came next, offering a refreshing take on the road movie, the action film, and the way women and men are represented in terms of their relations with one another. One of that film's stars, Geena Davis, went on to take the lead in the poorly executed pirate adventure *Cutthroat Island* (1995), then fared better in *The Long Kiss Goodnight* (1996). Written by Shane Black—the brains, with Joel Silver, behind the *Lethal Weapon* series and other high-octane action films—Davis' role as a super-assassin with amnesia became the template for subsequent female action roles, such as Angelina Jolie's CIA agent in *Salt* (2010) and Charlize Theron's MI6 agent in *Atomic Blonde* (2017). There is also a link to Steven Soderbergh's thriller *Haywire* (2011), starring Gina Carano as special agent Mallory Kane, who, like Uma Thurman as The Bride in *Kill Bill* (2003), runs circles around her male adversaries.

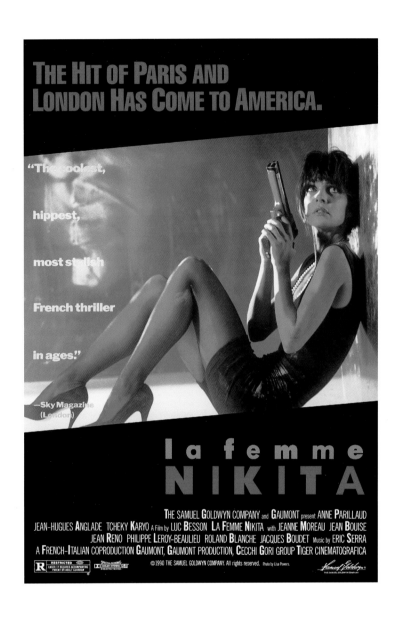

OPPOSITE

Aliens (1986)
Ripley is the star of James Cameron's sequel and the literal "poster girl" for the modern female action hero—not that the role completely extinguishes her maternal instincts.

ABOVE

La Femme Nikita (1990)
The ghost of Cinéma du look (see page 229) hovers over these neon blue hues. However, the contrast of Anne Parillaud's dress and shoes with her gun pose suggests a sly humor.

DIRECTOR STUDY
PEDRO ALMODÓVAR

OPPOSITE

Pepi, Luci, Bom and Other Girls Like Mom (1980)
A cartoon strip and a soap opera, Ceesepe's design has the actors introduce themselves and features frames that hint at the narratives the film encompasses. Like so many poster designs for an Almodóvar film, the color red looms large.

BELOW LEFT

What Have I Done to Deserve This? (1984)
Ivan Zulueta's downbeat design might be bleak, but it is in keeping with the filmmaker's desire to draw on Italian neorealism. There is humor here, but not as outrageous as it is in other artworks.

BELOW RIGHT

All About My Mother (1999)
Oscar Mariné's artwork for Almodóvar's superlative melodrama is one of the most minimal designs. But its focus on the central character, who most memorably appears in red, hones in on the film's emotional power.

Spanish filmmaker Pedro Almodóvar was a central figure in *La Movida Madrileña*, the art and cultural movement that emerged in the wake of General Franco's death in 1975. As a result, his early films celebrated sexual freedom as the Spanish people won democracy. But he soon branched out to become one of the key filmmakers of his generation.

The themes, artistry, and color of Almodóvar's films have always been present in the posters that promote them. He worked closely on their designs, and with some of Spain's finest graphic artists, in order that they best represent his work. An early collaborator was Carlos Sánchez Pérez—known by his pseudonym Ceesepe—who worked with the filmmaker on his breakthrough sophomore feature *Pepi, Luci, Bom and Other Girls Like Mom* (1980). Presented as a cartoon strip, the poster is playful yet hints at the country's patriarchal streak. Ceesepe later designed the poster for *Law of Desire* (1987), conjuring up an art deco image of domestic life. It is a stark contrast to Jean-Marc Haddad's almost Bressonian design for the French release of the film—a painting

of a bed with its pillow and covers slightly crumpled. But both artists place sex at the heart of their designs.

Another key Almodóvar collaborator was Ivan Zulueta, a filmmaker in his own right. Zulueta's designs for *Labyrinth of Passion* (1982) and *Dark Habits* (1983) are wildly inventive. The former features an arrow plunging into an image that is both a heart and a woman's buttocks. Below it, Hollywood stars comingle. *Dark Habits* sees a tiger don a nun's habit, its paw balancing a nightclub singer. Zulueta's work on *What Have I Done to Deserve This?* (1984) is bleaker, with Carmen Maura's character in front of a run-down apartment block and appearing to hold a lizard. The French and Italian designs for the film, which also feature a lizard, fall short of the complete vision that Zulueta's poster presents.

One of the most famous designs for an Almodóvar film not designed by his regular collaborator Juan Gatti (see overleaf) is Oscar Mariné's simple, beautiful drawing for *All About My Mother* (1999). Evocative in its caricature of Cecilia Roth's grieving mother, it nevertheless keeps the bold colors that tell us this is an Almodóvar film.

JUAN GATTI

Pedro Almodóvar's longest and most fruitful artwork collaboration has been with Juan Gatti. A *Vanity Fair* article once noted: "There are millions of people who have a Gatti in their house, and many do not even know it." His designs for Almodóvar's posters have become almost as fashionable as the films themselves.

Born in Buenos Aires in 1950, Gatti moved to New York in 1978, where he worked with the designer Kenzo Takada, before a trip to Madrid in 1980 led to the role of creative director at CBS Records. While working with the musicians of *La Movida Madrileña*, Gatti encountered Almodóvar, and their collaboration began with the Picasso-inspired poster for *Matador* (1986). The image is loosely based on a painting by the singer Carlos Berlanga, but Gatti's more radical interpretation accentuates the film's extremes.

The project that cemented the collaboration was also Almodóvar's international breakthrough. *Women on the Verge of a Nervous Breakdown* (1988) features a series of designs that draw on the work of Alexey Brodovitch for *Harper's Bazaar* in the 1950s—a combination of faces and lines. Gatti followed it with a no less bold approach to *Tie Me Up! Tie Me Down!* (1989), which recalls Saul

Bass' misshapen blocks of color, but far louder and more boisterous. One version of the poster replaces the cutouts with stills in the color blocks, highlighting the star status of Antonio Banderas and Victoria Abril.

High Heels (1991) and the controversial *Kika* (1993) found Gatti at his most mischievous. For the former, the stiletto of a shoe transforms into the barrel of a gun, and for *Kika* the cast are arranged in provocative poses. The understated *The Flower of My Secret* (1995) is sensuous in its use of roses designed like a heart, with the silhouette of a woman typing laid on top, but the golden bodies pressed against each other in the poster for *Live Flesh* (1997) highlights Almodóvar at his most sensual. If the image is subtle, the accompanying type is bold and forthright, hinting at the two dimensions of the director's lusty crime drama.

More recently, Gatti's designs for Almodóvar have run the gamut between the minimalism of *Bad Education* (2004) and the florid style of *Volver* (2006) and *Broken Embraces* (2009). They are designed around the films' star Penélope Cruz, but retain the signature style that defines Gatti's collaboration with the filmmaker.

BELOW LEFT

Broken Embraces (2009)
Red is a key color for Gatti and Almodóvar. Here, it appears in a more subdued form, while the Warhol-esque image of Cruz is a play on the malleability of personal identity.

BELOW RIGHT

High Heels (1991)
Autumn Sonata (1978) may have inspired this film, but it is unlikely Ingmar Bergman would have been happy with such an outrageous image. It implies everything is not always as it seems.

OPPOSITE
CLOCKWISE FROM TOP LEFT

Bad Education (2004)
This is one of Gatti's most effective designs. The red circle hints at a tragedy in the protagonist's past, destroying the innocence of childhood.

Live Flesh (1997)
Gatti's sensual image for Almodóvar's adaptation of Ruth Rendell's thriller appears to involve two figures. But the placement of the limbs suggests otherwise.

Women on the Verge of a Nervous Breakdown (1988)
Gatti's design rearranges the components of a woman's face and inserts a torso below the title. It creates an everywoman— the embodiment of the ensemble cast.

Volver (2006)
This film channels the Italian neorealist movies of the 1940s. The poster captures Penélope Cruz as Anna Magnani once was, with the flowers hinting at magical realist elements.

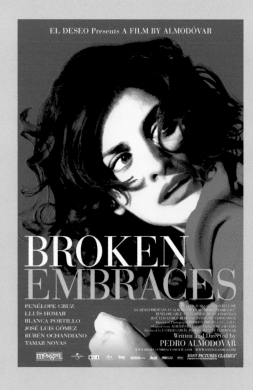

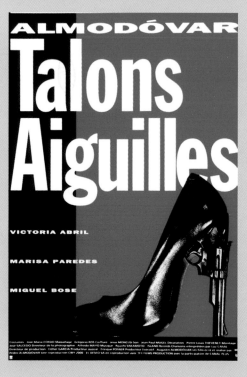

El Deseo présente, avec la collaboration de TVE et Canal+ Espagne

un film de
ALMODÓVAR

La Mauvaise Education

GAEL GARCÍA BERNAL   FELE MARTÍNEZ   DANIEL GIMÉNEZ CACHO
LLUIS HOMAR   FRANCISCO BOIRA   JAVIER CÁMARA
José Luis Alcaine   José Salcedo   Alberto Iglesias
Esther García   Agustín Almodóvar
Écrit et Dirigé par **PEDRO ALMODÓVAR**

Sony Music   www.lamauvaiseeducation-lefilm.com

CIBY 2000 PRESENTE
UN FILM DE ALMODÓVAR

EN CHAIR
ET EN OS

JAVIER BARDEM   FRANCESCA NERI   LIBERTO RABAL
ANGELA MOLINA   JOSE SANCHO   AVEC LA PARTICIPATION DE PENELOPE CRUZ ET PILAR BARDEM
D'APRÈS LE ROMAN DE RUTH RENDELL "LIVE FLESH" MUSIQUE ALBERTO IGLESIAS MONTAGE JOSE SALCEDO DECORATEUR ANTXON GOMEZ
COSTUMES JOSE Mª DE COSSIO MAQUILLAGE JUAN PEDRO HERNANDEZ PRODUCTEUR EXECUTIF AGUSTIN ALMODOVAR DIRECTEUR DE LA PHOTOGRAPHIE AFFONSO BEATO
DIRECTION DE PRODUCTION ESTHER GARCIA UNE COPRODUCTION CIBY 2000 / EL DESEO, S.A. / FRANCE 3 CINEMA
CIBY 2000   **ECRIT ET RÉALISÉ PAR PEDRO ALMODÓVAR**   CIBY Distribution

EL DESEO PRÉSENTE UN FILM DE
ALMODÓVAR

VOLVER

PENÉLOPE CRUZ   CARMEN MAURA   LOLA DUEÑAS
BLANCA PORTILLO   YOHANA COBO   ET CHUS LAMPREAVE
DIRECTEUR DE LA PHOTOGRAPHIE JOSÉ LUIS ALCAINE   MONTAGE JOSÉ SALCEDO
PRODUCTEUR EXÉCUTIF AGUSTÍN ALMODÓVAR   PRODUIT PAR ESTHER GARCÍA
inter   CANAL+   ÉCRIT ET RÉALISÉ PAR **PEDRO ALMODÓVAR**   WWW.VOLVER-LEFILM.COM

EL DESEO presenta

MUJERES
al borde de un ataque de NERVIOS

un film de
ALMODÓVAR

Carmen Maura
Antonio Banderas
Julieta Serrano

María Barranco
Rossy de Palma
Guillermo Montesinos
Kiti Manver
Chus Lampreave
Yayo Calvo
Loles León
Ángel de Andrés López
y la colaboración de
Fernando Guillén
fotografía José Mª de Cossío
sonido Gilles Ortión
producción ejecutiva Esther García
montaje José Salcedo
música Bernardo Bonezzi
director de fotografía José Luis Alcaine
producción Antonio Llorens
productor ejecutivo Agustín Almodóvar

guión y dirección
Pedro Almodóvar

el deseo

FIN-DE-SIÈCLE CINEMA

Science fiction was arguably the most dominant blockbuster genre in the 1990s. The subject matter and tone of these films varied greatly, but the one overriding theme dealt with the destruction of the Earth. With less than a decade before the end of the millennium, some filmmakers were indulging our appetite for end of the world scenarios.

No film better encapsulated imminent global catastrophe than *Independence Day* (1996). As with the majority of such disaster epics (these films were the 1990s incarnation of 1970s disaster movies), the United States was generally the focus of attention. This worked in director Roland Emmerich's favor with his story of a large-scale alien invasion, as it allowed him to destroy buildings that were recognized around the world. Most audiences were sold on the image of a vast spaceship hovering menacingly over Manhattan.

Terminator 2: Judgment Day (1991) began the decade with a distinctly 1980s style of marketing, emphasizing action star Arnold Schwarzenegger, but *Delicatessen* (1991) took a more subtle approach to an otherworldly place, with its image of a pig and a butcher's knife. It merely hints at the strange and dangerous world that exists in Jean-Pierre Jeunet and Marc Caro's film. Another French filmmaker, Luc Besson, had approached the end of the world as we know it with his directorial debut, *The Last Battle* (1983), but his *The Fifth Element* (1997) offers up a stylized vision of the future. It was made on the scale of a big-budget Hollywood film but was wilder, as evinced in its more abstract promotional artwork.

If *Gattaca* (1997) gives us hope for the future in Ethan Hawke and Uma Thurman's optimistic space adventurers, Kathryn Bigelow's *Strange Days* (1995) suggests that the world has already gone to hell, Terry Gilliam's *Twelve Monkeys* (1995) sees the end right around the corner, and Paul Verhoeven's celebrated trilogy of *RoboCop* (1987), *Total Recall* (1990), and *Starship Troopers* (1997) envisions our planet as a vast corporate police state. Even the jocular *Men in Black* (1997) has to deal with at least one global threat on a daily basis. And in *The Matrix* (1999), arguably the bleakest blockbuster to end the century, the Wachowskis pit leather-clad rebels against a computer system that has rendered us little more than a power source for its operating system.

Delicatessen (1991)
This minimalist design perfectly captures the surreal tone and the visually dark aesthetic of Jeunet and Caro's inventive, if grisly world. In particular, it hints at the film's blackly comic humor.

TOP

Independence Day (1996)
The 1990s science fiction equivalent of the 1950s biblical epic, Roland Emmerich's film is the mothership of the blockbuster alien invasion movies. This expansive image of an attack on New York highlights the scale of what is to come.

BOTTOM

The Fifth Element (1997)
Luc Besson's end of the world adventure is notable for its bold visual aesthetic. The poster for the film tones down the colorful cityscape in order to contrast it with the key elements of the plot.

THE ESSENCE OF SPIELBERG

Since the release of *Jaws* in the summer of 1975, the promotional campaigns behind Steven Spielberg's films have been fine-tuned to ensure their maxim impact with audiences. From the summer tentpole movies to the more serious dramas, his films have often been defined by a concept and distilled to their essence in order for them to achieve success.

After *Jaws* (see page 217) came *Close Encounters of the Third Kind* (1977), the poster for which features a bright light at the end of a straight road and hints at the presence of something otherworldly in our path. What isn't clear is its intentions. A single concept also drove John Alvin's main artwork for *E.T. the Extra-Terrestrial* (1982, see page 223)—human contact with alien life form. This time, the connection between an alien and a young boy underpins the bond of friendship.

Alvin was one of Spielberg's key collaborators throughout the 1980s. He designed the poster featuring the silhouetted images of Whoopi Goldberg's character in *The Color Purple* (1985) and Richard Dreyfus holding Holly Hunter against the spectral light of heaven for *Always* (1989). However, it was Alvin's artwork for *Empire of the Sun* (1987) that hinted at the way many

of Spielberg's films would be promoted in the future. A boy runs up a hill, carrying his toy plane, as a real fighter plane falls in flames from the sky and against a red and yellow sun. That single image defined *Empire of the Sun*'s narrative. Alvin designed something simpler for *Hook* (1991), giving viewers nothing but the image of the villain's hooked prosthetic.

Two years later, audiences became aware of *Jurassic Park* (1993) via its logo. In a similarly minimal way, *A.I. Artificial Intelligence* (2001) uses the outline of a boy to help compose the first two letters of the film's title. Names and numbers are traced across the design of *Schindler's List* (1993), but it is the contact between the adult and child's hands in Georgia Young's design that is key to the humanity of the film. Likewise, with the image of a single soldier appearing on the brow of a hill in the poster for *Saving Private Ryan* (1998), we see both one man's story and, as he is silhouetted, the story of millions who fought in World War II.

As such, although a film about a theme park populated by dinosaurs and a drama detailing some of the worst atrocities of humankind might seem worlds apart, they have something in common.

BELOW LEFT

Saving Private Ryan (1998)
Arguably the most effective of the silhouette designs for a Spielberg film, this presents a single US soldier as an everyman.

BELOW RIGHT

Jurassic Park (1993)
As one of the first blockbusters to fully explore the potential of CGI technology, the genius of the *Jurassic Park* campaign lay in its refusal to reveal anything.

OPPOSITE
CLOCKWISE FROM TOP LEFT

A.I. Artificial Intelligence (2001)
The logo is one of the cleverest for any Spielberg poster. It ponders on the idea that a sentient being could be engineered that might possess more humanity than its creators.

Schindler's List (1993)
Georgia Young's design was chosen over the more austere image created by Saul Bass. The simple gesture, overlaid with the names of the dead, hints at humanity amid the horror of the Holocaust.

Empire of the Sun (1987)
John Alvin's juxtaposition of a boy playing with his toy plane and the real plane crashing to Earth hints at Spielberg's approach to J. G. Ballard's Bildungsroman. It is a war film presented through the prism of childhood.

Hook (1991)
The main poster featured Robin Williams' grown-up Pan and Dustin Hoffman's aged nemesis. But this poster is an archetypal Alvin/Spielberg teaser, hinting at a revisionist take on J. M. Barrie's fable.

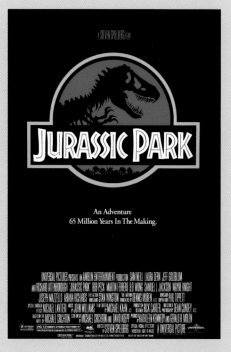

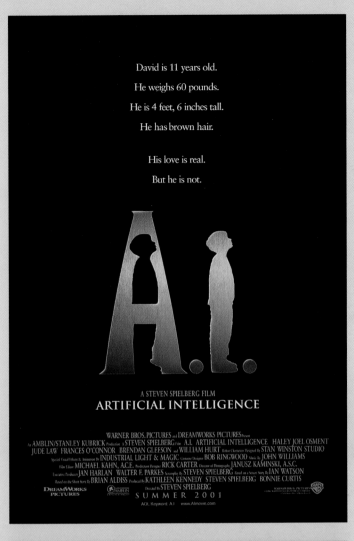

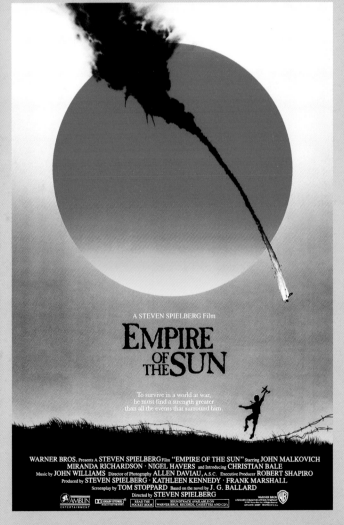

Someone has taken their love of scary movies one step too far.
Solving this mystery is going to be murder.

S C R E A M

DAVID
ARQUETTE
NEVE
CAMPBELL
COURTENEY
COX
MATTHEW
LILLARD
ROSE
McGOWAN
SKEET
ULRICH
and
DREW
BARRYMORE

DIMENSION FILMS PRESENTS A WOODS ENTERTAINMENT A WES CRAVEN FILM "SCREAM" MUSIC BY MARCO BELTRAMI EDITED BY PATRICK LUSSIER PRODUCTION DESIGNER BRUCE ALAN MILLER
DIRECTOR OF PHOTOGRAPHY MARK IRWIN A.S.C. CO-PRODUCER DIXIE J. CAPP CO-EXECUTIVE PRODUCERS STUART M. BESSER EXECUTIVE PRODUCERS BOB WEINSTEIN HARVEY WEINSTEIN AND MARIANNE MADDALENA WRITTEN BY KEVIN WILLIAMSON
WOODS PRODUCED BY CARY WOODS AND CATHY KONRAD DIRECTED BY WES CRAVEN DIMENSION
SOUNDTRACK AVAILABLE ON TVT SOUNDTRAX Visit DIMENSION FILMS on the web at: http://www.dimensionfilms.com

THE HIGHLY ACCLAIMED NEW THRILLER FROM WES CRAVEN

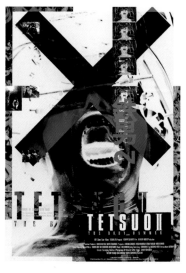

ABOVE

Scream (1996)
The figure in the poster for Wes Craven's smart exercise in postmodern horror could be Drew Barrymore's hapless victim. Or it could be the audience—victims of the film's upending of horror conventions.

TOP RIGHT

Tetsuo II: Body Hammer (1992)
Shinya Tsukamoto's cyperpunk original was a low-budget classic. Its sequel is bigger but just as difficult to pigeonhole. The artwork conveys a chaotic world and a man in a state of transformation.

BOTTOM RIGHT

Ring (1998)
The artwork for Hideo Nakata's superior version of the possessed videotape horror is ambiguous and unsettling. The ring here, with Sadako at its center, could be the focus ring of a camera lens.

A NEW BREED OF HORROR

From the late 1960s onward, the horror genre transformed at a rapid pace. By the 1990s, its legacy was ripe for reinvention or even parody, and witnessed a postmodern rehashing of familiar tropes. At the same time, there was international interest in the growing number of horror films emerging from Asia, offering a culturally specific and unsettling vision of the supernatural and undead.

The decade began with Jonathan Demme's psychological thriller *The Silence of the Lambs* (1991, see page 261) becoming the first horror film to win Best Picture at the Academy Awards. The following year, Francis Ford Coppola's *Bram Stoker's Dracula* (1992) offered horror on a lavish scale, but it was bloodless compared with Abel Ferrara's *The Addiction* (1995), whose simple poster promises something far bleaker and unsettling—a very modern vampire. Robert Rodriguez then spliced the thriller and vampire movie together with *From Dusk Till Dawn* (1996), but another horror film released that year experimented more formally with horror tropes.

Wes Craven had edged toward postmodern horror with his inventive *New Nightmare* (1994), but it was *Scream* (1996) that thoroughly deconstructed the slasher movie and horror genre. The poster—featuring nothing more than a terrified young woman—not only emphasizes the film's potential to scare but also plays on its knowingness. Similarly, *The Blair Witch Project* (1999) required little more than the fearful expression on its protagonist's face, but in a very different context. The low-budget hit harked back to the lost footage narrative that had been used in *Cannibal Holocaust* (1980). The publicity for the film implies that the events actually took place, and its success spawned countless imitations.

Although Shinya Tsukamoto hinted at a different kind of horror with his *Tetsuo* series (1989–2009), Hideo Nakata's *Ring* (1998) plays on the presence of an old world in modern technology and features the innovative use of filmmaking techniques to inspire fear. It was also significant in attracting international attention to the Asian horror film. With their focus on the presence of malevolent spirits in domestic spaces, films such as *Dark Water*, *The Eye*, *Ju-on: The Grudge* (all 2002), and *A Tale of Two Sisters* (2003) marked another stage in the development of the horror cycle.

ABOVE

The Blair Witch Project (1999)
The marketing for this ultra-low-budget horror made a virtue out of its no-frills imagery, and was bolstered by an Internet campaign that implied the events depicted in the film were real.

The key posters of the 1990s highlight the disparate nature of cinema over the course of the decade. There is no single movement or style, but each of the images represents a powerful cultural shift in some way.

The Silence of the Lambs (1991) wasn't just another horror film. Not since *The Exorcist* (1973) or *The Shining* (1980) had audiences been so drawn to the genre, as FBI agent Clarice Starling fights a battle of wills with Dr. Hannibal Lecter in the hunt for a serial killer. It was only the third film to win the "Big Five" Academy Awards (for Best Picture, Director, Leading Actress, Leading Actor, and Screenplay), and the chilling poster is no less impressive.

Ridley Scott's road movie pits Geena Davis' Thelma and Susan Sarandon's Louise against a restrictive and morally hypocritical patriarchal society. Written by Callie Khouri, *Thelma & Louise* (1991) tells the story of two women on a road trip who are, at various points, abused, attacked, robbed, and ultimately forced to defend themselves. With no options remaining, they turn to crime. The poster promises an open road, but it soon becomes a dead end.

Despite having only two director credits to his name, Quentin Tarantino was a ubiquitous presence in US cinema in the 1990s. If *Reservoir Dogs* (1991) was a fine example of low-budget filmmaking, *Pulp Fiction* (1994) cemented the director's credentials. Like its poster, the film mined US popular culture to produce a sprawling tale of criminal lives, which rattles along thanks to the sharp dialogue.

Of the French films produced in the 1990s, few caused as many waves as Mathieu Kassovitz's *La Haine* (1995), with its account of twenty-four hours in the lives of three young men from the banlieue. Located very much in the present (mid 1990s), Kassovitz's film can be seen as the French *Do the Right Thing* (1989): a tough and confrontational film that is unafraid to shine a light on racism and social segregation. Likewise, Danny Boyle's *Trainspotting* (1996) offers a sobering but fitfully funny account of the drugs scene in 1990s Scotland. Its various excursions into the surreal are countered with graphic depictions of drug abuse and its effects. Alongside the driving soundtrack, the poster helped make *Trainspotting* one of the defining British films of the decade.

BELOW

Trainspotting (1996)
Press screenings far in advance of a film release allowed distributors to include a review quote in the advance publicity. Here, a review caption is employed part of a bold advertising campaign for Danny Boyle's era-defining movie.

OPPOSITE
CLOCKWISE FROM TOP LEFT

The Silence of the Lambs (1991)
The image on the back of the death's-head moth is a miniature of the photograph *In Voluptas Mors* (1951) by Salvador Dalí and Philippe Halsman. Placed over Clarice's mouth, it resembles a death mask.

La Haine (1995)
The top image is fueled by rage. It is directed at the only kind of life the character has known, detailed in the images below the credits. It is confrontational and impossible to ignore.

Thelma and Louise (1991)
There is a sense of a journey beginning with this poster. The open road lies before the two women, and in the Polaroid they appear happy. The only constant, as their journey becomes bleaker, is their friendship.

Pulp Fiction (1994)
This is not so much a poster for a film as the adaptation of a cover for the kind of fiction that inspired Quentin Tarantino to create a world populated by colorful criminals from all walks of life.

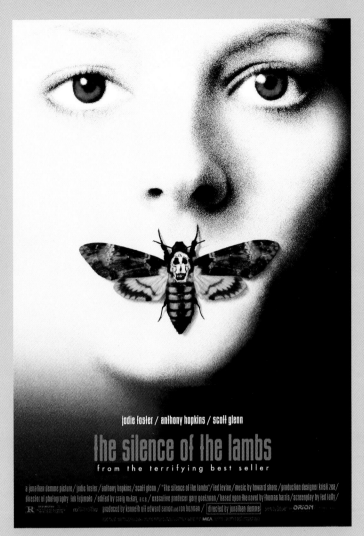

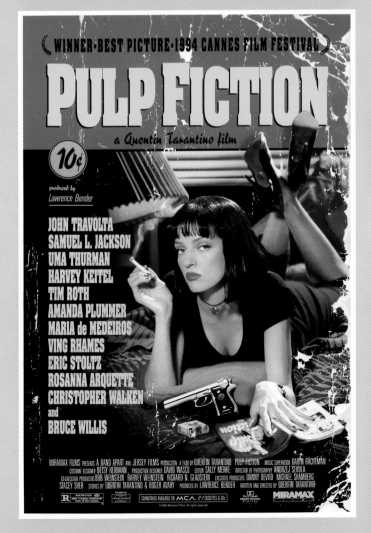

2000s

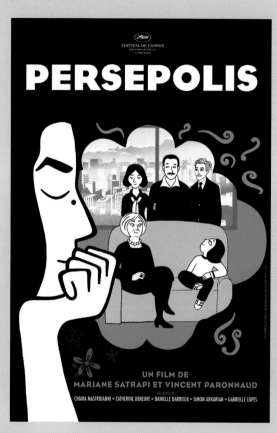

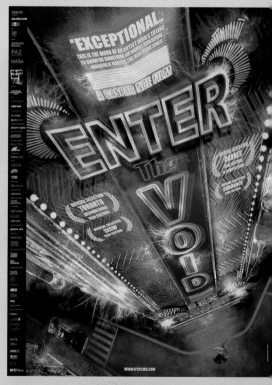

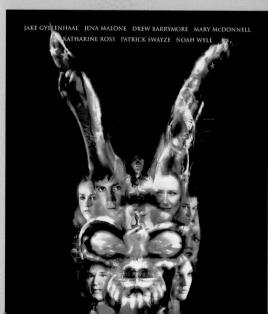

In the 2000s, the homogenization of movie poster design around the world became more prevalent. The escalation in the size of the budgets for mainstream Hollywood fare meant that success was not guaranteed by the box office results of the United States alone; a film also had to succeed in foreign territories. To ensure this, promotional campaigns were rolled out on a global basis.

The Marvel and DC superhero movies best exemplify the campaigns waged by major studios. Films often open on different dates across multiple, if not all, territories, and the marketing campaigns for them are planned like military campaigns. The aim is to find a common factor that appeals to as large a group of people as possible. Although the underlying idea behind the movie poster remains the same—to sell the film based on its star, genre, or concept—the desire to give it universal appeal led to a particular style of design that was replicated, albeit with the inclusion of a few changes, with each film.

There were exceptions to this approach, but they tended to exist as outliers—films with which studios could afford to take a chance because they were outside the main canon. In addition, there is the case of Christopher Nolan, whose singular vision, melded with his remarkable success, made him one of the few mainstream filmmakers to have an extraordinary degree of control over his films.

Unlike in previous decades, there were no clear design trends in the 2000s. Some films opted for a retro approach to their look, such as the Blue Note album cover design for *La La Land* (2016). Animation ran the gamut from the simple representation of characters to more complex hand-drawn images. Stars still featured heavily on posters around the world, particularly in India, where the most popular Bollywood actors now occupy the same revered position that Hollywood stars enjoyed in the golden age. However, there is no longer any strict methodology as to how they are presented. Technology has had a significant impact on poster design and its function, too, perhaps even redefining its role.

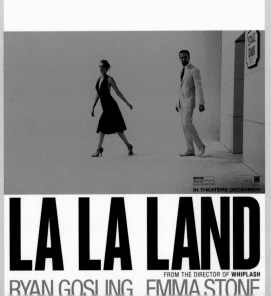

The lengthy nature of the filmmaking process means that responses to world events take time to appear on screen. The terrorist attacks on September 11, 2001, were no exception. Aside from the short film portmanteau *11'09''01 – September 11* (2002) and the speedily produced documentaries comprising footage shot that day, it was a few years before films dealing with the attack, the planning behind it, and its aftermath appeared in cinemas. However, they soon became a regular presence on the screen and led to other films that grappled with the trajectory along which the world has moved in the years since.

The films that relate to 9/11 can be divided into thematic categories. Some of the dramas deal directly with the events themselves. The most chilling is *United 93* (2006), directed by Paul Greengrass,which imagines the panic and terror aboard the plane before it crashes into a field in Pennsylvania, killing all on board. The poster for the film is understated, but the knowledge of what happened makes the seemingly innocuous image of a plane flying past the Statue of Liberty profoundly unsettling.

Oliver Stone's *World Trade Center* (2006) had a similar aim, but was filmed from the perspective of rescuers trapped in the rubble of the buildings. The poster is arguably more grandiose than the one for Greengrass' film: the twin towers are intact, with two figures standing between them. Stone emphasizes the importance of the human story in this tragedy, no matter its scale.

While *The Hamburg Cell* (2004) is one of the few films to examine the intense planning that led to the attacks and *Charlie Wilson's War* (2007) casts its gaze even further back in order to understand Afghanistan–American relations at the time of the Russian occupation of the country, other films look at events that have panned out since. The posters for *Rendition*, *Lions for Lambs*, and *In the Valley of Elah* (all 2007) feature their lead actors with somber expressions, underpinning the weight of the themes with which each film grapples. *Rendition* is arguably the most effective, the environment behind each character indicating their role in the complex drama.

Films such as *Reign Over Me* (2007), *The Space Between* (2010), *Remember Me* (2010), and *Extremely Loud and Incredibly Close* (2011) prioritize the personal

ABOVE

Zero Dark Thirty (2012)
Redacted text became a signifier of sanctioned covert military operations and is employed here to underpin the secrecy with which the operation to kill Osama Bin Laden was carried out.

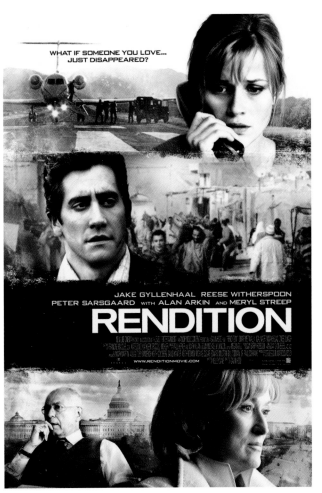

CLOCKWISE FROM TOP LEFT

World Trade Center (2006)
The image promoting Oliver Stone's film highlights the iconic status of the two main World Trade Center towers, while intimating the importance of the people trapped in them.

Rendition (2007)
A stock design for a Hollywood drama is given dramatic heft by the absorbing backdrops, which provide context to the worlds in which each of the characters exists.

Osama (2003)
The title was always going to attract attention, but its use becomes painfully resonant in detailing the plight of the eponymous girl. In this design, the title also acts as the bars that withhold her freedom.

over the political, and the posters for each film feature no direct reference to the attacks. *Reign Over Me* and *The Space Between* both employ sunlight as a metaphor for the darkness of the present and the hope that existed in the past or might exist in the future. In the case of the former, a seasonal shift denotes tumultuous change for Adam Sandler's character. The sun lights up the street behind him, presumably from when his wife was still alive, while the present and near future are cast in the gray light of a bleak winter.

Siddiq Barmak's *Osama* (2003) was the first film to be made in Afghanistan after the defeat of the Taliban, and it remains one of the most compelling and disturbing indictments of the regime. Set while the Taliban were still in power, it follows a young girl who pretends to be a boy in order to help her family survive. The poster depicts the main character locked behind her false name, an image that presages the character's grim fate in the film.

A similar design, featuring images within the film's title, was used for one of the posters promoting *Zero Dark Thirty* (2012), directed by Kathryn Bigelow. An alternative poster features only the film's title on a plain background, but the words are almost indiscernible as though they have been redacted. *Syriana* (2005), which attempts to grapple with Middle Eastern and Gulf affairs in the light of the attacks, follows a similar route with its artwork. George Clooney plays the character whom bureaucrats are attempting to silence, and his eyes and mouth are torn out from the poster image.

Genre cinema also entered the fray. The opening attack in *War of the Worlds* (2005) clearly references the images seen around the world, showing people walking through Lower Manhattan covered in dust after the collapse of the World Trade Center towers. *The Dark Knight* (2008) grapples more with the nature of terror and its impact upon the collective psyche, through the way in which Heath Ledger's Joker wreaks havoc upon Gotham. Frank Darabont's *The Mist* (2007) takes a Stephen King novella from 1980 and creates a powerful allegory regarding the rise in religious extremism. The film provides a razor-sharp satire of Bush-era America and tells a powerful horror tale whose ending makes *The Mist* one of the bleakest genre films of the decade.

Cloverfield (2008) remains arguably the most potent film to inflect the mood created by the 9/11 attacks within a genre narrative. It details an attack by an unidentified alien upon Manhattan, opening with Lady Liberty's head being lopped off and lobbed into a building near to a party attended by the film's protagonists. The film's poster, which echoes the artwork for *United 93*, can be seen as a sobering update of the paranoid science fiction movies of the 1950s.

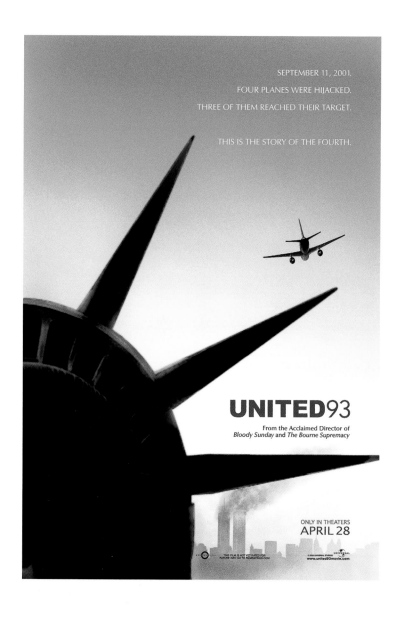

SOME THING HAS FOUND US

A BAD ROBOT PRODUCTION

CLOVERFIELD

PARAMOUNT PICTURES PRESENTS A BAD ROBOT PRODUCTION "CLOVERFIELD" LIZZY CAPLAN JESSICA LUCAS T.J. MILLER MICHAEL STAHL-DAVID MIKE VOGEL ODETTE YUSTMAN VISUAL EFFECTS BY DOUBLE NEGATIVE AND TIPPETT STUDIO
COSTUMES DESIGNED BY ELLEN MIROJNICK EDITED BY KEVIN STITT A.C.E. PRODUCTION DESIGNER MARTIN WHIST DIRECTOR OF PHOTOGRAPHY MICHAEL BONVILLAIN ASC EXECUTIVE PRODUCERS GUY RIEDEL SHERRYL CLARK PRODUCED BY J.J. ABRAMS BRYAN BURK WRITTEN BY DREW GODDARD DIRECTED BY MATT REEVES

 PG-13 PARENTS STRONGLY CAUTIONED
SOME MATERIAL MAY BE INAPPROPRIATE FOR CHILDREN UNDER 13
VIOLENCE, TERROR AND DISTURBING IMAGES

01·18·08

CloverfieldMovie.com

PRINTED IN U.S.A.

ABOVE

Up (2009)
An old man is an unexpected choice as the protagonist of a mainstream family-oriented animation, but *Up* constantly plays against expectations. His expression hints at the film's deadpan humor.

TOP RIGHT

My Life as a Zucchini (2016)
The expressions of the characters from the small French orphanage are wry at best, suggesting trouble in their past lives. This image reflects the subtlety of Claude Barras' sensitive animated drama.

BOTTOM RIGHT

Toy Story 3 (2010)
The gang is back, but this time they all find themselves in peril. There are villains throughout this adventure comedy, but what these characters fear most, evinced by the closing moments, is adulthood.

ANIMATION

Disney's golden age of animation ran from *Steamboat Willie* (1928) to *Sleeping Beauty* (1959). The budget overruns on the latter film were so great that something had to be done to cut costs. It was decided to replace traditional hand inking with Xerography, a process that was significantly cheaper but resulted in a noticeable loss in quality. This move seemed to reflect an era when expediency trumped high standards for many animation studios.

There were a number of significant moments in the world of animation between 1960 and the appearance of a revitalized Disney in the early 1990s. *The Flintstones* first aired on television in 1960 and ushered in a new platform for animators. However, the quality of most television animation remained average. *Watership Down* (1978) was a notable step forward, as it was the first animation to feature Dolby sound. However, the most important film from this period is arguably *Who Framed Roger Rabbit* (1988), which employed state-of-the-art effects to combine live action and animation in a loving homage to the Hollywood of old and the noir thriller.

Disney's *Beauty and the Beast* (1991) not only marked the beginning of a renaissance for the studio and signaled a shift toward computer animation technology, but it also witnessed a change in the way the films were promoted, thanks to John Alvin's softer designs. Since then, the animation world has continued to be in a state of dynamic change. Computer animation has dominated the work of studios such as Pixar Animation Studios and DreamWorks Animation, while other companies have opted for a more traditional approach with their films.

Founded in 1985 and based in Tokyo, Studio Ghibli is run by Hayao Miyazaki and Isao Takahata. It came into being after the success of Miyazaki's feature *Nausicaä of the Valley of the Wind* (1984) and has built a reputation for hand-drawn animation. Miyazaki is not averse to using computer technology, but it has always been employed to embellish upon detailed artwork. The artwork for each film conveys a sense of wonder that is reflected in its narrative, hinting at the magical, transportive nature of animated film. Many of Studio Ghibli's films touch on environmental issues and are not afraid to broach the impact of conflict on human lives, which has resulted in visually breathtaking imagery

ABOVE

The Incredibles (2004)
The poster for Pixar's superhero adventure now looks like an accurate forerunner of the countless designs that have defined the genre over the past decade, albeit with a more playful perspective.

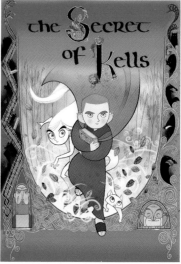

ABOVE

Persepolis (2007)
The artwork here, employing the style of Marjane Satrapi's celebrated graphic novel, plays with memory and the halcyon days of family life in Iran in the lead-up to and during the revolution.

TOP RIGHT

Waltz with Bashir (2008)
Take away the dog tags and gun, and this still from Ari Folman's animated recounting of the Lebanon War in 1982 could have been from a zombie movie in the style of *Land of the Dead* (2005).

MIDDLE RIGHT

The Secret of Kells (2009)
The poster for Tomm Moore and Nora Twomey's film works effectively on two levels: it underpins the beauty and simple style of their animation, and it channels the centuries-old text that inspired it.

BOTTOM RIGHT

Spirited Away (2001)
Chihiro's wide-eyed face underpins the clear lines of Studio Ghibli's house style. But her look of wonder, contrasting with the vast seascape below her, hints at the breadth of Hayao Miyazaki's imagination.

and stories of emotional heft. In 2003, Miyazaki was finally recognized by the Academy of Motion Picture Arts and Sciences and won a Best Animated Feature Academy Award for *Spirited Away* (2001). However, by that time Miyazaki, Takahata, and their studio had already established an enviable reputation for the peerlessness of their films.

A year after Studio Ghibli came into being, Pixar Animation Studios became incorporated, although another decade passed before it became a household name. This resulted from the release of the studio's first feature, *Toy Story* (1995). It was an extraordinary achievement, realized through the use of photorealistic 3D rendering software RenderMan, and Pixar soon became the benchmark to which all other major studio animated features were compared. *Toy Story*'s combination of striking visuals and imaginative storytelling became a feature of almost all Pixar's films, but the best works pushed the envelope of storytelling, to encompass the Chaplin-esque tale of a lonely robot cleaning a planet (*WALL-E*, 2008), a grieving old man who hasn't quite shaken his youthful spirit of adventure (*Up*, 2009), a suburban family coming to terms with their superhuman powers (*The Incredibles*, 2004), a young girl whose mental faculties are—literally—in a state of chaos (*Inside Out*, 2015), and, perhaps most movingly, the characters of *Toy Story* accepting that their owner has outgrown them.

While DreamWorks Animation, which became an independent entity in 2004, scored its own commercial and creative successes with *Shrek* (2001), *Madagascar* (2005), *How to Train Your Dragon* (2010), and their sequels, other, smaller production companies also pushed the boundaries of animation technology and storytelling. Richard Linklater's philosophical *Waking Life* (2001) used the rotoscope technique, wherein actors are filmed with digital video, which is then drawn over to create an animation. *Waltz with Bashir* (2008) also employed innovative techniques in its account of the Lebanon War in 1982, whereas the monochrome *Persepolis* (2007) returned to more traditional hand-drawn methods for its coming-of-age story set against the backdrop of the Iranian Revolution.

As highlighted in the posters for *The Triplets of Belleville* (2003) and *The Secret of Kells* (2009), the animation of both these films is also more traditional, in keeping with the classic feel of their stories. In contrast, the colorful stop-motion animation of *My Life as a Zucchini* (2016) belies the moving account of the children who live in a small French orphanage. Like the best animation, this film is the perfect combination of subject and form.

ABOVE

The Triplets of Belleville (2003)
Sylvain Chomet's animation plays with cultural caricatures and is often as melancholy as it is humorous. This is partly achieved through the muted palette of his backdrops, as highlighted in this poster.

THE SUPERHERO MOVIE

There may come a time in the future when people look back to the early 2000s and wonder why the superhero movie was the dominant form of entertainment. What began as an infrequent series of comic book adaptations has turned into a multi-billion-dollar entertainment industry. The artistry that goes into creating these worlds is impressive, but the way they have been sold has increasingly slipped into a well-trodden formula.

It would be easy to correlate the rise of the superhero film with the world post-9/11. Certainly, films such as *The Dark Knight* and *Iron Man* (both 2008) touch on the role terrorism now plays in our lives. But a trend for superhero movies had been building up before then, as evinced by *Blade* (1998), *X-Men* (2000), and *Spider-Man* (2002), the last of which was in production before 9/11 and whose initial artwork was withdrawn because it featured the World Trade Center's twin towers.

Visual effects had reached a point where films could convincingly represent each superhero's powers. But it was Christopher Nolan's *The Dark Knight* trilogy that gave the genre credibility. (Only M. Night Shyamalan previously attempted such a sober take with the novel superhero thriller *Unbreakable* of 2000.) The poster for *Batman Begins* (2005) hinted at what was to come; subsequent films were darker and their artwork bleaker.

Iron Man brought some brightness to bear on these worlds. The early preview posters featured Tony Stark's creation alone, but the main artwork created the template that most mainstream Marvel films have emulated. Like the classic *Star Wars* (1977) poster, the Marvel franchise artwork features the heroes and villains in action pose. The mood or arrangement of actors might shift, and accompanying artwork might depict individual characters, but the style mostly remains the same. The DC Comics cinematic universe is similar, although the *Justice League* (2017) poster, featuring head shots of the heroes, is particularly insipid.

Some superhero film artwork has been inventive. *Chronicle*'s (2012) flying schoolboys, *Logan*'s (2017) focus on two hands holding, and *Deadpool*'s (2016) sly parody of romantic drama tropes suggest a sly intelligence at work in a genre where more imaginative use of poster design would always be welcome.

CHRISTOPHER NOLAN

OPPOSITE
CLOCKWISE FROM TOP LEFT

Memento (2000)
Not only does this poster play on the idea of memory, but the fact that the images are unfocused suggests what we do see is never quite accurate. The title typography accentuates this lack of clarity.

Inception (2010)
As Nolan and his kind of cinema have become more popular, his stars—no matter how big they are—have become secondary to his vision. The artwork resembles a *Mission Impossible* episode directed by M. C. Escher.

Interstellar (2014)
Again, it is the world that Nolan creates that is the real draw of this journey into space. The vertical light that dominates other posters in the film's campaign is here seen in negative and horizontal, across the title.

RIGHT

The Prestige (2006)
The spiral hints at the magical world conjured up by Hugh Jackman and Christian Bale's illusionists, but also their descent into rivalry, deceit, and tragedy.

FAR RIGHT

Dunkirk (2017)
Like *Inception*, the backdrop is key here, but the solitary figure recalls the artwork for some of Steven Spielberg's films (see pages 256-257).

The elasticity of time, the fallibility of memory, and the proximity of chaos wend their way through the narratives of Christopher Nolan's films. A filmmaker who can command large budgets to produce intelligent mainstream entertainment, he occupies a singular position in contemporary Hollywood cinema. In addition, he is renowned for his oversight of every aspect of his films, including their promotional artwork. This is evident in the meticulous way each film's campaign hones in on the themes that Nolan explores.

Memento (2000) is typical of a Nolan poster. The image is deceptive. Playing on the Droste effect, Guy Pearce's character is pictured with a Polaroid of Carrie-Anne Moss' character who has a Polaroid of Guy Pearce, and so on. It perfectly sums up the playfulness of the film's narrative. One artwork for *The Prestige* (2006), Nolan's Victorian-era battle between two illusionists, has Christian Bale and Hugh Jackman face off against each other against a hypnotic spiral of light, which appears to be both behind and in front of them, thus suggesting nothing we see can be believed. A shaft of light dominates an image used for one of the *Interstellar*

(2014) posters, with the film's title taking the place of a rocket. With two figures standing at its base, it recalls the sense of wonder aroused by Steven Spielberg's *Close Encounters of the Third Kind* (1977).

Another poster for *Interstellar* features a visual theme that runs through a number of artworks for Nolan's film. Matthew McConaughey in a space suit walks through an arctic alien landscape whose sky is an inversion of the ground he walks on. It echoes the mind-altered city featured in *Inception* (2010)—a place where the only rules are those constructed by the person imagining them. The artwork for *Dunkirk* (2017) also plays with this visual metaphor—of a world falling apart—albeit with a lone soldier facing the destruction of a naval vessel in the very real combat of World War II.

Chaos also reigns in the filmmaker's *The Dark Knight* trilogy. The poster for *Batman Begins* (2005) intimates that Bruce Wayne's alter-ego is the physical projection of his fears (see page 273), and both *The Dark Knight* (2008) and *The Dark Knight Rises* (2012) take that projection further, portraying the rot of corruption through a city literally crumbling away.

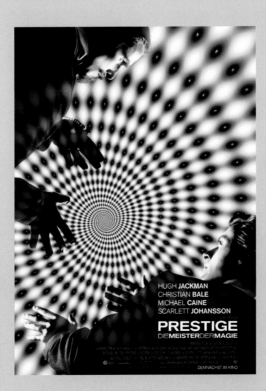

EUROPEAN CINEMA

A number of movements appeared throughout the 2000s that drew together key filmmakers and were notable for a distinct style. Although each is a loose grouping, whose definition was created by critics, there are certain thematic traits that link the films, particularly in the way they were promoted.

New French Extremity appeared at the end of the 1990s. The term was coined by the critic James Quandt and it defines a collection of transgressive films by a group of French directors who include Claire Denis, François Ozon, Leos Carax, Gaspar Noé, and Olivier Assayas. Not all the works made by these filmmakers fit into this group. The ones that do tend to employ sex and violence as a way of exploring the body politic. Noé's work in particular has attracted attention for its graphic content and the way his films are promoted.

New Turkish Cinema, whose filmmakers straddle the border between Europe and Asia, is an even looser collective term for those whose work has appeared since 2000. Indeed, there is no overriding theme among the films made by Yılmaz Erdoğan, Çağan Irmak, Derviş Zaim, and Zeki Demirkubuz, for example. However, the country's recent cinema has received significant focus because of the work of Nuri Bilge Ceylan. His films, comprising long takes, raise questions of identity and estrangement. He is an acclaimed photographer, and his images are often breathtaking in their beauty.

Romanian New Wave cinema is arguably the most cohesive and important of these recent movements. Comprising directors who mostly reached adulthood at the time of the country's move to democracy, films such as *The Death of Mr. Lăzărescu* (2005), *12:08 East of Bucharest* (2006), and *4 Months, 3 Weeks and 2 Days* (2007) highlight the hypocrisy of life in the Ceaușescu regime and chart the shift toward free-market capitalism. Like the films, which employ long takes and are shot in a realist style, the artwork tends to feature a simple still image from the film.

The Greek Weird Wave followed the economic crisis of 2008. Dominated by the work of Yorgos Lanthimos and Athina Rachel Tsangari, the films in this loose grouping explore notions of alienation in contemporary society, often through absurdist humor that can tilt toward the surreal.

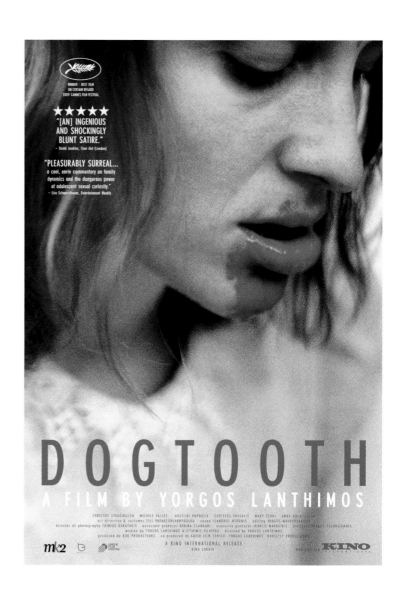

ABOVE

Dogtooth (2009)
The image appears to display the results of a violent act. But all is not what it seems. Like Yorgos Lanthimos' later *The Killing of a Sacred Deer* (2017, see page 284), ambiguity is everything.

OPPOSITE

Enter the Void (2009)
This poster image resembles an elaborate frontage to an old movie palace. But the perspective is key. It indicates how the film's protagonist views the world: overhead, out of body, and saturated with color.

NURİ BİLGE CEYLAN'DAN
BİR ZAMANLAR ANADOLU'DA
MUHAMMET UZUNER   YILMAZ ERDOĞAN   TANER BİRSEL

www.nbcfilm.com/uzuletta

THE MASTERMIND

THE LOOKOUT

THE RIGHT-HAND MAN

THE WILD CARD

THE STAR

THE BLING RING

Based on Actual Events
Written and Directed by SOFIA COPPOLA

THEBLINGRING.COM   A24

OFFICIAL SELECTION
COMPETITION
FESTIVAL DE CANNES

THE LOBSTER

**COLIN FARRELL   RACHEL WEISZ   JESSICA BARDEN   OLIVIA COLMAN   ASHLEY JENSEN
ARIANE LABED   ANGELIKI PAPOULIA   JOHN C. REILLY   LÉA SEYDOUX   MICHAEL SMILEY   BEN WHISHAW**

A CURE FOR WELLNESS

COMING SOON

If one looks only at the artwork for the average blockbuster release over the course of the past two decades, it is not unreasonable to assume that the future of the poster is uncertain. From superheroes to transforming robots and the first re-boot of a decades-old space opera, the shining chrome of the most insipid CGI creations appears to have made its influence felt on movie artwork. And yet, in other areas, the film poster has thrived—from world and independent cinema to the fringes of the mainstream and the work of auteurs.

Few contemporary directors attract as much controversy, acclaim, and ire as Lars von Trier. His early *Europa* trilogy was accused of proto-fascism, and its posters were as bleak in their worldview as the films. The artwork for *The Idiots* (1998), von Trier's contribution to the Dogme 95 movement, is clear in its explicit content, while the poster for the provocatively titled *Antichrist* (2009) features a demonic orgy and the promotional campaign for von Trier's two-part *Nymphomaniac* (2013) comprises a series of posters showing each of the film's

cast members in a state of sexual release. The poster for *Dancer in the Dark* (2000) is, by comparison, restrained—but also enticing.

Obliqueness dominated the promotional campaigns for a number of key films of the 2000s. One of the best was for Alexander Payne's *Sideways* (2004), a lyrical road movie-cum-buddy comedy set in California's wine-growing region. It pairs two unlikely friends on a stag trip that gradually descends into farce. A plain green backdrop on the poster represents the lush verdant landscape of the film's location, while the increasingly uncomfortable and strained relationship between the two men is encapsulated by a simple, but effective, line drawing. Likewise, the strange events that unfold at a remote sanatorium in Gore Verbinski's *A Cure for Wellness* (2016) are perfectly represented by a young woman floating in a medicine bottle.

One of the designs for Harmony Korine's *Spring Breakers* (2012) features the Day-Glo contents of a rucksack laid out in perfect order upon a bed: sneakers,

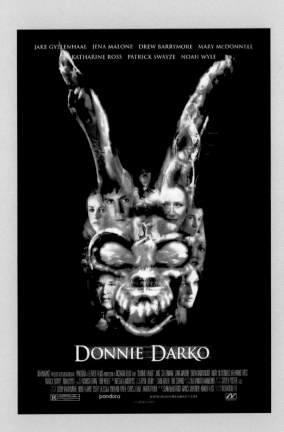

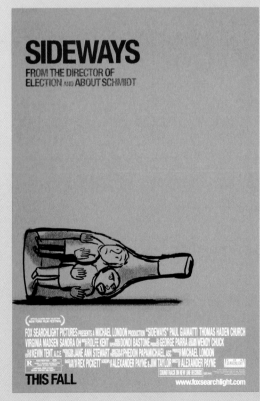

D
AN
CER
IN THE
DARK

A LARS VON TRIER FILM

BJÖRK   CATHERINE DENEUVE

BEST
PICTURE
PALME D'OR
CANNES
FILM FESTIVAL

OFFICIAL SELECTION

OPENING NIGHT · THE 38TH NEW YORK FILM FESTIVAL

FALL 2000

BJÖRK
BEST FEMALE
PERFORMANCE
CANNES
FILM FESTIVAL

MUSIC COMPOSED AND PERFORMED BY BJÖRK

SELMASONGS   MUSIC FROM THE MOTION PICTURE "DANCER IN THE DARK" AVAILABLE ON CD ON ONE LITTLE INDIAN RECORDS AND ELEKTRA ENTERTAINMENT GROUP

R RESTRICTED
UNDER 17 REQUIRES ACCOMPANYING
PARENT OR ADULT GUARDIAN

WWW.DANCERINTHEDARKMOVIE.COM

FINE LINE FEATURES
A Time Warner Company
© 2000 FINE LINE FEATURES

hot pants, sunglasses, money, smart phone, necklace, knuckle dusters, balaclava, and two revolvers. The following year, Sofia Coppola's *The Bling Ring* (2013) featured a similar design, in a minimal mode, highlighting the main protagonists' materialism. Both posters worked, but Coppola's benefited from less clutter.

No less inventive is the design accompanying the release of Spike Lee's *Bamboozled* (2000). Confronting the prejudices still prevalent in the United States, the poster depicts older racist stereotypes in popular culture as a reflection on the present. Lee returned to a similar theme in the mockumentary *C.S.A.: The Confederate States of America* (2004). Imagining the South won the Civil War, the poster features a NASA photograph of an astronaut standing on the moon next to a Confederate flag.

The belated success of *Donnie Darko* (2001) had much to do with its artwork. The film opened to little initial success in the United States, but it was well received in the United Kingdom. Word of mouth boosted the film, along with the depiction of a strange rabbit that appears to foretell the events that happen around the main character. The outline of the rabbit became the dominant image for the film, with all the characters appearing inside it. Defying easy categorization, the poster allowed *Donnie Darko* to exist in its own space, beyond genre.

Todd Haynes' *I'm Not There* (2007) also defies easy classification. It is a mythical, fictional biography of Bob Dylan, which finds him played in various stages of his life by six different actors. The artwork cleverly tackles this with a multi-faceted design that hints at Saul Bass without recalling his work directly. It has a retro look, and employs text cards in the same way that Dylan did in his music video for "Subterranean Homesick Blues" (1965).

The artwork for Nuri Bilge Ceylan's films has often accentuated the beauty of his cinematography. For his slow-burning crime thriller *Once Upon a Time in Anatolia* (2011), the artwork for the Turkish release plays upon the location of a body that the police and the suspect are searching for amid the vast Anatolian landscape. Its subtlety is matched by the intimation of longing in the acclaimed artwork for Yorgos Lanthimos' *The Lobster* (2015), a film that skirts the science fiction genre and whose dissection of human relationships and the nature of loneliness its poster underpins.

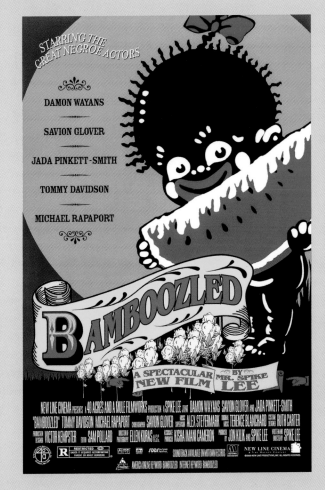

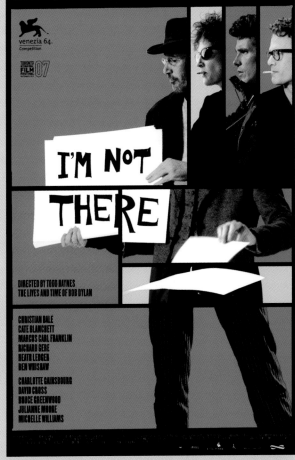

THE FUTURE

The future of the movie poster is uncertain. The speed at which technology is changing and how people consume films are likely to have an impact on the way movies are sold to audiences. The use of portable devices means that people who enjoy the same kind of entertainment are likely to be consuming it at different times and in different formats. Some films are not even showing in cinemas at the time of their release. So where does that leave the poster?

The business of movie poster collecting remains lucrative. In 2012, an original poster for Fritz Lang's *Metropolis* (1927) sold for US$1.2 million. It is one of only four remaining originals. Posters for monster and horror movies of the early 1930s, such as *Frankenstein*, *Dracula* (both 1931), *King Kong* (1933), and *The Black Cat* (1934), have each sold for more than a quarter of a million dollars. Early Bond posters, or any iconic artwork by one of the spy series' most notable designers, Robert E. McGinnis, are guaranteed to fetch a significant price—provided, of course, that the posters are genuine. As in any market, knowledge is the richest commodity and the only guard against purchasing a poster of no monetary value.

As for posters advertising new releases, changes in the past two decades have shown how technology is pushing certain non-electronic media toward obsolescence. However, it has also brought billboards to life. Initially, the space allocated to one poster underwent a mechanical change so that a simple roller or Venetian blind design could allow two, three, or more posters to occupy one space on rotation. Digital screens take this concept further. It is now possible to see a trailer, a clip for a film, or a moving image within a space previously occupied by a poster. The world might be only a few innovations away from a *Minority Report* (2002) scenario, in which billboard signs advertise a specific film in order to cater to the tastes of the person walking past. Likewise, magazine apps no longer have to feature a poster for an upcoming release. They can offer a reader or viewer anything from a trailer to an interview with a film's stars in order to entice them to watch it.

There is also a more fundamental threat to film posters, in the way they are now created. Whereas artwork was once the remit of a designer working with a film studio, today there can be many voices airing their

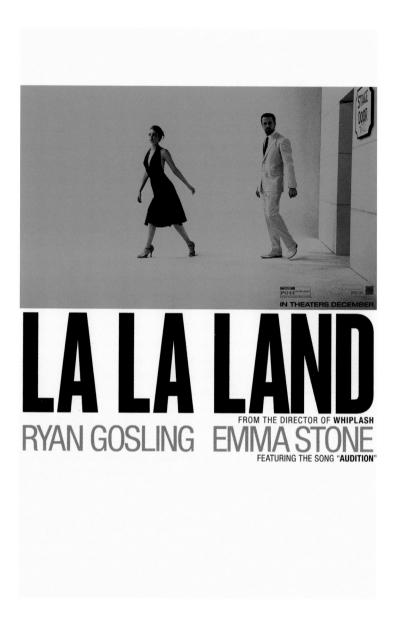

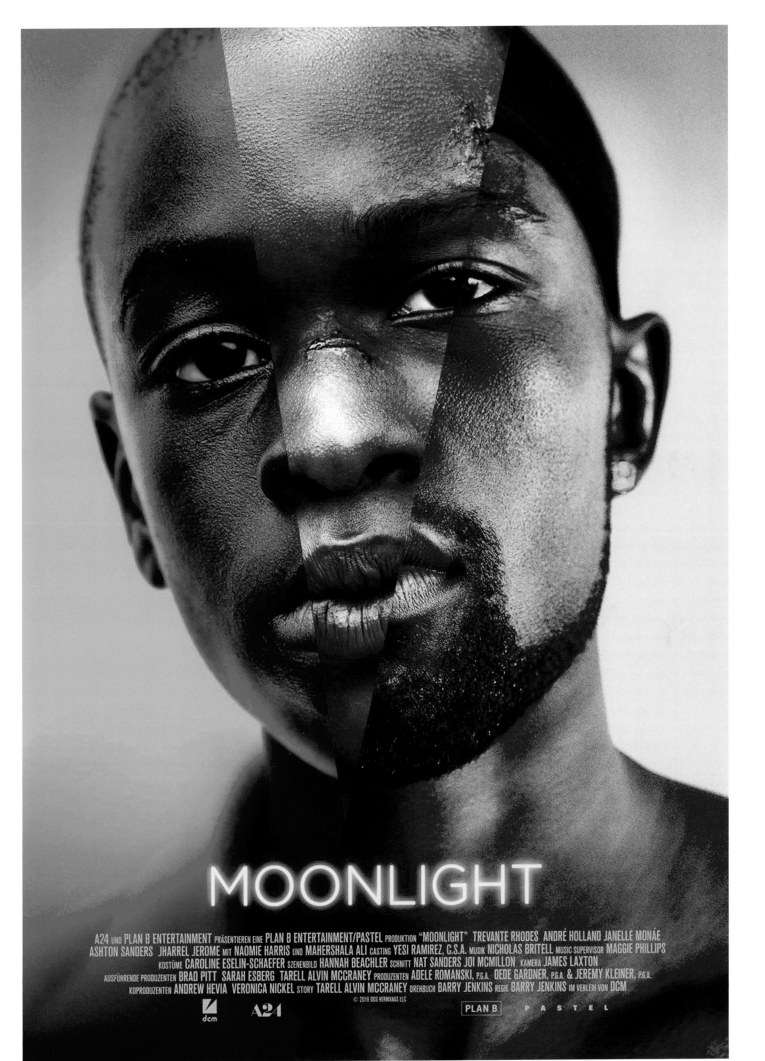

MOONLIGHT

A24 UND PLAN B ENTERTAINMENT PRÄSENTIEREN EINE PLAN B ENTERTAINMENT/PASTEL PRODUKTION "MOONLIGHT" TREVANTE RHODES ANDRÉ HOLLAND JANELLE MONÁE
ASHTON SANDERS JHARREL JEROME MIT NAOMIE HARRIS UND MAHERSHALA ALI CASTING YESI RAMIREZ, C.S.A. MUSIK NICHOLAS BRITELL MUSIC SUPERVISOR MAGGIE PHILLIPS
KOSTÜME CAROLINE ESELIN-SCHAEFER SZENENBILD HANNAH BEACHLER SCHNITT NAT SANDERS JOI MCMILLON KAMERA JAMES LAXTON
AUSFÜHRENDE PRODUZENTEN BRAD PITT SARAH ESBERG TARELL ALVIN MCCRANEY PRODUZENTEN ADELE ROMANSKI, P.G.A. DEDE GARDNER, P.G.A. & JEREMY KLEINER, P.G.A.
KOPRODUZENTEN ANDREW HEVIA VERONICA NICKEL STORY TARELL ALVIN MCCRANEY DREHBUCH BARRY JENKINS REGIE BARRY JENKINS IM VERLEIH VON DCM

© 2016 DOS HERMANAS LLC

dcm   A24   PLAN B   PASTEL

opinion, creating competition between the visions of a director and producer, a studio or production company's marketing department, stars whose PR agencies demand their name is prominent in the artwork, and the person designing the poster. True, some of these conflicts are not new. The more high profile a film, the more people in various positions want a say in how the film is promoted. Sometimes, it is a simple case of ensuring that the placement of the credits appeases the film's stars. This happened on *The Towering Inferno* in 1974 (see page 209). Steve McQueen and Paul Newman were both major stars. Newman had more screen time and was arguably the principal character among a stellar cast, but McQueen was no less a box office draw. The solution was to have McQueen's name first, with Newman's appearing after it, albeit slightly higher on the poster. Likewise, McQueen's head shot was positioned to the left of the image of the burning tower, with Newman to the right. In this instance, everyone was satisfied, but design by committee can often result in blandness. In a similar vein, the proliferation of sequels and franchises can often lead design down a creative-free rabbit hole in a studio's desire to give audiences more of the same.

The passion for original and bold poster design isn't hard to find. A general search online for movie posters reveals a world of designers, artists, and enthusiasts creating posters for their favorite films. Some revel in their obliqueness, while others playfully riff on original designs. Many are inspired, and some are better than the original posters for the film.

There is hope that the poster will remain a key element for selling a movie. Indeed, there are still noteworthy posters being produced for new films. Some ooze cool, like the car firing out of a gun in the stylish artwork for *Baby Driver* (2017; see page 209), while others look back to an earlier time, such as the retro Blue Note album cover-style poster for *La La Land* (2016). It gives the film a modishness that contrasts with the main poster's echoing the heyday of the classical Hollywood musical. The *Moonlight* (2016) artwork cleverly employs three images of its lead actors, all playing one character at different ages, to suggest an exploration of identity and race. While the glacial image of a hospital room underpins the emotional chill of *The Killing of a Sacred Deer* (2017), the exaggerated height of the room hints at something absurd—a twisting of reality. Although the artwork for Michael Haneke's *Happy End* (2017) might initially appear underwhelming, its power lies in the juxtaposition between the image and the film's title. All these posters engage and entice us, hinting at the possibility of what lies in store if we watch the film. If we do, they will have served their purpose.

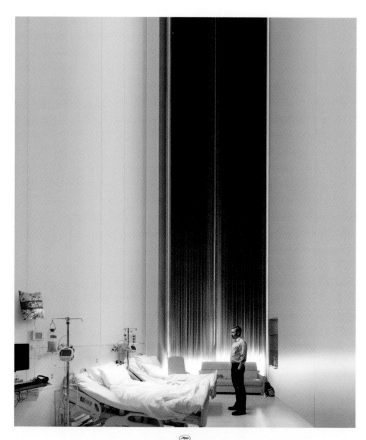

The Killing of a Sacred Deer (2017)
Each Yorgos Lanthimos film exudes a unique style when it comes to promotional artwork. This image, one of two used for *The Killing of a Sacred Deer*, might not hint at the film's humor, but it succeeds in suggesting the director has once again created a strange world.

OPPOSITE

Happy End (2017)
This image, taken from the film's final moments, suggests a bleak world view. For one central character, it is the only road open to them, while the smartphone button icons imply that we are seeing this picture through the eyes of another.

INDEX

Page numbers in *italics* refer to illustrations

286

PICTURE CREDITS